Globalizing Democracy and Human Rights

In her new book, Carol Gould, the author of the highly regarded and successful *Rethinking Democracy*, addresses the fundamental challenge of democratizing globalization, that is, of finding ways to open transnational institutions and communities to democratic participation by those widely affected by their decisions.

The book develops a framework for expanding such participation in crossborder contexts, arguing for a strengthened understanding of human rights that can confront worldwide economic and social inequalities. It also introduces a new role for the ideas of care and solidarity at a distance. Reinterpreting the idea of universality to encompass a multiplicity of cultural perspectives, the author takes up a number of applied issues, including the persistence of racism, the human rights of women, the democratic management of firms, the use of the Internet to enhance political participation, and the importance of empathy and genuine democracy in understanding terrorism and responding to it.

Clearly and accessibly written, this major new contribution to political philosophy will be of special interest to professionals and graduate students in philosophy, political science, women's studies, public policy, and international affairs, as well as anyone who wants to more fully comprehend the dilemmas of a globalized world.

Carol C. Gould is Professor of Philosophy and Government and Director of the Center for Global Ethics at George Mason University.

Globalizing Democracy and Human Rights

CAROL C. GOULD

George Mason University

PUBLISHED BY THE PRESS SYNDICATE OF THE UNIVERSITY OF CAMBRIDGE
The Pitt Building, Trumpington Street, Cambridge, United Kingdom

CAMBRIDGE UNIVERSITY PRESS
The Edinburgh Building, Cambridge CB2 2RU, UK
40 West 20th Street, New York, NY 10011-4211, USA
477 Williamstown Road, Port Melbourne, VIC 3207, Australia
Ruiz de Alarcón 13, 28014 Madrid, Spain
Dock House, The Waterfront, Cape Town 8001, South Africa

http://www.cambridge.org

First published 2004

Printed in the United States of America

Typeface ITC New Baskerville 10/13 pt.   *System* LaTeX 2$_\varepsilon$ [TB]

A catalog record for this book is available from the British Library.

Library of Congress Cataloging in Publication Data

Gould, Carol C.
Globalizing democracy and human rights / Carol C. Gould.
p. cm.
Includes bibliographical references and index.
ISBN 0-521-83354-X – ISBN 0-521-54127-1 (pbk.)
1. Democracy.   2. Globalization.   3. Human rights.   1. Title.
JC423.G663   2004
321.8–dc22   2003068730

ISBN 0 521 83354 X hardback
ISBN 0 521 54127 1 paperback

In memory of Marx W. Wartofsky,
and for our son, Michael Gould-Wartofsky

Contents

Acknowledgments

The work on this book was initiated under an NEH Summer Stipend in 1992 and an NEH Fellowship for College Teachers held during a sabbatical year in 1993–1994. It was also supported during that period by a Fulbright Senior Scholar Award in France, where I was fortunate to be appointed a Research Associate at the C.R.E.A. group at the École Polytechnique, an affiliation that continued for many years thereafter. Concluding work on the volume was undertaken during a second sabbatical in 2000–2001, when I held the Fulbright Florence Chair at the European University Institute and subsequently was a Fellow at the Woodrow Wilson International Center for Scholars in Washington, D.C. The opportunities for discussion and research provided by those institutions were invaluable to me. I would also like to thank Stevens Institute of Technology for its support during my sabbatical leaves.

I presented earlier drafts of many of these chapters at various conferences and seminars and am grateful to the participants in those meetings for their trenchant and helpful comments and criticisms. "Hard Questions in Democratic Theory: When Justice and Democracy Conflict" was originally given to the Princeton University Department of Politics and appeared as a Working Paper of the University Center on Human Values. The chapter "Two Concepts of Universality and the Problem of Cultural Relativism" was presented as the Keynote Address of the Annual Conference of the North American Society for Social Philosophy. I originally read "Embodied Politics" to the Society for Women in Philosophy, New York Chapter, and then to the Fordham University Philosophy Department, and "Racism and Democracy" was read to a session of the Radical Philosophers Association at the American Philosophical Association

Eastern Division meetings. I originally presented "Cultural Identity, Group Rights, and Social Ontology" at the IVR World Congress in Bologna, and in revised form at a national conference of AMINTAPHIL. "Conceptualizing Women's Human Rights" was given to the Gender Working Group at the European University Institute in Fiesole, Italy. "Evaluating the Claims for Global Democracy" was given in early form to the Department of Political and Social Sciences at the European University Institute, and in revised form as the Presidential Address of the Metaphysical Society of America. I originally presented the chapter "Are Democracy and Human Rights Compatible in the Context of Globalization?" as a Work-in-Progress at the Woodrow Wilson International Center for Scholars, and in a subsequent version at the NEH Seminar on Supranationalism at Columbia University, sponsored by the Carnegie Council on Ethics and International Affairs. A version of "The Global Democratic Deficit and Economic Human Rights" was presented to the 2003 Annual Meeting of the Canadian Philosophical Association. "Democratic Management and the Stakeholder Idea" was presented at the Conference on Ethics across the Curriculum at the University of Florida, "Democratic Networks: Technological and Political" was given in early form at a Stevens Conference on Technology Studies: New Frontiers, and the final chapter, "Terrorism, Empathy, and Democracy," at a joint session of the Society for Philosophy and Public Affairs and the Committee on the Status of Women of the American Philosophical Association. All of these opportunities for scholarly interchange provided valuable feedback and criticisms, which I hope I have taken into account in the revision of this work.

The author expresses appreciation to the University Seminars at Columbia University for their help in publication. The ideas presented have benefited from discussions in the University Seminar on Political & Social Thought and the University Seminar on Political Economy & Contemporary Social Issues.

Acknowledgment is also due to the readers of this book for Cambridge University Press, for their discerning comments and suggestions. I am indebted as well to my editors at the Press, Terry Moore and Stephanie Achard, for their helpful direction and wise guidance.

Earlier versions of Chapters 2, 4, 5, and 10 have appeared previously, and I would like to acknowledge those original publications. An initial version of Chapter 2 was included in the volume I coedited with Pasquale Pasquino titled *Cultural Justice and the Nation-State* (Lanham, MD: Rowman & Littlefield, 2001), 67–84. Chapter 4 is a revised version of

"Racism and Democracy Reconsidered," published in *Social Identities*, Vol. 6, no. 4 (2000): 425–439. Earlier versions of Chapter 5 appeared as "Group Rights and Social Ontology," *The Philosophical Forum*, Special Double Issue on "Philosophical Perspectives on National Identity," Vol. XXVIII, nos. 1–2 (Fall–Winter 1996–1997): 73–86; and in revised form in *Groups and Group Rights*, eds. Christine Sistare and Larry May (Lawrence: University Press of Kansas, 2001), Chapter I, 43–57. Finally, an earlier version of Chapter 10 was published under the title "Does Stakeholder Theory Require Democratic Management?" in *Business & Professional Ethics Journal*, Vol. 21, no. 1 (Spring 2002).

I am deeply grateful to my professional colleagues and friends, including Ross Zucker, John Lango, Virginia Held, Frank Cunningham, Peter Caws, Joan Callahan, Sibyl Schwarzenbach, James Sterba, Alistair MacCleod, Chris Morris, William McBride, and Jim Cohen, for many helpful discussions and insightful comments over the years, and for their personal and professional support at various stages of this work. I would also like to thank Andrew Gould, Jon Gould, James Scow, Salvatore Prisco, Susan Schept, Michel Paty, Joelle Proust, Tony Alterman, Lisa Dolling, Bill Tabb, and Nettie Terestman for their understanding and encouragement. I received many keen comments on my approach from several of my students at the School of International and Public Affairs and in the graduate school at Columbia, and from students and faculty at the European University Institute. In addition, I would like to thank Justin Marshall, my intern at the Woodrow Wilson Center, for his capable editorial and bibliographical assistance.

Most especially, I am profoundly grateful for the extensive commentary, critique, and editorial help that I received from my late husband, Marx Wartofsky. His constant support and encouragement, together with the inspiration he provided as a first-rate philosopher, a political thinker of exceptional passion and integrity, and as my partner over the years, were invaluable to this work, as to all my other work. I would also like to thank my philosophically minded son, Michael Gould-Wartofsky, for numerous insights and editorial suggestions that have improved this work considerably. Michael's deep commitment to the development of a theory and practice for a more just and democratic society mirror those of his father and were important in the elaboration of my ideas and in the revision of the manuscript. I dedicate this book to both of them.

Introduction

Between the Personal and the Global

This book attempts to bring philosophy to bear on a set of crucial practical problems: How can increasingly globalized political and economic institutions, as well as emerging transborder communities, be opened to democratic participation by those widely affected by their decisions? In view of the inequalities attendant on globalization and the corporate aggrandizement it entails, how can people's rights to the fundamental conditions that make for an adequate standard of living be fulfilled? And given the increases we have seen in global interconnectedness, is there a way to retain cultural and social differentiation at the level of local communities, while protecting against violations of human rights in the name of the diversity of cultures?

In the face of these challenges, it is clear that new modes of thought are required. We need to clarify how far broader reaches of people can take part in the decisions of powerful global institutions and what the limits of such participation might be. Thus, in addition to long-standing demands for a greater say in decisions in local contexts, there are growing discussions about democratic participation across regions (as with the European Union), about instituting democratic accountability in the supranational bodies that play an important role in steering the course of economic globalization (e.g., the International Monetary Fund and the World Trade Organization), and about possible uses of the Internet and other technologies to facilitate democratic decision making. Clearly, too, the reach and meaning of human rights have to be more coherently and forcefully articulated, including the question of establishing a global rights structure to which people can appeal, even against decisions by their own governments. And it is evident that, beyond these questions about making politics and institutions more responsive, new modes of feeling and intercultural understanding are now necessary. It seems that if we are to function in increasingly cosmopolitan ways, we also need to feel empathy and even solidarity with those at a distance. We would have to show that such feelings of concern can be extended more globally, instead of applying only to those close to us.

What sort of theoretical framework, then, can help to guide these globalization processes – economic, political, and technological, as well as cultural and personal – in more humanistic and justice-regarding ways? How should democracy and human rights be specifically conceived so as to facilitate increased cooperation in economic, ecological, and security matters? This book proposes a way to address these questions by focusing on the key issue of interpreting and interrelating democracy and human rights. It draws on the traditions of political philosophy and critical social theory, and on more recent feminist theorizing, to delineate a new perspective on these pressing contemporary issues. From this perspective, the sort of globalizing that is required entails an expansion of democratic modes of decision making and of human rights themselves, not only internationally but also beneath the level of politics, so to speak, in social, economic, and even personal life. Also needed is an increased attention to differences, especially as concerns the diversity of cultural groups and their interaction. It is apparent, too, that democracy and human rights, viewed as global norms, cannot be interpreted simply along the conventional Western lines with which we have long been comfortable, if they are to win more universal assent and measure up to their universal aims.

In this work, I start from the principles introduced in my earlier book *Rethinking Democracy*. The view of democracy proposed there was rather distinctive among contemporary approaches in putting a conception of human rights at the core of democratic theory, and I develop this aspect further in what follows. *Globalizing Democracy and Human Rights* thus proposes that to guide current practice we need an enlarged conception of democracy taken within a strengthened framework of human rights. It suggests how the implementation of these norms demands changes in both personal relations and at a more global level, and not only an intensified realization of traditional political democracy operating with a limited set of rights protected by a national constitution.

In this view, democracy is seen to be based on reciprocal and empathic personal relations and extends through plural social and cultural contexts to a transnational and indeed global level. I call such a conception *intersociative democracy*, to emphasize crossborder decision making and the need for transborder solidarity, along with new intercultural associations. In each of its contexts of application, such democratic decision making is conceived to be grounded in a strengthened conception of human rights, going beyond customarily emphasized civil and political ones to economic, social, and cultural rights, where these merit increased recognition in emerging international law. Moreover, when democratic decision making and human rights are considered from the perspective of a multiplicity of cultures, we will see that they require rights for minority groups, although these can be understood as based on a set of cultural human rights rather than as intrinsically group-based rights.

A philosophical approach of this sort can, I trust, play a helpful clarifying role in regard to social movements that seek to make globalization more people-centered and democratic, in place of the perpetuation of its current modes of functioning, which, despite the claims of its exponents, largely benefit powerful economic interests and wealthy nation-states at the expense of less-well-off groups and developing countries. It is apparent that globalization has shown positive dimensions as well, especially in the technological facilitation of increased communications worldwide, in the political and legal internationalization so far achieved between and across nation-states, and incipiently in new forms of economic cooperation across borders. Yet it has also proceeded in the absence of democratic forms of organization at transnational levels and with attention to a bare subset of human rights, without adequate regard for the economic and social well-being of large segments of the world's population, perhaps especially women and children.

In this problematic situation, it is suggested that the proposed conception of democracy, based on justice, can apply in new ways to decision making in emerging transnational communities and organizations. Questions of the scope of such decision making – in particular, who has a right to participate in which decisions – play an important role in this work. Clearly, too, by *globalizing democracy*, I mean more than extending current forms of rather emaciated political democracy to other nation-states. Rather, the activity of globalizing calls for new intersociative democratic relationships to develop along with the growth of transborder interdependence, not limited to those close to us or to political societies as such. I introduce the concept of *democratic networks* in this connection. The more cosmopolitan outlook required for such a globalization of democracy, in which we are attuned to the needs of those at a distance, is also articulated in what follows.

A key concern here is to investigate the nature of the deep relation between democracy and human rights, beyond the truism that democracy is one of the human rights or that "liberal democracies" are committed to both democratization and a set of civil and political rights. Instead of simply conceiving human rights as incorporated within a given country's constitution, I provide an argument supporting their expanded regional and global implementation and for the legitimate constraint that they can pose on democratic decision making. Interestingly, the potential impact on people's human rights will also be seen to provide an important criterion for deciding when democratic participation in global institutions is required. I also propose that the fulfillment of human rights, including access to means of subsistence, sets relevant goals for democratic societies and for their economic functioning. Finally, an exploration of the complex dialectical relations between democracy and human rights confirms the idea that democratic participation provides one of the main ways in which people can protect their human rights, while conversely the protection of such rights is itself a condition for widespread democratic participation. I consider some of the problematic philosophical issues raised by the interrelation of these norms.

In this work, as in *Rethinking Democracy*, I draw on what I have named *social ontology*, as a theory of the nature of social reality. Specifically, this approach gives priority to a conception of human freedom and to socially understood *individuals-in-relations* as the basis for the extension of democratic decision making to all contexts of common activity, whether political, economic, or social. Human rights have a fundamental place here, inasmuch as they reflect the basic claims people can validly make on each other for the conditions that make each one's freedom achievable. Thus, although this work stresses the centrality of democratic and cooperative forms of decision making, it does not see this as the genesis of human rights and of justice themselves, norms that are, rather, at its foundation. In addition, feminist approaches to the idea of care and empathy as important values, to women's equal rights and the corollary critique of domination, and to the idea of embodiment importantly suggest ways to personalize and, in this sense, to transform both democratic politics and human rights doctrine, and these possibilities are developed here. The proposed theoretical basis is also seen to have substantial implications for some issues in applied ethics, including democratic management in firms, the potential uses of the Internet for democratic participation, and current matters of international concern, including the analysis of terrorism and the response to it.

The approach in this book thus aims to hold together and indeed to integrate certain strains in political theory that have most often been developed separately – for example, justice and care, or again, individual freedom and extensive social cooperation. It does so from the standpoint of a rather systematic political philosophy, in the conviction that such theorizing is necessary, and indeed beneficial, if we are to make our way through unjust social practices. In this respect, this approach contrasts with efforts to devise purely "political," or "consensual," approaches to political principles, which propose minimalist approaches to such principles as a way of gaining widespread agreement about norms. Yet the social ontology at work here is evidently not "metaphysical" either, in that it avoids appeal to religious or natural foundations and is anti-essentialist in its rejection of the older idea of a fixed human nature. Although this view grounds political norms in human agency and interaction, it sees these latter as marked by change and sociocultural differentiation, and as transforming themselves historically. Furthermore, such an approach leaves room for multiple (and sometimes conflicting) values in political philosophy, while aiming for a degree of coherence in the overall account. Yet, as understood here, philosophical approaches have to be closely linked with social critique and developed with an eye to the emerging possibilities of practical change.

In several ways, then, this book goes against the grain of much current political theorizing. But because its methodology is dialectical, it attempts to retain the strengths of the prevailing views. This method involves beginning from a critical consideration of leading approaches to key concepts for politics and then attempting to preserve crucial insights of these alternative approaches, while avoiding their defects, within a new and consistent synthesis. This way of proceeding also draws on both continental and Anglo-American approaches in philosophy without endorsing one at the expense of the other, while facilitating further revision from non-Western perspectives. Because of this synthetic character, the framework should be judged, I think, not only in terms of the effectiveness of the individual arguments given but also by the degree to which it succeeds in providing an original, coherent, and illuminating approach to the substantial range of issues it addresses.

The structure of the work is as follows: Part I presents much of the theoretical basis for the process of extending democracy and human rights, to be elaborated in novel ways in subsequent chapters. (Important elements of this theory are also developed in Chapters 3, 5, 8, and 9 as well as implicitly throughout the work.) Chapter 1 addresses rather systematically some of the hard normative issues concerning the concepts of democracy, justice, human rights, and care. The chapter begins by taking up three main models, or "ideal types," of the (sometimes conflictual) relation between democracy and justice, as exemplified to various degrees in the well-known and highly developed approaches of John Rawls, Robert Dahl, and Jürgen Habermas. I offer a critique of procedural and discursive approaches to democracy and justice, while appreciating their emphasis on deliberation, and then go on to argue that an alternative sense of democracy, grounded on a conception of justice as equal positive freedom, is better able to take account of the centrality and, indeed, the priority, of human rights. I also introduce other features of this theoretical framework that refine it in various ways – specifically, the ideas of reciprocity, empathy, and attention to differences.

Chapter 2 examines how human rights themselves can be regarded in more pluralistic ways, given the diversity of cultures and the treatment of women within them. A conception of universality is introduced that differs from the abstract one normally used to discuss human rights; I call this alternative "concrete universality." I also discuss some of the difficulties that attend the determinate lists of human functioning that have been proposed – by, for example, Martha Nussbaum – and attempt to chart a path between such determinateness, on the one hand, and cultural relativism, on the other. This requires a new and more social account of value creation and brings into play considerations of empathy and solidarity.

Part II, "Democracy and Rights, Personalized and Pluralized," addresses the important issues of extending these basic conceptions to interpersonal contexts beneath and beyond the political and of interpreting them in more diversified ways than is usual. Thus, Chapter 3 begins by taking up a central conception that has emerged mainly from feminist theory as it pertains to politics – namely, the idea of embodiment – and I situate the approach adopted here in relation to alternative interpretations of the role of the body in politics. I focus especially on the concept of need and the function of meeting differentiated needs as being among the aims of political and economic cooperation. This chapter, along with others in this part, pursues the connection, introduced earlier, of politics to reciprocal and empathic modes of personal interaction, through which differences between individuals and groups can be adequately recognized and effectively taken into account in the public domain.

Although it is by now commonplace to criticize traditional liberal democracy for its abstract individualism, in which differences other than those of political opinion are ignored or overridden and assigned to the private sphere, the alternative approach that would take differences seriously requires further development. Some basic questions arise here: What differences should be recognized, and why these rather than others? Which differences should be ignored, and which would it be pernicious to recognize? Does the emphasis on the recognition and representation of differences violate equal rights as a norm of justice? Clearly, in addition to recognizing the diversity of existing social and political communities – along the lines of individual and group differences, including sex, race, ethnicity, and so forth – we need to extend democratic theory to the variety of such communities worldwide.

Part II goes on to address these issues by, in the first instance, analyzing the conceptual relations between the understanding of race and cultural identity, in which a social constructivist approach plays a prominent role, and between the critique of racism and the normative requirement for democracy. I then proceed to delineate a model of cultural identity and intercultural democracy, in which certain group rights of minority cultures can be recognized, while seeing them as derived from individual human rights to cultural self-development. Here, I rely on a social-ontological conception of groups as constituted entities. I lay out alternative relations that the public sphere can take to the cultures within it, and I also briefly consider the interpretation of the concept of a nation in this connection.

The issue of the pluralization and personalization of rights is pursued further in Chapter 6, the final chapter of this part, on women's human rights. In personal terms, taking human rights to apply to the private sphere and generally to the concerns of women, as recent feminist theory has suggested, leads to a reconceptualization of them in several important respects. In this context, I also propose that such a reformulation reveals how human rights are based on relations of care and concern for others, extending to those at a distance, as much as they are on more conventional considerations of justice.

In Part III the book turns to the crucial topic of globalizing democracy and puts the earlier theoretical discussion of democracy and human rights, conceived now in more pluralistic ways, into contemporary applied contexts of decision making in regional, multilateral, and global institutions. In fact, readers who are strongly interested in questions of relating democracy and human rights to the conditions of globalization may want

to read this part first. In Chapter 7, I begin with a descriptive characterization of economic and political globalization and with the correlate
emergence of supranational and multilateral bodies such as the International Monetary Fund (IMF) and the World Trade Organization (WTO),
and I discuss the problem of the lack of democratic participation in the
workings of these bodies. The various models of global democracy advanced by David Held and several other contemporary political theorists
are then categorized and evaluated, followed by an analysis of various
possible criteria that can be used to demarcate the proper scope of a
democratic community. This analysis provides the basis for discussing
the increased role – and modalities – of transnational or crossborder decision making, the place for fully global democratic communities, and
the difficult issue of ways to democratize the supranational bodies that so
affect contemporary economic and political globalization.

Such processes of globalization are increasingly recognized to require
a normative framework of human rights, and we see the beginnings of
what has been called a "global human rights regime." As is already the case
in Europe, citizens worldwide would be able to appeal to regional and
international rights bodies for protection of their human rights (even
of their economic, social, and cultural rights) against actions of their
own nation-states. This poses for us the interesting and difficult problem
of possible constraint by this rights regime not only on sovereignty but
also on democratic decision making at national and local levels. The
legitimacy of this constraint, and the issue of the compatibility of such an
extensive human rights regime with decision making within democratic
communities, is the topic of analysis in Chapter 8. It is suggested there that
the approach put forward in earlier chapters – particularly concerning
the philosophical relation between the concepts of democracy and of
human rights, and the more substantive model of democracy used in this
work – helps to resolve the question of this compatibility in the affirmative.

In light of these considerations, I turn in Chapter 9 to the project
of democratizing globalization and approach the democratic deficit in
multilateral institutions such as the WTO and the IMF in relation to what
I call the "justice deficit," or the discrepancy in the realization of economic and social human rights in different societies. I consider some
of the proposals for increasing democratic input into decisions by such
organizations as well as in the new crossborder contexts. I also take up
recent pragmatic proposals, along with the territorially based and functional approaches to such democratization considered in Chapter 7, the
first chapter of this part. A closer analysis and interpretation of the idea

of being importantly affected by decisions is advanced as a supplement to the idea that those engaged in common projects or networks of interdependence should have opportunities to provide input into these more global decisions. The chapter goes on to consider several of the essential and complex interrelations between human rights, particularly the economic and social ones, and such democratic decision making.

Part IV addresses three issues in applied ethics that can helpfully be approached using the framework introduced in the earlier sections; the discussion of these current applications also helps to concretize it in various ways. In Chapter 10, I take up the issue of democratic management in firms and show how it is implied both by the normative requirement to extend democratic decision making to economic life, as proposed earlier in the book, and by the dominant approach in current business ethics, namely, stakeholder theory. This latter approach holds that managers ought to take into account not only the interests of stockholders but also the interests of all those groups who are affected by and affect the corporation, including employees, customers, suppliers, the local community, and so on. I examine the stakeholder criterion of "those affected" by corporate decisions and consider the normative justifications advanced for this approach, as for the older view that calls for workplace participation. On this basis, I attempt to specify the sense in which stakeholder theory requires some form of participative, or what I call democratic, management, and to consider which stakeholders in fact have a right to such participation.

Chapter 11, on democratic networks, addresses the question of the degree to which, and the ways in which, democratic decision making can be enhanced by the Net (or the global information infrastructure). Keeping in view the normative principles for computer networking introduced in my earlier work *The Information Web*, I consider the increasing rate of globalization in the scope and uses of information and communication technologies and their role in facilitating transnational communities of certain sorts, and I ask what new issues have to be taken into account in developing democratic uses of these media. The pronounced "digital divide," along with "cyberimperialism," necessarily qualifies our optimism about the power of information networks to facilitate such cyberdemocracy. I introduce a distinction among three types of online communities and suggest that the Net is especially well suited to expanding the participation of crossborder or regional groups in political decisions.

Finally, I turn to a central issue in current international ethics – namely, the normative understanding of terrorism and appropriate responses to it – and consider this difficult issue from the standpoint of the book's earlier account of empathy and its interpretation of democracy. After briefly discussing the definition of terrorism, I take as my focus certain recent terrorist acts directed against noncombatants or civilians. Given that these acts manifest not only injustice and the violation of human rights, but also a wholesale lack of human fellow feeling, I consider how the concept of empathy as developed in feminist ethical theory can further illuminate this sort of case. In this connection, I make use of Hannah Arendt's account of thinking and judging – and specifically, the role of imaginatively presenting to oneself the situation and perspective of the other – and suggest that inasmuch as they do not identify with the common human needs of their victims, such terrorists cannot properly be understood as altruists, as is implied by some theories of terrorism. I go on to suggest that empathy and transborder solidarity can also play a role in responding to terrorism, by helping us to understand and address the conditions that may contribute to its emergence. Finally, opportunities for democratic participation can be seen to provide important means for effectively addressing these conditions, and the book closes with a consideration of the import of democracy in this very contemporary context.

By way of conclusion, we can see that the "between" in the title of this introduction – "*Between* the Personal and the Global" – is not intended to demarcate a delimited region between the two extremes in which democracy and human rights are rightly bounded. Rather, the "between" is meant in an active sense, in which it includes both extremes and connotes a going back and forth between the various levels of the personal, the plural, and the global. It suggests that if we are to succeed in re-envisioning democracy at national or more global levels, we need to focus on personal relations of reciprocity, care, and empathy, while, conversely, these latter are fostered only by a social and political environment – within a recognized human rights framework – organized inclusively and cooperatively.

PART I

THEORETICAL CONSIDERATIONS

1

Hard Questions in Democratic Theory

When Justice and Democracy Conflict

I want to begin by considering some hard questions in the theory of democracy that center on this issue: When is it legitimate to constrain democratic decision making in the interest of justice? If democracy is a central value in political and social life, what can justify limiting or overriding the decisions arrived at by the democratic process? Wouldn't any constraint undercut the very essence of democracy? On the other hand, justice is also a central value for politics, economics, and society. Can our commitment to democratic process allow for decisions or laws democratically arrived at that violate the requirements of justice? Where these two values conflict, what is the basis for judgment as to which will prevail? Even if we agree that in certain cases democracy should be constrained in the interest of justice, who has the right or the authority to determine this? Worse yet, if democracy is itself understood as that procedure that most fully realizes the principle of justice (by recognizing equal rights of participation in decision making), how can it in turn need to be constrained by the requirements of justice? In short, how can democracy as a just procedure itself violate justice?

Liberal theorists, most notably John Rawls and Robert Dahl, have discussed these issues principally in the context of political democracy. The primary constraint on democratic decision making has typically been seen as a constitutional framework that sets the boundaries of legitimacy for democratic decisions by protecting the rights or basic liberties of individuals and by specifying, limiting, and balancing the powers of government. Even in this political context, however, the issue of legitimate constraint on democratic decisions is not settled, and it raises significant conceptual questions. It becomes still more problematic if democracy is taken to extend to social and economic life (as I have previously argued it should be[1]). For in these contexts, there is only an informal structure of decision making, not defined by the making of laws and usually not governed by a formal constitution. Moreover, norms of economic and social justice that could possibly serve to limit the scope of democratic decisions in these areas are not usually the subject of general agreement in the way in which the norms of political and legal justice more often are. Therefore, what may be in contention is not whether the demands of social justice should override democratic process, but rather what exactly the demands of social justice are.

In contemporary political theory, we can observe that in the main there have been two relatively separate conversations: one about justice and one about democracy. On the one hand, there has been an extended philosophical discussion about theories of justice that makes passing reference to democracy and its place within such theories. On the other hand, there has been major renewed interest in democratic theory, but often without explicit reflection on the relation of democracy to justice.[2] There has, of course, been recognition of the relation between these two concepts in traditional theories of political democracy and in their contemporary versions. Thus, the protection of individual rights as a requirement of justice and the protection of minority rights against the potential injustices of majority rule are seen to be essential constraints on democratic decision making, constraints embodied in a constitutional framework and in the process of judicial review. Likewise, it is recognized that democratic procedures may eventuate in unjust laws despite these constitutional protections, because of the limitations of human knowledge and judgments and because of conflicts of interest between majorities and minorities. Nonetheless, it is often argued that there is an obligation to obey even unjust laws if they are duly instituted, in the interest of preserving social stability and out of respect for the abiding institutions of democracy.

Another conceptual difficulty or hard question arises here: While different theories of justice have grounded individual liberties and rights in various ways, it has remained less than clear whether the introduction of constitutional guarantees by a democratic or consensual procedure is what legitimates these rights, in which case they would be grounded in the

---

[1] Carol C. Gould, *Rethinking Democracy: Freedom and Social Cooperation in Politics, Economy, and Society* (Cambridge: Cambridge University Press, 1988), Chapters 1, 4, and 9.

[2] There are of course exceptions – for example, the book by Ian Shapiro, *Democratic Justice* (New Haven, CT: Yale University Press, 1999).

value of democracy; or whether these rights have a normative claim that is independent of, or external to, such procedures. That is, are such rights constituted as rights by their democratic or consensual recognition, or is the imperative to institute them based on their prior and autonomous status as rights? In other terms, are such rights procedural or substantive? This question is further complicated by the fact that several theories of justice have themselves framed the principles of justice in terms of some consensus (e.g., Rawls, Habermas), which may seem to put these principles themselves in the context of a quasi-democratic decision procedure. If that is the case, then rights entailed by or derived from these principles of justice might themselves ultimately be social constructs internal to, or constituted by, a democratic or quasi-democratic process and thus not independent of such procedures. It would not be clear, then, why the results of one democratic procedure would have the normative authority to constrain another.

This question, like the previous one, is what I have characterized as a hard question – namely, one that presents a conceptual bind or else a conflict between two equally justified values, a conflict that appears to be difficult or impossible to resolve. In this work, where I am concerned to analyze the relation between democracy and human rights, it is especially important to consider how democratic decision making is related to a framework of rights, not only as a set of rights pertaining to citizens within a given state but also to human rights more generally. In the second part of this chapter, I delineate a view that gives these rights a fundamental role, and indeed a stronger one, I think, than in the alternative conceptions I consider in the first part. I also analyze their basis in action and reciprocal modes of social interaction, and suggest an interpretation of rights that takes differences seriously.

The relation between justice and democracy remains deeply problematic and needs greater attention than it has thus far received. That is not to say that it has not been discussed at all. In fact, there are significant approaches to this question from the one side and the other, especially by Rawls from the standpoint of his theory of justice and by Dahl from the standpoint of his elaboration of his democratic theory. There is also an interesting perspective on this question in the work of Habermas in the development of his theory of communicative action, as well as in his more recent writing on law and democracy, and in the work of Joshua Cohen, Iris Young, and others. Although I discuss some of these views specifically, I analyze the theoretical alternatives principally in terms of three ideal types, which these views exemplify in varying degrees.

Concerning the relation between the norms of democracy and justice, then, some theorists (1) take the requirement for democratic decision making to follow from a conception of justice, that is, as realizing one of its basic desiderata. Others, conversely, (2) see justice as required for the sake of democracy, namely, as a set of rights necessary for the protection and viability of democratic processes. Still others (3) see the value of democracy instrumentally as the best way to achieve just outcomes, where such outcomes are understood either as (a) in conformity with standards of justice independently defined or as (b) whatever is produced by some ideal democratic or consensual procedure itself. In the latter case, I propose, democracy and justice are assimilated to each other.

In what follows, I review these theoretical alternatives as background for the articulation of my own argument concerning the relation of justice and democracy. This permits a response to the hard question concerning the respects in which the demands of justice, including, in my view, human rights themselves, can legitimately delimit democratic decision making. Hopefully it also resolves the apparent paradox in which democracy as a requirement of justice would need to be constrained in the interests of justice. Within this framework, I go on to consider the second hard question, namely, what legitimates the constitutional protection of rights and therefore the constraints on democratic processes if the authority of the constitution itself derives from a democratic process of adoption. This is what I call the "constitutional circle." Here, too, my approach sees the rights that constrain democratic processes as including not only civil and political rights within a nation-state but also the more general set of human rights that extend beyond borders. This aspect of my view, introduced here, is developed more fully in later chapters of this book.

Alternative Conceptions of the Relation of Justice and Democracy

As suggested earlier, theoretical formulations of the relation of justice and democracy can be divided into three main views. The first sees democracy as required by justice. In such an account, *justice* is taken to be the prior value from which follow democratic rights of participation in political processes or self-governance. Justice is understood here as entailing either equal liberty or equal consideration of interests. *Equal liberty* can be defined as freedom of choice protected against external interference (negative freedom) or, again, as the equal freedom of self-development (equal positive freedom). On these views, equal liberty is seen to entail certain basic rights of self-determination or self-rule. Thus the legitimation of democracy is that it is required as the expression of the equal freedom of individuals, which constitutes an essential part of the norm of justice. Rawls's early discussion of his first principle of justice in *A Theory of Justice* – that is, the principle of equal liberty – suggests an account of this sort, insofar as it requires the right to vote and to stand for elective office.[3] Dahl, in one formulation, also proposes grounding democracy in the prior value of equal personal autonomy and the equal consideration of interests.[4]

The second theoretical approach, by contrast, takes democracy to be the prior or basic value and sees civil liberties and equal rights as necessary for the preservation and viability of democracy. On such a view, even the requirements of social and economic justice are seen as means for preserving or enhancing democracy. In this type of approach, the unalienable and primary right is that of democratic self-governance itself. Dahl most often seems to favor this sort of position. Thus he speaks of "fundamental political rights as comprising all the rights necessary to the democratic process."[5] Or again he writes,

What interest, then, can be justifiably claimed to be inviolable by the democratic process, or, for that matter, any other process for making collective decisions? It seems to me highly reasonable to argue that no interest should be inviolable beyond those integral or essential to the democratic process.[6]

The third conception of the relation between justice and democracy sees democracy as the best means for arriving at just outcomes in decision making or legislation. Thus democracy is legitimated instrumentally in this view. In contrast to the first case, where equal liberty requires equal opportunities to participate in decision making independent of the outcome of the decisions, here it is the fact that democracy conduces to just legislation or to just outcomes of decision making that recommends it. Rawls presents such a view in arguing that the institutions of a constitutional democracy satisfy the principles of justice and they do so because "[i]deally, a just constitution would be a just procedure arranged to insure a just outcome."[7] Iris Young has given a different version of this view in

---

[3] John Rawls, *A Theory of Justice* (Cambridge, MA: Harvard University Press, 1971), 60.

[4] Robert Dahl, *Democracy and Its Critics* (New Haven, CT: Yale University Press, 1989), 97–105.

[5] Robert Dahl, *A Preface to Economic Democracy* (Berkeley: University of California Press, 1985), 25.

[6] Dahl, *Democracy and Its Critics*, 182.

[7] Rawls, *A Theory of Justice*, 197.

suggesting that political democracy modified by procedures of group representation offers the best prospect for arriving at just outcomes, defined in terms of social and economic justice.[8]

Within this instrumentalist view, there are two readings: On the first, the criterion for the justness of the outcomes of democratic decision making is not merely the appropriateness of the procedure itself, because even with properly democratic procedures, unjust outcomes are possible. But this means that the standard of justice is independent of the procedure. Rawls's conception of constitutional democracy in *A Theory of Justice* is of this sort. Thus he writes,

Clearly any feasible political procedure may yield an unjust outcome. In fact, there is no scheme of procedural political rules that guarantees that unjust legislation will not be enacted. In the case of a constitutional regime, or indeed of any political form, the ideal of perfect procedural justice cannot be realized. The best attainable scheme is one of imperfect procedural justice.[9]

The second reading holds that an outcome is just if it is produced by some ideal democratic decision procedure. That is, there is no appeal to any independent criterion of justice beyond what the ideal democratic procedure would yield. Iris Young has written along these lines:

A theory of communicative democracy thus claims a strong connection between democratic processes and just outcomes. Because there is no theological or socially transcendent ground for claims about justice, just norms and policies are simply those that would be arrived at by members of a polity who freely communicate with one another with the aim of reaching an understanding.[10]

Along somewhat similar lines, Joshua Cohen has introduced a conception of democracy as an ideal deliberative procedure that legitimates outcomes, but he does not define outcomes in terms of their justness.[11]

---

[8] Iris Marion Young, "Justice and Communicative Democracy," in *Radical Philosophy: Tradition, Counter-Tradition, Politics*, ed. Roger S. Gottlieb (Philadelphia: Temple University Press, 1993).

[9] Rawls, *A Theory of Justice*, 198.

[10] Young, "Justice and Communicative Democracy," 130.

[11] Joshua Cohen, "Deliberation and Democratic Legitimacy," in *The Good Polity*, eds. Alan Hamlin and Phillip Pettit (New York: Blackwell, 1989), 18–27. In a subsequent article, however, Cohen seems to draw a connection between democracy and just outcomes, insofar as deliberation aims at defining a common good, and this in turn is understood in terms of Rawls's difference principle. See Joshua Cohen, "Procedure and Substance in Deliberative Democracy," in *Democracy and Difference*, ed. Seyla Benhabib (Princeton, NJ: Princeton University Press, 1996), 106.

In this sense, Cohen does not here present an explicit conception of the relation of democracy to justice.[12]

Habermas gives an interesting perspective on this issue. In his earlier work, prior to his magnum opus *Between Facts and Norms* (discussed later), he tended to refer to democratic forms as merely a question of political organization, as a practical question of "[which] mechanisms are in each case better suited to bring about procedurally legitimate decisions and institutions."[13] This seems like a purely formal and procedural characterization of democracy, with no particular normative content. However, he also characterized "procedurally legitimate decisions and institutions" as those that "would meet with the unforced agreement of all those involved, if they could participate, as free and equal, in discursive will formation."[14] But the counterfactual condition of free and equal participation sounds very much like equal liberty as a traditional principle of justice. In these remarks, Habermas can be said to straddle the first and third conceptual alternatives and to adduce without explicit acknowledgment an external and independent normative criterion, itself not constituted as a consensual norm but instead presupposed for "procedurally legitimate decisions." A further complication is that insofar as Habermas gives an account of the genesis of norms or of "discursive will formation" in an "ideal speech situation," which constitutes a notion of justice, this seems to tacitly make an appeal to a quasi-democratic notion of consensus. By *quasi-democratic*, I mean to point to the kind of free agreement among "reasonable" people in a situation of equality that is not strictly the outcome of a voting procedure but rather one in which differences are overcome and a common view adopted or decided upon through this process of coming to agreement. But then what is essentially an ideal of democratic procedure – namely, a rational agreement among free and equal participants – itself defines the norm of justice. In such a formulation, the concepts of justice and democracy would seem to be assimilated

---

[12] In his 1996 article, Cohen argues that deliberative democracy requires the "liberties of the moderns" – for example, religious liberty and free expression – as well as the participatory "liberties of the ancients" as conditions for its requirement of citizens being able to give reasons to each other for their collective choices. This view gives central place to democracy itself or to political autonomy as the basis for rights and thus comes closer to the second model of the relation of justice and democracy discussed earlier. See Joshua Cohen, "Procedure and Substance in Deliberative Democracy," 95–119.

[13] Jürgen Habermas, *Communication and the Evolution of Society* (Boston: Beacon Press, 1979), 1–6.

[14] Ibid., 1–6.

to each other, and justice would lose its critical force against democratic decisions that we might want to say violate it.

This also holds for Rawls on a certain interpretation. Consider the following argument: According to Rawls, imperfect procedural justice presupposes an independent criterion of justice that a democratic process may fail to meet so that it is possible to arrive at an unjust outcome by democratic procedures. However, this independent criterion, namely, the principles of justice, is itself the outcome of rational consensus or, as subsequently conceived, an overlapping consensus (or again, a "reasonable overlapping consensus"). These principles are then instituted as political constraints by a founding constitution. Although this consensus is not simply a de facto one and is distinguished from a mere "modus vivendi," it nonetheless may suggest that the principles of justice themselves are constituted by a quasi-democratic procedure that gives them their authority and, in Rawls's constructive sense, their objectivity.[15] On this interpretation, then, what was supposed to be an independent criterion distinct from the democratic process that it constrains would seem to derive its own authority from a sort of democratic process.

On the other hand, the original procedure, as Rawls describes it, presupposes that the individuals in the original position are free and equal (or, in a more qualified later version, that they conceive of themselves as free and equal) and thus, in effect, that they share an equal right to participate in the setting up of the principles, as well as an equal rationality. Even if, as Rawls originally puts it, a single person could reason to the principles of justice, this would counterfactually entail that any one or more of such persons would reach the same agreement. The principles themselves therefore presuppose a procedure that embodies the very same basic liberties and rights that the principles then come to express. On such a reading, the argument on the independent criterion of justice would beg the question, inasmuch as it presupposes what it sets out to establish. Although this is not a new insight about what might be called Rawls's circle, in the particular case here it suggests that the distinction seems to vanish between a substantive external criterion of justice and a democratic process or procedure that may fail to meet it. If so, we have a situation in which the principles of justice, which are supposed to be independent of the democratic process that they constrain, derive their own authority from a quasi-democratic process of consensus formation; at the same time, the authority of the quasi-democratic process is based

---

[15] See John Rawls, *Political Liberalism* (New York: Columbia University Press, 1993), 119f.

on a tacit appeal to the very same principles of justice that emerge from it. To the degree that this in fact characterizes their arguments, both Rawls and Habermas seem to hover between a substantive justification of procedure and a procedural justification of substance.

If, instead, the independent criterion of justice tacitly appealed to in the case of imperfect procedural justice were understood as itself established by some other legitimating procedure, then we would have the constraint on one process – legislative democracy – by another prior and privileged process – the consensual formation of the principles of justice. These principles are given political authority by a founding convention that embodies them in the constitution. This constitution sets out both the forms of legislative democracy and the constraints on unjust decisions arrived at by means of such democracy; and in Rawls's early model, which closely follows the American political structure, it also introduces the process of judicial review, which is authorized to make judgments about the authority of the democratic decisions in terms of the principles of justice articulated in the constitution. In short, the independence of the criterion of justice would then not be the independence of substance over procedure but rather would be the priority of one procedure over another, namely, the procedure of consensus formation of the principles of justice over the subsequent legislative procedures of political democracy. Although this seems intuitively acceptable in the historical sense in which a constitution is taken to have priority over the outcomes of the democratic political process operating within it, such acceptance would seem to beg the question of what gives greater authority to one procedure over the other, namely, the constitutional over the legislative. That it has such authority is a matter of historical and political fact, but that is not itself a normative argument as to whether it ought to have such authority.

Yet Rawls indicates that he has provided such a normative argument in his account of reasonable and overlapping consensus and in the content of this consensus, as agreed-upon principles of justice. The normative force of Rawls's argument in his later work seems to depend in great part on the notion of reasonableness.[16] This reasonableness falls short of the normative force of claims to truth, cognitive or moral. But not only does it suffice as a political norm for Rawls, but it is also the most that a political norm should attain to in a pluralist society where mutually exclusive comprehensive doctrines, if pursued to their limit, would lead to political strife and instability. Thus far, then, this is a norm of a pragmatic

[16] Ibid., 48–66, 127–129.

sort, and in this sense it sets the limits to what the normative content of the principles of justice could reasonably be. But Rawls has sometimes claimed more for it than this. For example, he cites such apparently moral claims as that slavery is unjust or tyranny is unjust as "moral facts" from which general principles of justice can be constructed. But it is more than a little puzzling as to what their status is, or what the normative force is of calling such cases of injustice "facts." It seems to me that something more needs to be said about this. Furthermore, it certainly doesn't seem to be a procedural view about justice to take it to be a conception reasonably constructed from such facts.

Beyond this, Rawls does make the claim that the reasonable overlapping consensus is based on substantive, in the sense of comprehensive, views, and one may think that the consensus is therefore not procedural but substantive in content. Rawls sometimes seems to say just that, namely, that "the political conception is affirmed as a moral conception and citizens are ready to act from it on moral grounds."[17] But in Rawls's account, these may be, and indeed usually are, different and even mutually exclusive moral grounds. This is a somewhat peculiar appeal to substance over procedure, however, for if the alternative comprehensive views are incompatible with each other, as Rawls agrees they may well be, then as far as substantive grounds go, they cancel each other out and what remains is the consensual agreement on liberal principles of justice. These principles seem to constitute a second-level sort of political substance, a set of values endorsed by "public reason," which is at the very least compatible with the alternative comprehensive doctrines. This "secondary substance," if one may borrow the Aristotelian usage, then has a strange mode of existence, somewhere between the full-blown substance of comprehensive doctrines – moral, metaphysical, or religious – and the more shadowy status of merely procedural justice.

Robert Dahl, in his *Democracy and Its Critics*, is quite happy to reject the distinction between substantive rights and interests, on the one hand, and "merely" procedural democratic processes, on the other. In considering "the possibility that the democratic process may impair important substantive rights or other requirements of justice," he argues that "any alternative to a perfect or imperfect democratic process for making collective decisions will require some other process for making collective decisions. . . . What began as substance versus process turns out to be

---

[17] Ibid., 168.

process versus process."[18] To the question of whether there are any inviolable substantive rights or interests that should be protected by constraints on the democratic process, he says in effect that only those rights or interests that are integral to or necessary for the democratic process itself are inviolable. But they are inviolable only because were they to be violated the process would not be democratic. Thus he writes,

> It seems to me highly reasonable to argue that no interests should be inviolable beyond those integral or essential to the democratic process. A democratic people would not invade this extensive domain except by mistake and such a people might also choose to create institutional safeguards designed to keep mistakes from occurring.[19]

In short, Dahl argues that unjust outcomes of democratic process either are failures of democracy, in which case they are not the outcomes of democratic process at all, or else they are "mistakes." The latter should not be protected against by any external constraints (e.g., constitutional or judicial protections – what he calls "quasi-guardianship") but rather by "improving the operation of the democratic process: to make it more truly democratic."[20] But this might suggest to us a magical disappearing act, in which the problem of the conflict between democracy and justice seems to disappear with the wave of a wand. On such a reading, there is no conflict because if it is not just, it is not democratic by definition, in that the basic rights and liberties are simply those essential to or necessary for democracy. Democracy cannot violate them and still be democracy. To complicate matters further, there are "mistakes" in democratic decision making. In that case, it is still democracy in spite of an unjust outcome, but improvement is necessary so that the mistakes will not happen next time. The thrust of Dahl's argument here is that a democratic people will learn from its mistakes in the long run and will institute protections and improvements to safeguard the basic rights needed for democracy. He is thus highly optimistic about the prospects for the evolution of democracy as a self-correcting system.

It is clear that for Dahl, democracy as the right to self-governance is the fundamental value and that the only requirements of justice that can be held inviolable are those required by democracy itself. But even these cannot be protected by any means other than the democratic process.

---

[18] Dahl, *Democracy and Its Critics*, 176.
[19] Ibid., 182.
[20] Ibid., 174.

Thus Dahl expands the concept of democracy to include not only the so-called formal or procedural requirements but also "all the general and specific rights – moral, legal, constitutional – that are necessary to it,"[21] as well as "all the resources and institutions necessary to it,"[22] presumably including social and economic conditions. Not only does the problem of the relation of justice to democracy dissolve because all these matters are assimilated to democracy, but also there is no way to protect any rights apart from the procedures of majoritarian democracy itself. This is indeed a design for radical democracy, dependent on the judgment and good will of majorities.

A similar problem emerges in some accounts of the relation between justice and democracy that are influenced by Habermas's model of communicative action and discursive ethics. I have already noted Iris Young's claim to the effect that justice is whatever an ideally democratic body decides after due discussion. She has argued that there is no independent criterion of justice apart from such a decision procedure, but in effect this would mean that there can be no appeal against the injustice of any decision, since "injustice" would remain undefined here. What we have in this case is what Rawls has called pure procedural justice. In her more recent book *Inclusion and Democracy*, Young analogously claims that "[w]hat counts as a just result is what participants would arrive at under ideal conditions of inclusion, equality, reasonableness, and publicity."[23] At other points in that work, however, she suggests that justice can be defined in a more independent way in terms of "the institutional conditions for self-development and self-determination of a society's members."[24]

In the more purely deliberative or procedural view that Young seems most inclined to, the justness of outcomes in a deliberative decision procedure derives in large part from the proper constitution of the *demos* – the body politic. To achieve such an adequately democratic body, she has proposed including in the political process a sort of compensatory representation of groups that have been previously discriminated against. Like Dahl, Young here appears to build the normative principles of justice – namely, the basic liberties and rights, as well as fair decision

---

[21] Ibid., 175.

[22] Ibid., 175.

[23] Iris Marion Young, *Inclusion and Democracy* (Oxford: Oxford University Press, 2000), 31. Or again, "The theory says that justice is nothing other than what the members of an inclusive public of equal and reasonable citizens would agree to under these ideal circumstances" (33).

[24] Ibid., 33.

procedures – into both the character of the decision-making body and its deliberative or communicative procedure. And this presumptively guarantees that the outcomes are just. In effect, the justice in the consequent is already contained in the antecedent of this political proposition, so that the just outcome follows analytically, so to speak.[25] But suppose one were to object to a particular decision of such an ideal democratic body that it is unjust. This would seem to be meaningless, inasmuch as there could be no appeal beyond the correctly constituted and functioning procedure.

We can generalize this difficulty, inasmuch as it seems to apply to Habermas's own earlier discourse theory, on a certain interpretation. As suggested, the preconditions for coming to an agreement about norms or generalizable interests by means of discourse or argumentation include the reciprocal recognition by the participants of their equal roles and of their equal freedom to enter into the discussion. But this again builds norms of justice into the very discursive activity that generates and validates the norms. If so, it would not be surprising that the norms of a communicative ethics or of justice that emerge from this procedure should be precisely the norms that characterize the procedure in the first place. On such a reading, what we have here would seem to be a circle.

Habermas's intention, at least in his earlier theory, was in fact to find some ground in human practices for the emergence of moral norms. Yet he does not want to presuppose what these norms themselves would be substantively but rather wants to consider what would motivate the process of arriving at some consensus on "generalizable interests" in order to coordinate actions. In earlier work, he had sought what he called "quasi-transcendental" grounds for various norms in characteristic modes of human action and interaction. Subsequently, his main focus has been on norms implicit in discursive or linguistic practices and in particular what he calls "communicative action," which is the domain in which moral norms emerge. The aim of this sort of action, according to Habermas, is that of reaching an understanding or coming to agreement about what ought to be done.

Although a certain ambiguity has been noted between the weaker sense of "understanding" as grammatical or linguistic comprehension of an utterance and a stronger sense of a common understanding that reaches agreement, Habermas's notion of communication or of "communicative

---

[25] Young discusses the circularity between justice and democracy in the deliberative view in her *Inclusion and Democracy*, 34–36, but she does not address the theoretical problem here directly.

competence" signifies an ability to arrive at a rational consensus by means of argument in an ideal speech situation. This is an ideal-normative model of a procedure, in which norms are considered, validated, and agreed to solely by the force of the better argument. In short, it is a model of discursive practice, or of moral practice interpreted in terms of discourse – specifically, a conversation or dialogue – as a way of arriving at norms for social action or dealings with others. Therefore, the justness of the actions or dealings thus undertaken derives from the way in which they were agreed to and from the acknowledgment of the universality of the principles governing them, and not from conformity to any extrinsic rights or entitlements. Instead, such normative claims to equality, or to freedom or autonomy, or respect, are all built into the preconditions of the discourse – for example, that any speaker is free to enter into the discussion and is not to be hindered by compulsion, that speakers take up reciprocal dialogue roles, and so on.

While Habermas did not originally present this discursive practice or dialogue about norms as a model of democracy, it clearly has analogies to such a model, for example, in his formulation that all who are affected by the consequences of adopting a norm should be able to participate in the argument about it and should find it acceptable; and his views have been interpreted in these terms by others. Somewhat analogous models of deliberative democracy have been developed by others, including Joshua Cohen, Iris Young, and Seyla Benhabib. Yet, when interpreted as accounts of democratic practice, deliberative or discursive models can sometimes have an air of unreality about them. This occurs insofar as they give central place to the requirement for consensus, which would seem to be too stringent for the practical business of reaching political decisions, at least in anything larger than a Quaker meeting.[26] This stringency consists primarily in its requirement of full agreement, which not only is unrealistic but also can at times even be coercive in its effect on participants. In addition, because of the priority accorded to reason-giving in the course of deliberation, such an approach seems to regard democracy as something like a discussion among philosophers. Returning to Habermas's original interpretation, however – in which consensus is a fully counterfactual norm of agreement, and not an actually attainable decision point – we

---

[26] In his 1996 essay, Joshua Cohen suggests that "even an ideal deliberative procedure will not, in general, produce consensus." See "Procedure and Substance in Deliberative Democracy," 414. For a critique of reliance on consensus, see Thomas Christiano, *The Rule of the Many* (Boulder, CO: Westview Press, 1996), 19, 37ff.

can say that it nonetheless remains what I earlier characterized as quasi-democratic, as was Rawls's procedure for reasoning to the principles of justice, and this poses the various issues for us that I have presented.

Habermas's early approach looks to human action and interaction as a basis for norms and therefore seems to appeal to something beyond the mere procedure as its ground. However, the interaction turns out to be understood as itself procedural, that is, in terms of discursive modes of coming to agreement. Manifestations of reciprocity or of reciprocal recognition are taken as forms of discourse or linguistic interaction. In this context, the freedom and equality of the participants pertain only to their dialogue roles and in this way are defined relative to the procedure, and these individuals have no independently characterized status beyond this that could provide a ground for rights. The implication for social norms of such an exclusive emphasis on discursive practices is that the whole domain of nondiscursive activity that is also norm-governed plays no significant role in the understanding of freedom and equality or as a basis for rights. Such nondiscursive activities, which may involve discourse but are not themselves activities of discourse, include individual action and joint action oriented to the realization of goals, such as at work; expressive or creative activity, such as in the arts; scientific activities of discovery and invention; as well as the range of caring relations among family, friends, and citizens, and even across borders. Furthermore, the requirement for rational argumentation as definitive of communicative action in its norm-generating aspects seems a narrow account of such communication and of rationality, one that excludes emotion from its purview.[27] Moreover, such an account raises serious questions about the representation of the interests of those who are unable or unwilling to measure up to this standard. It is at this point that Habermas's approach seems most culturally relative.

I would also suggest that in its emphasis on agreement as the goal of discourse and the arriving at generalizable interests, Habermas offers too exclusively social an account of interests. This view does not leave enough room for the recognition of individual differences in contexts of social and political interaction and in the norms themselves. It seems to regard individual difference primarily as an obstacle to be overcome on the way to consensus rather than as something that is normatively significant.

---

[27] See the discussion in Chapter 3. A related point is made in Young, *Inclusion and Democracy*, 39.

In his more recent work on law and democracy, Habermas sharply distinguishes between the domain of morality, on the one hand, and that of law and democracy, on the other, discussing justice in connection with the first of these. He regards the principle of discourse as underlying both of them, such that both moral principles and democratic procedures can in a sense be regarded as specifications of that more general and more abstract "discourse-theoretic" perspective. The discourse principle is a so-called freestanding principle of "communicative reason" that lays out the requirement of "procedural rationality" or that "explains the point of view from which norms of action can be impartially justified."[28] Habermas states the principle as follows: "D: Just those action norms are valid to which all possibly affected persons could agree as participants in rational discourses."[29] Although this still seems to have a democratic resonance, it is no longer possible to regard it as a democratic principle (which is instead one specification of it). Hence, any assimilation or interdefinition of justice and democracy is ruled out. Furthermore, Habermas now holds that moral principles, although they rightly can have an effect on the domain of politics, are not the foundation of the legal nor of the political, where the latter is also to be understood as legally constituted. On his view, law and politics, although susceptible of being organized normatively in terms of democracy and a set of rights, are taken to constitute a separate domain from that of morality.

The import for us primarily concerns Habermas's development of the conceptions of democracy and the fundamental civil liberties and political rights of citizens, which he refers to as human rights. Since rights, on his view, emerge in a domain of law rather than morality, they are not to be understood in the sense given to them by the traditions of natural law or natural rights. Human rights do not have a claim on us prior to the institution of such a legal domain. Instead, the classic rights of life, liberty, and property, as Habermas refers to them, are to be understood as coming into being along with the idea of popular sovereignty itself, but not simply as requirements for it. As he suggestively puts it, the ideas of personal autonomy and public autonomy are posited together and mutually presuppose each other.

In this conception, democracy arises as a procedure for a legally constituted political domain of citizens. According to Habermas, "the

---

[28] Jürgen Habermas, *Between Facts and Norms* (Cambridge, MA: The MIT Press, 1996), 108–109.

[29] Ibid., 107.

principle of democracy should establish a procedure of legitimate law-making. Specifically, the democratic principle states that only those statutes may claim legitimacy that can meet with the assent (*Zustimmung*) of all citizens in a discursive process of legislation that in turn has been legally constituted."[30] It cannot be said to pertain to extralegal relations, in, say, economic or social life, nor does it even rightly characterize all of politics, which consists of administrative power as well. Extralegal social life, while not itself susceptible of democratic organization, contributes to a public sphere in which the multifarious associations of civil society can generate ideas and opinions that influence political representatives, as they do to a degree at present.

Thus, for Habermas, democracy itself arises when the discourse principle is given a legally institutionalized form, and this in turn can be seen as a "logical genesis of rights," as he puts it, where rights themselves arise in this sphere of law. He further explains that such rights result from "applying the discourse principle to the general right to liberties – a right constitutive of the legal form as such – and ends by legally institutionalizing the conditions for a discursive exercise of political autonomy."[31] Or again, "This system [of rights] should contain precisely the rights citizens must confer on one another if they want to legitimately regulate their interactions and life contexts by means of positive law."[32] Note, then, that, for Habermas, private and public autonomy are brought into reciprocal relation within this domain of law.

But there remain some questions that we can ask about Habermas's newer approach. It is not clear whether the changes he has introduced eliminate the circularity described earlier that seems to lie at the heart of discursive proceduralism, or instead whether separating an abstract discourse principle from both morality and legality simply reduplicates it in both domains. Whereas, originally, conceptions of freedom and equality of participants, presumably already normative in some sense, are presupposed in the discursive genesis of norms for action, we find a similar presupposition in the spheres of law and democracy. The question is, what is the basis for attributing this freedom and equality to participants? Why, in turn, does it apply to all members? Habermas aims for a "subjectless," "postmetaphysical," and fully intersubjective justificatory point of view, and he eschews any natural foundation for rights, which would

---

[30] Ibid., 110.
[31] Ibid., 121.
[32] Ibid., 122.

presumably also bar appeals to the nature of human action itself. In that case, though, it is not yet clear what the basis is for the human rights that "must be presupposed."

Habermas further indicates that these human rights extend to citizens or members of a polity, thereby contravening the original idea of "the rights of man." Despite other criticisms we might want to make of this latter idea, the notion that human rights are claims that people can make on each other independent of their nation-state is lost in his account (although he would insist on certain moral claims that people can make in this more general social context). As we have seen, because of the relatively sharp separation that he makes between morality and legality, rights – including human rights – now distinguished from justice, can apply only in the domain of legality and institutions. It thus remains unclear on his view how human rights can be completely general and universal, which many have appealed to as the source of their strength. The implication, instead, is that their extension beyond given nation-states is based not in any universality that they entail but only through international agreements that would newly constitutionalize them on such a global level.

Moreover, these human rights remain narrowly defined in Habermas's account. As noted, they center on rights of life, liberty, and property for citizens and extend to political rights of participation. But "basic rights to the provision of living conditions" are required only contingently, that is, "insofar as current circumstances make this necessary if citizens are to have equal opportunities to utilize" their basic civil rights.[33] This would seem to leave the economic, social, and cultural rights in present declarations of human rights in a somewhat precarious theoretical position.

Habermas's account of democracy is also problematic from my standpoint in its restriction in principle to only a part (although an important part) of the political domain; it is of necessity legally constituted. The sense in which democratic decision making can apply to institutions in social and economic life, as well as the sense in which democratic modes of decision can be informally applicable in our daily lives, is blocked in his account. Rather, his conception of democracy remains tied exclusively to the recognizable and familiar forms of legislation and political representation, although he proposes that these need to be more genuinely implemented and rendered fully legitimate, especially in regard to becoming more open to rational considerations. Finally, we can question

[33] Ibid., 123.

whether democracy should be understood wholly procedurally as in his account, where it is taken as a specification of the more general procedural requirements of a discursive conception of communicative reason, or whether it needs to be given a more substantive interpretation as well. This question, along with the central ones concerning the relation of democracy to justice and to human rights, is considered in the next part of this chapter.

More generally, we have observed how, emphasizing the fact that democracy as the form of self-governance always involves discussion, deliberation, or communication among the participants in this self-governance, deliberative theorists of democracy have focused on the discursive element and have tended to downplay the element of joint decision making and of the self-governance that it enables. However, while free and equal participation in public discourse in an ideal model may well help to shape public opinion (although in practice public opinion is often shaped by other means), public opinion by itself does not govern. Since governance in a democracy is self-government by means of participation and representation in contexts of decision making, an important issue that remains to be addressed is how to make these forms themselves more fully democratic.

The Requirements of Justice and the Limitation of Democracy

Our review of the approaches to conceiving the relation of justice and democracy shows them to be, in the main, procedural. I have suggested that they do not provide an independent basis for the existence of human rights of individuals that a strong conception of justice would demand. In the remainder of this chapter and in other parts of this work, I want to argue for a conception of democracy that allows for a more secure basis for human rights than is provided by discourse theory, deliberative democracy, or Rawlsian theory. Furthermore, as will be evident, even though the conception of democracy here values deliberation, it sees it as part of a democratic process and not as norm-constituting nor as the source of justice, but rather as subject to human rights themselves. Later sections of the book, particularly Part III, which concerns the globalization of democracy, go on to consider some of the other complex interrelations between these ideas of democracy and human rights.

In the views analyzed in the first part of this chapter, then, rights are seen largely as being authorized by one or another procedure; or they are presupposed as necessary for discursive or democratic procedures, or by appeal to our particular moral or social intuitions. But if we grant that a democratic procedure, however justified, may still arrive at an unjust outcome, then there must be some independent criterion of justice, the appeal to which cannot be, circularly, to a democratic or quasi-democratic procedure in turn. Instead, it must be grounded in some substantive features of human practice or of human existence if it is to have the normative force required. This then proposes a quasi-foundational although nonessentialistic approach to the grounding of rights, liberties, and entitlements, and this is what I have developed in my previous work.[34] I have designated this approach social ontology.[35] The reason I call it quasi-foundationalist is that it is distinguished from traditional foundationalisms, which appeal to some systematic metaphysical grounds and are essentialistic in their commitment to natural kinds. By contrast, a social ontology makes no appeal to a transempirical or transcendental moral reality but rather is based on what I believe to be experientially or phenomenologically well-evidenced features of the action and interaction of human beings. Moreover, this is a regional ontology, which does not make claims about the nature of being or reality as such but rather addresses itself exclusively to the domain of individuals in their social relations. Furthermore, my suggestion is that every social and political theory has an ontological commitment of this sort, whether recognized or not.

The claim here, then, is that rights involve the recognition of features of human action and interaction and that therefore an argument for or a justification of such rights can be made on these grounds. Thus it is not based simply on what people like us would agree to nor on an appeal to our moral intuitions. Such an approach does not, however, deny that procedures themselves are necessary and normatively justified in giving rights an institutional existence, as I discuss later in connection with the constitutional circle.

Here I want to bring in the normative framework that I developed in *Rethinking Democracy* insofar as it relates to the specific issues discussed in this chapter. This framework also serves as a basis for subsequent arguments in this book, which, however, will expand that construction in novel ways, particularly in integrating in it conceptions of "concrete universality," care, empathy, and solidarity. As elaborated in the earlier work,

---

[34] Gould, *Rethinking Democracy*, and *Marx's Social Ontology: Individuality and Community in Marx's Theory of Social Reality* (Cambridge, MA: The MIT Press, 1978).

[35] "Social ontology" is a term I coined nearly thirty years ago in a series of lectures at the C.U.N.Y. Graduate Center titled "Marx's Social Ontology," March 1975.

the common root or the common foundation that normatively grounds the conceptions of both justice and democracy is freedom, understood as the criterial or distinguishing feature of human action. *Freedom* has a complex sense here: It is, on the one hand, a bare capacity for choice among alternatives; on the other, it is the exercise of this capacity – individually or together with others – in the realization of long-term projects and the development of abilities. In this sense, freedom is an activity of self-development or self-transformation as a process over time, and I interpret this as the characteristic mode of human agency or life activity.

Although it is necessarily the self-development of individuals, which I take to be the ontologically primary entities in social life, this transformative process both requires social interaction and is often expressed in common or joint activities oriented toward shared goals. Thus these individuals are to be understood ontologically as individuals-in-relations or as social individuals. In this view, the characteristic mode of being of these individuals, that is, their activity, essentially involves their relations with others. Individuals are who they are, or become who they are, through such social relations, and in this sense these relations can be said to constitute them as being who they are. However, this does not mean that individuals are wholly constituted by their relations. As agents, they choose and can also transform many of these relations, either individually or jointly with others, and they can be said to have a capacity for purposeful activity that is not a function of these relations. Furthermore, as concretely existing beings who are the bearers of their relational properties, they cannot be reduced to their relations, which, moreover, do not exist independently of the individuals who have them. In earlier work, I have suggested how such a social ontology avoids the defects of one-sided views that emphasize either agreements among externally related individuals or else holistic accounts of society as determinative of individuals within it. This approach thus attempts to integrate an account of free individuality with one that recognizes the central role of sociality in self-development and in the account of rights and democracy.

Central to this approach is the observation that self-transforming activity requires not only the making of choices but also the availability of the means or access to the conditions necessary for making these choices effective. Thus the freedom of individuals to develop, as what has been called positive freedom, requires access to the material and social conditions of such activity. Among the material conditions are means of subsistence and the means for carrying out the activities, and among the social ones are freedom from domination and, correlatively, reciprocal recognition by the agents of each other's freedom. However, since free choice is necessary for self-developing activity, so-called negative freedom, or the absence of constraint on people's choices, is also normatively required. Furthermore, the exercise of this capacity for choice carries with it a normative imperative in that it is the activity by which we confer value on the objects of our choice and by which we reflexively acknowledge the value of the activity of choosing.[36] But the full realization of the bare capacity for choice lies in the process of self-development, which is thus posited as a normative requirement in the act of choice itself.

There is another step to the argument here that takes us to the conception of justice: Since freedom as agency or the capacity for choice characterizes all human beings as human and since the exercise of this agency in self-development is a normative imperative, and furthermore, since this exercise requires conditions, I argue that there is an equal and valid claim – that is to say, a *right* – to the conditions of self-development on the part of each human being. (The argument here thus follows Feinberg's characterization of 'rights' as valid claims.[37]) On this view, to recognize others as human beings is in the first place to acknowledge their agency (whether individual or joint) and, correlatively, to recognize that this capacity remains abstract and empty unless it is exercised in concrete cases; and furthermore, that this exercise requires conditions, both material and social, if it is to be realized as self-transforming activity. The validity of the claim to the exercise of this capacity and to its conditions and therefore its status as a right is thus ingredient in our recognition of the other as human. I call this principle of equal rights to the conditions of self-development *equal positive freedom* and take it to be the principle of *justice*. This is of course a telescoped version of the argument developed in the earlier book,[38] but it serves to introduce the essential connection between justice and democracy.

I argue that the principle of justice thus conceived as a (prima facie[39]) equal right to the conditions of self-development requires *democracy* as the

---

[36] For this argument, see Gould, *Rethinking Democracy*, especially 129–130.

[37] See, for example, Joel Feinberg, "The Nature and Value of Rights," *The Journal of Value Inquiry*, Vol. 4 (Winter 1970), reprinted in *Rights*, ed. David Lyons (Belmont, CA: Wadsworth, 1979), 78–91, and the discussion in Gould, *Rethinking Democracy*, 62–66.

[38] For fuller development of this argument, see Gould, *Rethinking Democracy*, 60–71.

[39] Equal rights are qualified as prima facie inasmuch as there are other principles that potentially conflict with them and may qualify them in certain ways. See Gould, *Rethinking Democracy*, 66, 153–156, 166–170, and 190–214.

equal right to participate in decision making concerning the common activities in which individuals are engaged. For engaging in such common activities involving shared goals is itself one of the main conditions for individuals' self-development, the opportunity for which requires that they be self-determining in this activity. If, instead, an individual's actions were determined by others in such contexts, it would not be an exercise of the agency that is required for self-transformation. However, since such common or joint activity necessarily involves acting with other individuals, the exercise of individuals' agency in this context must take the form of codetermination of the activity, that is, rights to participate in decision making about it.

Although such democratic decision making characteristically involves procedures of majority vote, it need not be defined so narrowly but may encompass other forms of deliberation and decision and a range of procedures that allow for equal participation by those engaged in common activities. Such an open concept of democracy is particularly important in order for us to avoid a cultural bias restricting it to the most familiar Western forms of representative democracy.

One obvious alternative case here is consensus or near-consensus decision making, found in many traditional African communities and in indigenous populations in the Americas and elsewhere, as well as in dissident movements today within larger liberal democracies. In these diverse cases, democracy is often direct and, although it sometimes involves representation, is neither electoral nor majoritarian. For example, among the Bugandans in Uganda, the Zulu in South Africa, and the Akans in Ghana, participation at lower levels may be combined with representatives at a council level, who consult with community members to solicit their views on the issues under discussion; these representatives then strive for consensus within the council on what is to be done, a consensus that often involves compromise by all concerned.[40] Similarly, the autonomous communities characteristic of many indigenous peoples of the Americas, in which they exercise control over their own affairs, whether political, economic, or cultural, can exemplify democracy in the crucial sense of codetermination of joint activity. Such communities would need to adopt an inclusive understanding that grants full rights of participation to its members – an understanding that in some cases appears rooted in past indigenous practices. Among the examples offered

[40] Kwasi Wiredu, "Society and Democracy in Africa," *New Political Science*, Vol. 21, no. 1 (1999): 33–44.

of inclusive autonomous communities are the Aymara, with its ayllu system of government, developed before the Inca and Spanish conquests in
what is presently Bolivia, and currently undergoing a resurgence;[41] and
the Haudenosaunee, or the Iroquois Confederacy, with its own democratic model and its Great Law of Peace, pre-dating the period of colo-
nization.[42] On the grounds of this concept of democracy, it also follows
that such autonomous communities have a right to be free from domination or control by outside communities or states. Needless to say, such
inclusive autonomous communities are an ideal, probably nowhere fully
realized in practice today; yet it must be granted that they are not necessarily more elusive than are fully representative liberal nation-states,
which accord with the dominant Western model of democracy.

Alongside its openness to diverse cultural forms, then, the conception
of democracy advanced here remains normatively quite demanding, in
taking democracy to require equal rights of deliberation and participation and, optimally, equally effective rights rather than purely nominal
ones.[43] In addition, such a view of democracy does not imply that the
particular procedures chosen are indifferent. Clearly, some procedures
may be more suited to realizing the equal participative rights than others,
in both familiar national contexts and the newer global ones. In Part III,
I consider some of the transformations in the conception of democracy
required for crossborder and global associations, and I analyze how to
incorporate within it the idea of democratic input into decisions by people who may not be members of a given institution or political society
(and thus may not have fully equal rights of participation) but who may
be crucially affected by its decisions.

In the philosophical construction advanced here, we have seen that
the principle of democracy is derived from the principle of justice, understood as prima facie equal rights to the conditions of self-development,
where it is taken to apply to common or joint activities. This principle
of justice is ultimately based on the primacy of freedom as a value and,

---

[41] Taller de Historia Oral Andima, *Ayllu: Pasado y Futuro de los Pueblos Originarios* (La
Paz: Aruwiyiri, 1995), and Silvia Rivera, "Liberal Democracy and *Ayllu* Democracy in
Bolivia: The Case of Northern Potosí," *Journal of Development Studies*, Vol. 26, no. 4
(1990): 97–121. The work of Maria Eugenia Choque, former director of the Taller
de Historia Oral Andina (Workshop of Andean Oral History), is summarized at
http://www.ashoka.org/fellows/viewprofile1.cfm?PersonId=134.

[42] See John Mohawk, "The Great Law of Peace," as cited in *Communitarianism: A New Public
Ethics*, ed. Markate Daly (Belmont, CA: Wadsworth, 1994), 165–178.

[43] See also C. B. Macpherson, *Democratic Theory: Essays in Retrieval* (Oxford: Oxford University Press, 1973), especially Chapter 3.

specifically, on the equal freedom of each agent.[44] Understood in this way, justice therefore has normative priority over the requirement of democracy. In this sense, justice may legitimately constrain the democratic process when it leads to outcomes that violate the equal freedom of individuals. It is clear, then, that this account falls under the first model of the relation of justice and democracy sketched earlier, namely, the model that takes democracy to be required by justice.

The particular theory of positive freedom and justice delineated here gives rise to a conception of certain rights that need to be recognized as *human rights* – that is, as rights that people possess simply by virtue of being human and, therefore, equally and universally. These are the valid claims, which all individuals make on all others, to the conditions necessary for freedom, understood as self-development or self-transformation. What perhaps needs to be made clear here is that this conception of rights does not reduce to some atomistic distribution of rights to individuals considered as isolates – a charge sometimes brought against rights conceptions in general.[45] Human rights are always rights of individuals, based on their valid claims to conditions for their activity, but individuals bear these rights only in relation to other individuals and to social institutions. Right is in this sense an intrinsically relational concept. Furthermore, although these rights are in principle claims by each on all the others, yet since most of these rights cannot be satisfied by each human being acting separately, and since the conditions for the self-transformation of any individual are most often social ones that can be met only by a community or society, then it can be said that individuals hold these rights against society in general. Later in this work, I consider the question of the scope and implementation of these rights in the more applied contemporary contexts of globalization.

---

44 This suggests also that it is a mistake to separate freedom from equality in the justification of democracy, as Christiano does, and to derive it from only one of these, specifically in his case "equal considerations of interests" and the related equality of resources. In fact, I would argue that his own account tacitly appeals to a conception of freedom in his claim that a collective decision-making procedure is "what makes the pursuit of private aims in a just environment possible" (*The Rule of the Many,* 79). Likewise, his idea of equality of resources (including in politics) – in a way somewhat analogous to the conception of equal positive freedom as equal rights to the conditions of freedom that I have introduced – takes these resources "as tools, instruments, or means for pursuing our aims" (63).

45 See the discussion of this issue in Mary Ann Glendon, *Rights Talk: The Impoverishment of Political Discourse* (New York: The Free Press, 1991), which is oriented primarily to the context of American discourse about rights.

One can distinguish among human rights between rights to the conditions that are minimally necessary for any human action whatever – these can be referred to as *basic* rights – and rights to those conditions that are required for the free and self-developing activity beyond this minimum; these we can call *nonbasic* rights. Thus, for example, life and liberty are basic rights, whereas high levels of education or training may be nonbasic, although they may well still be human rights. Human rights generally, as the expression of equal freedom, should not be violated by any democratic procedure, and serve to specify the constraints on democracy. We can say that they constitute rights against majorities in contrast to the majority rights inherent in democratic decision making.

It might appear from this that the authority of democratic decision making is so delimited by such constraints that it makes democracy a marginal thing indeed. For if the latitude of choice is so narrow because of the prescriptions set by human rights, it would seem that democratic decision procedures, properly exercised, would be primarily a ratification of what is normatively predetermined. Likewise, if democratic decisions are overturned by the courts to protect these rights when they are constitutionally guaranteed, then the democratic process would again seem to be an exercise in freedom of choice only when it is "correct." Yet if democracy, as the right to participate in decision making, is required by justice and in fact constitutes one of the human rights, then it cannot be so reduced as to become trivial.

One might try to answer this claim, about the marginalization of the freedom of democratic choice by constraints in the name of justice, in two ways. The response requires the introduction of the distinction between formal and substantive democracy. The first part of the argument might go something like this: *Formal* democracy – namely, the actual procedures of democratic decision making and the act of participation – remains unaffected when a particular outcome of this decision procedure is overridden by the courts in the interests of justice. For example, when the U.S. Supreme Court declares a piece of legislation unconstitutional, it does not thereby delimit Congress's formal power to make laws. But it delimits those laws that are taken to be in violation of the Constitution. Formal democracy, then – for example, civil liberties and political rights – is not subject to constraint.

One may object to this that if many or most decisions came to be knocked down in this way, this formal freedom would tend to be a quite empty exercise. In answer to this objection, the counterargument might be that the exercise of democracy deserves to remain empty when its outcome is such that it violates the very rights and liberties for the sake of which democracy itself has been instituted. For if democracy is a requirement of justice, its outcomes cannot be permitted to undercut its own foundation.

But this second part of the argument now makes appeal to what one may call a conception of *substantive* democracy. This refers to the practice of democracy as an activity of self-development on the part of the participants in which agents reciprocally recognize each other's freedom and equality in the process of making collective decisions. A democratic decision that violates these very conditions in effect is inconsistent with democracy itself in this sense and undermines it. For the function and justification of democracy as we have seen are that it serves freedom, understood as self-development. Hence, democracy cannot in principle undermine its own function with any normative justification. Therefore, the constraints that arise from the demands of justice do not delimit democracy in this substantive sense.

Between the danger of the marginalization of democracy by overzealous judicial constraints and the danger of democratic abuse of the freedom of decision making to violate the rights of certain individuals or groups, there is a fine line of good judgment, a balancing act, for which the principles of justice and constitutional protections of rights and liberties can only be a guide. For there is nothing either in the formal procedures of democracy or in the substantive constraints of a constitutional framework and judicial review that will guarantee that the outcomes of democratic practice will be just.

The Constitutional Circle

We can now consider how this analysis of the relation of justice and democracy bears on the second hard question raised at the outset, which I have called the constitutional circle. This concerns the justification of the constitutional guarantees of rights that delimit or constrain democratic decisions. The process by means of which these constitutional guarantees are to be instituted is some kind of constitutional convention or an equivalent decision procedure. Short of the authoritarian or dictatorial determination of these guarantees by fiat on the part of a ruler, the constitution-making decision must itself involve some democratic or consensual procedure. But if these rights are instituted to limit or to constrain any democratic decision that would violate them – that is, if these rights have normative priority over the democratic process itself – then the question arises as to whether there are also rights that limit the very democratic or consensual process that determines the constitutional guarantees in the first place. Wouldn't there then have to be a prior determination of the rights that delimit the initial democratic process of constitution making, in order to introduce constitutional guarantees of rights? In short, is there an infinite regress here?

Alternatively, isn't there a circularity involved in the establishment of constitutional guarantees of rights by means of a consensual or democratic procedure that in turn itself presupposes some of the very rights to be institutionalized? For the very idea of consensus implies the free and equal status of those who entered into the agreement, and it is this freedom and equality that give the consensus its authority. Without this free and equal agreement to accept as binding what is agreed upon, the consensus has no force and is merely verbal. Thus it would seem to presuppose the very rights that it would authorize.

There would indeed be a regress if it were supposed that the rights established by the agreement were constituted as rights only in the agreement and had no prior status, and therefore that there had to be a prior authorization by a preconstitutional convention of the rights that apply to the constitution-making decision process itself. It would be circular if the rights that were instituted by the constitutional convention were the same rights that authorize the process of constitution making. The regress ends and the circularity is avoided, however, if we take the democratic or consensual determination of constitutionally guaranteed rights as a recognition of those rights that are ingredient in human action and, more specifically here, as a recognition that it is these rights that are at the basis both of the authority of the democratic or consensual procedure that sets constitutional guarantees and of the democratic structures of self-governance that the constitution itself establishes. This is not simply a presupposition of rights that are presumed to have their basis in the constitution-making process itself. For here, the constitution (or the law) is understood as articulating and formalizing what is already recognized in social life (although it also has a role in advancing or helping to promulgate such recognition).

This then is an argument for the normative priority of these rights vis-à-vis the democracy that exercises and protects them. On this view, then, these rights as valid claims exist whether or not they are explicitly recognized; and they are recognized as rights prior to their institutionalization. It is this recognition that is brought to the consensual determination of these rights as constitutional. So, for example, in a society where slavery is legal, as in ancient Rome or in the American South prior to the Civil War, the rights of the slaves to be free and to be treated as equals existed whether or not such freedom and equality were fully recognized, and these certainly were recognized as rights by those who undertook to institutionalize them and to end slavery. The alternative view would be to argue that slaves had no rights of freedom and equality until these were institutionalized and that rights therefore are brought into being by some decision procedure.

Rights and Reciprocity

What I propose here is an account of rights and of the principle of justice based on a social-ontological characterization of human action and of human beings. I have suggested that the evidence for such a claim is experiential or phenomenological; that is, it presents itself to us in the structures of everyday action and social interaction. What reveals these rights, practically speaking, is the daily and recurrent recognition by individuals of others as being like themselves, namely, as agents with claims to the conditions for their self-developing or self-transformative activity. This recognition characteristically takes place in several ways: first, in the basic reciprocity in which individuals make claims on one another to be free from harm and from constraints on their actions; and in exchange grant this same recognition of negative freedom and equality to the others; or else expect a benefit in return for benefit done. This level of instrumental or tit-for-tat reciprocity acknowledges the right of the other by virtue of an assertion of the reciprocal validity of one's own claim; that is, in asserting one's own right, one acknowledges the validity of the other's claim as a right by virtue of reciprocally recognizing it as like one's own.

Beyond this minimal reciprocity, a more socialized recognition of the other as having rights develops in the context of shared activity with others in pursuit of commonly agreed-upon ends. Where there is social agency or cooperation required in joint activity oriented toward common goals, the reciprocity is one of mutual recognition of those common rights that apply to such cooperative activity – notably, rights of participation in the determination of common goals and of the process of achieving them. When such informal modes of social interaction become more formalized and institutionalized, then these rights can come to be articulated explicitly in codes of conduct or in laws – for example, as equal rights or as voting rights. It is thus by the elaboration of such contexts of social activity, in both political and economic life, that the elements of the democratic process begin to emerge.

Third, still another context in which the recognition of rights proceeds in everyday experience is our ubiquitous personal relations with other individuals as selves, or as persons worthy of respect, and this is incipiently or explicitly a recognition of the worth or needs of the other. It expresses at the same time the worth or self-respect that we take ourselves to command as persons. This type of reciprocity among individuals goes beyond the instrumental recognition of the first type and applies to the domain of affective personal and moral life.

It can be added that these contexts of reciprocity are not presented here as a scheme of fixed stages nor as a historical account of the development of reciprocity. Still, as ingredient in action and social practices, these modes of reciprocal interaction provide a basis for the emergence of a full-fledged norm of reciprocity that supplements the norm of equal rights, where both can be seen as prerequisites for equal positive freedom. Reciprocity here is understood as an intentional relation of reciprocal recognition in which each person recognizes the other as free and self-developing.[46] In this sense, it is most obviously applicable to face-to-face relations among individuals and in direct democratic participation and deliberation. But in representative contexts as well, a tacit, if not explicit, recognition by each citizen of the other's equal rights is required in regard to political rights and liberties, such as voting, eligibility for office, and free speech.

Care and Democratic Community

In the account of forms of reciprocity, I have not included that mode of reciprocity that can be called *mutuality*, which goes beyond the recognition of the equal freedom, needs, and worth of others to an active concern with enhancing their well-being. Such mutuality is usually thought to fall outside the domain of politics and is probably not a requirement of democracy. However, the related concept of *care*, which has been discussed extensively in feminist moral and political theory, does in fact have implications for democracy and a conception of democratic community.

---

[46] Carol C. Gould, "Beyond Causality in the Social Sciences: Reciprocity as a Model of Non-Exploitative Social Relations," in *Epistemology, Methodology and the Social Sciences: Boston Studies in the Philosophy of Science*, Vol. 71, eds. R. S. Cohen and M. W. Wartofsky (Boston and Dordrecht: D. Reidel, 1983), 53–88; and Gould, *Rethinking Democracy*, 71–80.

These implications are noted here and enter in various ways later in this work.

Care – an idea originally articulated on the basis of women's experiences in the practice of mothering but clearly of more general application – encompasses a range of characteristic dispositions, such as concern for the other not out of duty, but out of empathy; attentiveness and sensitivity to the needs of others, and, more strongly, taking the others' interests as equal to or more important than one's own; attention to the growth of the other; and an orientation to the common interests of the family or of those who are close or related to one.[47] These feelings and dispositions are directed, at least initially, to particular others rather than universally, and so they tend to contrast with traditional notions of universal and impartial principles and obligations.

There is a presumption that these experiences and dispositions lend support to notions of community and to a richer conception of democracy. The question is how to interpret caring, attentiveness, and concern for common interests in the family, for the case of democracy. In one sense this seems obvious: The ways of expressing concern for others and for their needs that characterize the relation of care in intimate personal relations and in certain familial relations would seem to match a democratic community's requirement for relations of reciprocity and especially for reciprocal respect, although not all relations of care are reciprocal. Furthermore, the notion of common interests seems to be capable of extrapolation from the commonality of family feeling to a larger community or polity. In principle, at least, a shared or common interest both provides the context for democratic decision making and is elaborated in the process of deliberation that is supposed to lead to decisions. Likewise, the typical emphasis on providing for the specific needs of others associated with mothering or parenting, or with family relations more

---

[47] For a more extensive treatment, see my "Feminism and Democratic Community Revisited," in *Democratic Community: NOMOS XXXV*, eds. John Chapman and Ian Shapiro (New York: New York University Press, 1993), 396–413, and the discussion by Jane Mansbridge in "Feminism and Democratic Community" in that volume. Some sources of the feminist analysis are Carol Gilligan, *In a Different Voice* (Cambridge, MA: Harvard University Press, 1982); Nel Noddings, *Caring: A Feminine Approach to Ethics and Moral Education* (Berkeley: University of California Press, 1984); the essays in *Women and Moral Theory*, eds. Kittay and Meyers; Virginia Held, "Non-Contractual Society: A Feminist View," in *Science, Morality and Feminist Theory*, eds. M. Hanen and K. Nielsen (Calgary, Canada: University of Calgary Press, 1987); Sara Ruddick, *Maternal Thinking* (Boston: Beacon Press, 1989); and Iris M. Young, *Justice and the Politics of Difference* (Princeton, NJ: Princeton University Press, 1990).

generally, can usefully be imported into the larger democratic community in terms of a focus on meeting the differentiated needs of individuals and not simply protecting their negative liberties, as is discussed in the concluding part of this chapter. In this way, care translates into a responsiveness to the particular needs and interests of individuals or groups at the social level. It also has a political parallel in the concern for providing the economic and social means for the development of individuals and not only in refraining from impeding their choices.

A second source for modeling care theory, beyond the experience of mothering or parenting, has been relations of love or intimate personal relations more generally. Whereas mothering involves nurturance of the vulnerable child and thus in many ways is not a reciprocal relation, love relations are quintessentially reciprocal. However, to the extent that these and other personal relations such as friendship manifest mutuality, as a relation in which each individual consciously undertakes to enhance the other, they go beyond the less demanding sense of care and empathy involved in social reciprocity or the reciprocity of respect, where these are properly applicable to relations among members of a community who are neither lovers nor friends.[48] In the case of the family, characterized by common concern or common interest in the well-being of the family unit, we may also find what I have called *cooperative reciprocity*, as a relation among individuals engaged in activities toward common ends. It is therefore easy to see how the family metaphor came to be commonplace in the history of political thought, although historically it has been mostly given a patriarchal interpretation, with the king or the state as father.

Yet, the limitations on the extension of the concept of care to political or institutional contexts of democratic communities are also apparent in this account of its various models. As noted, even though the maternal or parental model includes important elements of reciprocity, parenting is in some central respects a nonreciprocal relation; by contrast, a democratic community is based (at least in principle) on reciprocal relations among equals who share authority by virtue of their equal rights to participate in decision making. Another limitation of the parental model, as of the model of love or friendship, is the particularism and exclusivity that are characteristic of such relationships. Presumably, fairness in politics requires equal rights and equal consideration of interests, independent of any particular feelings of care for given individuals. In fact, it

---

[48] Cf. Jacques Derrida, "The Politics of Friendship," *Journal of Philosophy*, Vol. LXXXV, no. 12 (1988): 632–645.

is an acknowledged violation of democratic equality to act on the basis of favoritism or special interests, or to permit personal alliances to violate standards of fairness. (Of course, the domain of politics, like those of the economy and social life, has its own modes of exclusivity and particularism, some warranted and others not; for example, citizenship itself is an exclusionary category, at least as states are now constituted. Similarly, ethnicity connotes not only belonging but also exclusion.) Yet, despite these limitations with the care model, I consider in Chapter 2 how the practice of care, along with the related feelings of empathy and solidarity, can in fact be extended in more universalistic ways.

We can summarize here the features of the care model that can usefully be generalized to the larger context of democratic communities: first, the concern for the specific individuality and differences of the other found in social reciprocity or the reciprocity of respect, which involves an empathic understanding of the perspective, feelings, and needs of the other and thus expresses a relation of care. Social relations of this sort distinguish deliberation or decision making in politics, or the workplace, from mere compliance with democratic procedures. However, reciprocal concern neither presupposes nor requires that the individuals have any personal affection for each other, only what we might call political feelings. Second, in the case of cooperative reciprocity, caring about the achievement of a shared end presumably gives rise not only to concern for each other's participation in this common activity but also to concern about their own responsibility for the joint undertaking. Third, there is the concern for the vulnerable, as a type of political and social care, that entails support of, or participation in, programs that provide for the welfare of the sick, the aged, the unemployed, and other dependent members of a community. Here, as in mothering, one of the aims of care is the elimination, where possible, of the conditions of dependence.

It is further evident that the concept of democratic community, particularly in view of the care model, goes beyond the traditional and thinner notion of democracy as simply a matter of political representation and equal voting rights. These latter are most often understood to require a mediation of individual differences or interests, that is, a fair method of adjudicating among them. Although this thinner democracy is compatible with a notion of a common interest, at least in an aggregative sense, and presupposes a minimal procedural common interest in this method of decision making itself, liberal democratic theory generally stops short of a notion of community. I have suggested instead that the very notion of equal rights of participation in shared decision making connotes a common interest in the common activity, as well as in the process of decision making about that activity.[49]

The idea of democracy, in itself, therefore presupposes community in a minimal sense, namely, that people in a democratically operating institution have a common interest in shared ends, in pursuit of which their cooperation is voluntary and not merely constrained by law or habit or effected by coercion. Such a community is constituted by the decisions of agents to engage in the determination of these ends and by free cooperation toward attaining them. But we need to maintain a distinction between a democratic community in this sense and the more organic and tradition- or culture-defined notions of community implied by Tonnies's concept of *Gemeinschaft* or by some contemporary communitarian ideas. As used here, a democratic community is also to be understood as an internally differentiated community, along individual and cultural lines, as is explicated in Chapters 4 and 5. And the complexities introduced into the ideas of both democracy and community, both by increasing globalization and by the networking it facilitates among multiple communities, are explored in Parts III and IV of this work.

Justice, Rights, and Difference

In view of this analysis of reciprocity and care, we can see that recognition of differences plays a key role in the principle of equal positive freedom and in the correlate account of rights. Whereas classic liberal theory was for the most part difference-blind in that principles of equal rights mandate a sameness of treatment, the principle of equal positive freedom as a principle of justice builds a recognition of difference and responsiveness to individuated needs, as well as the protection of the rights of difference, into its basic conception.[50] Thus, if there are to be equal rights to the conditions of self-development, justice requires not the *same* conditions for each one but instead *equivalent* ones determined by diverse needs. Thus, instead of merely adding a conception of nonstandard interests – for example, of the vulnerable – to the standard interests that the liberal theory of justice acknowledges, this principle introduces differentiation into the basic requirement of just treatment.

---

[49] For a further discussion of common interests, see Carol C. Gould, "On the Conception of the Common Interest: Between Procedure and Substance," in *Hermeneutics and Critical Theory in Ethics and Politics*, ed. Michael Kelly (Cambridge, MA: The MIT Press, 1990), 253–273.

[50] Gould, *Rethinking Democracy*, especially Chapters 1, 4, and 5.

Needless to say, this principle of justice as equal positive freedom presents a number of difficulties in its application: First is the necessity of a criterion of relevant versus irrelevant differences; not every need has an equal claim in the context of self-development. Second, at the policy level, it is difficult to make or implement policy that is radically individuated. Practically speaking, people often have to be treated in terms of their group characteristics. Still, as a regulative principle, such a conception of justice leads to efforts to accommodate differences both in distributive contexts and at the level of rights. Its import for group rights and women's rights is elaborated in Chapters 5 and 6.

Taking difference seriously in public life requires more than a reformulated principle of justice. The suggestion here is that it requires a radical increase in opportunities for democratic participation in all contexts of common activity, including not only in the discourse and associations of the public sphere but also in the institutions of economic, social, and political life. (The especially challenging proposal for participation in decision making in firms is considered in Chapter 10.) In this range of smaller-scale contexts for participation, difference can be directly expressed by individuals or groups and concretely recognized in their social interactions. Here, difference is directly presented and not simply talked about. In these cases, too, effective action can be taken on behalf of the specific needs and interests among members. Furthermore, participation can contribute to individuals' and groups' recognition and articulation of their own concerns. A multiplicity of contexts for such participation can also facilitate the elaboration of a range of individual capacities.

The value of such a diversity of contexts and its contribution to the development of individuals was recognized by some earlier pluralist theorists of democracy and of culture, notably by John Dewey. As Dewey puts it in *The Public and Its Problems*, democracy as a way of life is "a wider and fuller idea than can be exemplified in the state even at its best. To be realized it must affect all modes of human association, the family, the school, industry, religion. And even as far as political arrangements are concerned, governmental institutions are but a mechanism for securing to an idea channels of effective operation."[51] In consonance with his view, I have proposed an interpretation of democracy that extends

---

[51] John Dewey, "The Public and Its Problems" (1927), in *The Later Works of John Dewey, 1925–1953* (Carbondale: Southern Illinois University Press, 1981–1991), 2:325, as cited in Robert B. Westbrook, *John Dewey and American Democracy* (Ithaca, NY: Cornell University Press, 1991), 319.

it beyond politics or government and beyond its role as a procedure for setting policy or settling disputes. It is also, as Dewey held, a form of social organization that permits the expression of individuality in contexts of "associated individuals, in which each by intercourse with others somehow makes the life of each more distinctive."[52] Yet the view here does not follow Dewey's linkage of democracy to metaphysics in the context of an inclusive philosophy, in which he sought a resonance between human association and nature. The view here necessarily remains agnostic on this issue.

These pragmatist emphases on democracy as a form of society and on the self-development of individuals within it are themes pursued by C. B. Macpherson – for example, in his *Democratic Theory: Essays in Retrieval*[53] – and the conception of democracy developed in my earlier work and in this book owes much to his approach. I appreciate and pursue his focus on people's activity in developing their capacities, which in turn requires equal effective access to the means for such activity.[54] Macpherson also points to the fact that the exercise of capacities has to be under an individual's conscious control and not under the direction of another.[55] This recognition supports a requirement for democratic participation, in a way that I have attempted to articulate in my own arguments for the justification of democracy.

However, Macpherson suggests that one needs a conception of essential human capacities in order to spell out what equal effective development of powers amounts to,[56] and this is not a direction I choose to take, for reasons that will be elaborated in Chapter 2, in connection with alternative conceptions of universality. In addition, Macpherson seems to build in the requirements of adequate provision of means of life and other of what we would now regard as human rights into the conception of democracy itself.[57] While this may be acceptable for the broadest use of the term "democracy" as characteristic of a form of society or, in Dewey's terms, "a way of life," I am hesitant to conflate democracy and human rights for more ordinary uses of the terms, where democracy refers to

---

[52] John Dewey, "Philosophy and Democracy" (1919), in *The Middle Works of John Dewey, 1899–1924* (Carbondale: Southern Illinois University Press, 1976–1983), 11:53, as cited in Westbrook, *Dewey and American Democracy*, 364.

[53] Macpherson, *Democratic Theory: Essays in Retrieval*, 51.

[54] Ibid., especially Chapters 1–3.

[55] Ibid., 56.

[56] Ibid., 54.

[57] See, for example, ibid., 51.

decision making concerning common activities. It is evident that effective democracy requires considerably more equal access to resources than is available at present, but to build the conception of human rights into that of democracy does not preserve the possibility of appealing to human rights where democratic decisions may violate one or another of them, as I have discussed in this chapter. The account here thus seeks to preserve a certain separation among the concepts of freedom, human rights, and democracy, yet holds that democratic participation is based on a fundamental conception of positive freedom and on the equal claims people can make to it and to the conditions that make it realizable.

To summarize the thrust of this chapter, then: After considering leading theories of the relation of justice and democracy, I argue for the priority of justice and human rights in principle over the authority of democratic decisions. Yet, inasmuch as the argument for democracy is based on the requirements of justice as equal freedom, itself one of the human rights, it follows that interventions on behalf of justice should be carefully delimited, and specifically to cases where fundamental rights have been violated. Rights in turn are understood in a relational context and are tied to conceptions of reciprocity evident in interaction. An account of care and attention to differentiated needs concludes the account.

In Chapter 2, I take up this concept of needs in connection with the idea of an embodied politics and elaborate the idea of a pluralization of both democracy and rights. But first, I want to turn to the important theoretical issue of how to conceive of the universality of the normative perspective introduced, especially in the face of the diversity of cultural practices and norms. I am also concerned to develop a new conception of universality in this context, drawing in part on the ideas of care as well as empathy and solidarity.

2

Two Concepts of Universality and the Problem of Cultural Relativism

In Chapter 1, I sketched a conception of democratic participation framed by human rights, deriving from a fundamental notion of equal positive freedom. I pointed there to the need to see democracy and human rights themselves as open to multiple interpretations from diverse cultural perspectives, but I suggested as well that the conceptions of equal freedom and human rights have universalistic aspects. The potential conflict between such universalist norms and the multiplicity of varying and sometimes conflicting cultural traditions and practices has generated considerable discussion among philosophers in recent years. It is of course desirable to avoid a relativism of fundamental norms to cultures, but it is also important to see these values as drawing strength not only from our own but also from other, sometimes quite different, people, cultures, and traditions. In this chapter, I analyze the idea of universality that is ingredient in the conception of equal freedom and human rights and consider two of its possible meanings.

Universalist norms have recently been appealed to in order to come to grips with the existence of cultural practices that violate human rights or that oppress women or minorities, or again, in order to deal with the problems of persistent poverty and disregard of basic needs in less developed countries. Several philosophers have argued that we have to return to a fundamental conception of human beings and their functioning, in place of prevailing views that emphasize differences in cultures, genders, and so forth. This universalism has been advanced in a particularly clear way by Martha Nussbaum and Amartya Sen, Nussbaum using it primarily to provide a way to criticize the oppression of women (e.g., in opportunities for work, in dress, or even in regard to female genital mutilation), and Sen using a capabilities approach to human functioning to criticize the unequal treatment of women as well as the existence of widespread poverty and the lack of adequate levels of well-being in societies such as India.[1]

Here, I begin with some questions about this move to return to – as I characterized it in earlier work – an abstractly universalist conception of human beings, where this remains essentialist in specifying a determinate list of human characteristics shared by all and only humans. Despite the helpful nuances and qualifications that Nussbaum has recently emphasized to the effect that such universals are open-ended and subject to consensus and historical interpretation,[2] I suggest that this approach remains subject to the older critique that has been made of essentialist approaches by feminist theorists and theorists of race and class, especially concerning the historically and culturally biased inclinations of such lists and their basis in characteristics of dominant groups, whether they be male, or white, or class-based. These criticisms are even more telling, I argue, when such essentialist conceptions are put forward as a basis for development and for human rights, because they may import Western liberal conceptions of norms of development and rights under the guise of the universally human. Indeed, this can in turn permit cultural relativists to correctly object that other cultures have very different conceptions of human characteristics and functioning and of the claims humans make on each other, and that these conceptions are systematically excluded by such universalist approaches.

In the second part of this chapter, I go on to contrast this understanding of universality with an alternative conception of concrete universality,[3] which, I argue, can also make room for universal norms such as equal freedom and human rights. In that section, I go on to propose a more social approach to value creation and analyze the concepts of empathy and solidarity to which it appeals.

---

[1] This universalist perspective can be found, for example, in their essays in the collection *Women, Culture, and Development*, eds. Martha Nussbaum and Jonathan Glover (New York: Oxford University Press, 1995), 61–104, 259–273.

[2] Martha Nussbaum, *Sex and Social Justice* (New York: Oxford University Press, 1999), 40.

[3] This conception, influenced by Hegel's original presentation of it in his *Logic*, was developed in my "The Woman Question: Philosophy of Liberation and the Liberation of Philosophy," in *The Philosophical Forum*, Special Issue on Women and Philosophy, eds. Carol C. Gould and Marx W. Wartofsky, Vol. V, nos. 1–2 (Fall–Winter 1973–1974), reprinted with a new introduction as *Women and Philosophy: Toward a Theory of Liberation*, eds. Carol C. Gould and Marx W. Wartofsky (New York: G. P. Putnam's, 1976), 5–44.

Abstract Universality, Human Beings, and Development

Martha Nussbaum, Amartya Sen, Susan Okin, and other feminist theorists have criticized the postmodernist emphasis on multicultural differences and its apparent lack of a basis for objecting to oppressive cultural practices. From the feminist side, practices common in certain cultures – such as clitoridectomy, the requirement that rape victims marry their rapists, or wife battery as a penalty for committing adultery – have struck these theorists (rightly, I would say) as deeply oppressive to women. Given the commitment to women's equality, such practices cannot be tolerated on the grounds of respect for diverse cultures. Again, in the area of development, theorists such as Sen have argued for the need for common standards in assessing development and for establishing priorities among its aspects – for example, regarding the importance of the provision of adequate nutrition and health care. From this standpoint, cultural relativist views – which may even be critical of the concept of development itself insofar as it connotes a Western notion of modernization, or which recognize irresolvable diversity in standards of development – are held to be inadequate.

Consider a few examples of these criticisms: In the context of a critique of the concept of group rights, Susan Okin writes as follows in *Is Multiculturalism Bad for Women?*

Most cultures are suffused with practices and ideologies concerning gender. Suppose, then, that a culture endorses and facilitates the control of men over women in various ways (even if informally, in the private sphere of domestic life). Suppose, too, that there are fairly clear disparities of power between the sexes, such that the more powerful, male members are those who are generally in a position to determine and articulate the group's beliefs, practices, and interests. Under such conditions, group rights are potentially, and in many cases actually, antifeminist. They substantially limit the capacities of women and girls of that culture to live with human dignity equal to that of men and boys, and to live as freely chosen lives as they can.[4]

Because of this, Okin concludes that respect for cultural practices must be subordinated to the requirement of women's equality. Her objection, we might add, is primarily from the standpoint of liberal theory, suitably modified by feminist concerns, rather than from a concern with a universalist perspective, say, one of human rights.

---

[4] Susan Moller Okin, *Is Multiculturalism Bad for Women?* (Princeton, NJ: Princeton University Press, 1999), 12.

The objection to cultural practices oppressive to women has also been made from the standpoint of universality itself. Thus Nussbaum provides examples of views of which she is critical: an American economist who urges the preservation of traditional ways of life in a rural area of India. Nussbaum explains:

[W]hereas we Westerners experience a sharp split between the values that prevail in the workplace and the values that prevail in the home, here, by contrast, there exist what the economist calls "the embedded way of life"; the same values obtaining in both places. His example: just as in the home a menstruating woman is thought to pollute the kitchen and therefore may not enter it, so too in the workplace a menstruating woman is taken to pollute the loom and may not enter the room where looms are kept.[5]

Another interesting example that Nussbaum provides is that of a French anthropologist who "expresses regret that the introduction of smallpox vaccination to India by the British eradicated the cult of Sittala Devi, the goddess to whom one used to pray in order to avert smallpox."[6] Assuming that the anthropologist was actually bemoaning the vaccine, this would indeed be a case of cultural relativism run wild. "Would the residents of India feel this way?" we might be prompted to ask. In any case, we soon turn to the question of whether cases of this sort require Nussbaum's essentialist/universalist response, that is, Nussbaum's specific version of an appeal to universal characteristics and norms.

A third example of pernicious cultural practices is provided by Amartya Sen, who focuses on women's status in developing countries as part of an argument for working out standards or bases for assessing and comparing levels of development worldwide. In the positive freedom tradition, Sen articulates a conception of "freedom to achieve" as the basis of this standard and proposes to represent this idea in terms of capabilities to function in various ways, which in turn anchors his approach to justice (which he thinks involves aggregative considerations as well).[7] His leading example of pernicious cultural practices is the phenomenon of missing women, according to him more than 44 million in China, 37 million in India, and a total exceeding 100 million worldwide.[8] Who

---

[5] Martha Nussbaum, "Human Capabilities, Female Human Beings," in *Women, Culture, and Development*, 64.

[6] Ibid., 26.

[7] See Amartya Sen, "Gender Inequality and Theories of Justice," in *Women, Culture, and Development*, especially 266–267.

[8] Ibid., 259.

are these missing women? They are the women lost to morbidity and mortality, mainly in Asia and North Africa, by comparison with the ratio of women to men that reflects their biological advantage (as high as 1.05 to 1 in Europe and North America). Sen observes that this severe relative inequality of women worldwide is unjust and leads him to criticize any culturally relativist perspective that shies away from bluntly saying so.

Nussbaum's alternative to a cultural relativist perspective draws on Sen's positive freedom account of capabilities in her treatment of development; but she synthesizes it with her own Aristotelian theory of the general characteristics of human beings and their virtues, or good human functioning. The result is a challenging account of universality and of its relevance to the debates about development. Of course, universalistic perspectives are not new where development and intercultural comparisons are concerned. It is standard to appeal to universal human rights as a basis for criticizing unacceptable actions and practices in cultures worldwide. But before reconsidering these rights in a more expansive view, we can consider how Nussbaum's Aristotelian version of universality fares as an alternative to the postmodernist or cultural relativist positions that she roundly rejects. I focus especially on her initial presentation of this position in her article "Human Capabilities, Female Human Beings," and I take brief note of the revision and reinterpretation she gives to these ideas in *Sex and Social Justice*.

As Nussbaum and others have argued, it is necessary to avoid cultural relativism, which may be ingredient in certain postmodernist accounts of differences; but is the move we need to make that of a straightforward humanism or even essentialism? Do we need a conception of universality in the Aristotelian tradition of the sort Nussbaum proposes? This is how she puts it in her article: "My proposal is frankly universalist and 'essentialist'. That is, it asks us to focus on what is common to all, rather than on differences (although, as we shall see, it does not neglect these), and to see some capabilities and functions as more central, more at the core of human life, than others."[9] In her account of "the most important functions and capabilities of the human being, in terms of which human life is defined," she puts the question this way: "The basic idea is that we ask ourselves, 'What are the characteristic activities of the human being? What does the human being do, characteristically, as such – and not, say, as a member of a particular group, or particular local community?'"[10] (In

9 Nussbaum, "Human Capabilities," 63.
10 Ibid., 72.

passing, we are reminded of Marx's question in the *Grundrisse*: Does the human being exist as such apart from his or her community?[11])

Nussbaum daringly answers this question with a list of basic functions and capabilities that define the human form of life – from mortality, to the body with its needs for food, drink, shelter, sex, and mobility; to the capacity for pleasure and pain; the cognitive capabilities of perceiving, imagining, and thinking; early infant development; practical reason; affiliation with other human beings; relatedness to other species and to nature; humor and play; and to what she calls "separateness" (each of us feels our own pain, and so forth) and "strong separateness" (each life has his or her own peculiar context and surroundings and, as Heidegger put it, is in each case mine). This list represents what Nussbaum calls the first threshold, a level of capability to function "beneath which a life will be so impoverished that it will not be human at all."

There are some obvious questions here, already raised by others: Is a developmentally delayed child or a profoundly malnourished child who cannot play not human? These characteristics cannot really be definitional or criterial for the human, for then someone lacking some important sort of perception or mobility would not be human. Surely this would be too strong (what about Helen Keller, for example?), and Nussbaum would have to clarify the interpretation of these functions to rule out this implication. But let us presume that this can be done.

The second threshold is the higher one, which she claims is the main concern of public policy (but, we might object here in passing, such policy must also be concerned with the basics), namely, the level "beneath which those characteristic functions are available in such a reduced way that, though we may judge the form of life a human one, we will not think it a good human life."[12] This second threshold is then specified by a list of ten basic capabilities to function, at which societies should aim for their citizens. These range from being able to live to the end of a life of normal range to having good health and being adequately nourished to having adequate shelter, and so on (all, by the way, grouped as one point of the ten); to having pleasurable and not painful experiences; being able to perceive, think, and reason (again, one number); being able to have attachments to things and other persons; being able to form a conception of the good; being able to live for others, also with concern for nature; being able to laugh and play (very important to Nussbaum, seemingly

---

[11] See Karl Marx, *Grundrisse* (New York: Vintage, 1973), 265.
[12] Nussbaum, "Human Capabilities," 81.

equal to food, clothing, shelter, and reproduction put together); being able to live one's own life and no one else's (which refers to the possibility of free choice); and finally, along with this, being able to live one's own life in one's own surroundings and context, with free associations and personal property.[13]

This is a very rich theory indeed, but too rich perhaps for those who may find this approach to be culturally relative – that is, expressive of a Western, indeed U.S., late-twentieth-century view. While this objection does not yet amount to much, it gives us pause. Somehow, such lists or specifications of the essential – from Aristotle to Locke and Kant (with rationality as central, but in different senses) or Rousseau, or in a different tradition Fichte (with freedom as central) to, in yet another tradition, Marx and Engels (with productive activity as central), to Nussbaum (whose list is fuller than most of these but crucially highlights separateness and strong separateness, at least in the initial presentation of the approach) – inevitably strike us as culturally biased in an important way, if not ideologically one-sided or distorted (and this is not even to speak of the gender, racial, or class perspectives often evident in such views). Why is this the case, and can it be remedied within this sort of essentialist theory? Is the problem simply that we have not gotten the essential properties correct, or is there a difficulty with this very enterprise of the construction of a universal characterization of human beings?

In my 1974 article "The Woman Question: Philosophy of Liberation and the Liberation of Philosophy," I argued that it is precisely the conception of what I called "abstract universality" at work here that is the source of the problem. (I return shortly to the question of whether Nussbaum herself employs such a conception.) Such a criterion of universality attempts to characterize what is common to all human beings or to all societies at all times and abstracts from differences between them; in this way, it does not attend to merely local or accidental aspects of the human or social. In the classical view, it studies the human qua human, or human nature as such. Furthermore, in strong versions of this essentialist position, the universal properties must also be necessary – those without which the individuals would not be members of the given class – and therefore are properties that make them the kinds of things they are. On this view, in which differences are taken to be accidental, it would follow that, in considering the human, all historical and social differentiation drops out and only those abstracted properties that remain invariant for

[13] Ibid., 83–85.

all humans and in all societies count as essential. These characteristics are seen as fixed instead of as historically changing. In my use, the term "abstract" is contrasted with its opposite, "concrete," where "concrete" denotes those properties that individuate human beings or societies or that differentiate them, that is, make them the particular individuals or societies they are.

Aside from the many well-known philosophical critiques that can be made of the abstract universalist position,[14] the more practical criticism in this context is that the use of this criterion to determine essential or general human properties is apparently not a value-free, but rather a value-laden one, that it tends to reflect the interests, needs, and prejudices of particular social groups. (Moreover, the rank order of essential traits tends to be determined by the relative roles and priorities that these properties have in a given social system.) This is problematic especially because essentialism tends to mask the particular interests under the guise of universality and therefore is deceptive. On my view, it is the very abstractness of the criterion that in fact opens it to such distortion, by way of its exclusion of concrete social and historical differences as accidental and therefore philosophically irrelevant. In the earlier critique, I showed that various great philosophers chose those properties as universally human that the philosophers themselves either explicitly identified as male properties, or that were associated with roles and functions in which males predominated.[15]

In establishing global standards for conduct and for development, it seems possible that contemporary theories may similarly be introducing local characteristics from a particular social context under the guise of general human ones. When one hears of strong separateness as a basic human good, or play as a basic capability (a concept owing a great deal to Schiller, Freud, and other relatively recent thinkers), one is led to reflect on the apparently inevitable selectivity and perspectival character of such lists. This is not to say that Nussbaum is wrong about the importance of strong separateness or play, only to put in question the universality of the list. We could ask, why isn't it also characteristic of human beings to want love or security or to live in a community? These are presumably covered under other headings – love and community under affiliation, security under the need for shelter or early infant development or perhaps

---

[14] This was also a focus in my article "The Woman Question: Philosophy of Liberation and the Liberation of Philosophy."

[15] Ibid., especially 5–25.

property – but this raises the issue of the level and description of the characteristics. Why these and not others? And if we are simply looking for general characteristics and not only good characteristics, perhaps we should add some negative capabilities that are characteristic capabilities of many, if not most, people, such as jealousy or selfishness or even violence. According to TV talk show host Jerry Springer, everyone is a voyeur; perhaps this trait should count. Isn't the list in fact socially, historically, and culturally very deeply variable? And, as both Marxists and postmodernists would point out, such lists tend to miss the connection to power and the powerful in a given social context. If so, do not such attempts to characterize the human, particularly as a basis for public policy (and not only as a philosophical theory), end up being coercive, to the degree that they impose the standards of one particular culture on others? This might be especially so in the area of development policy. Would it not be better, we might suggest, to see both development and the self-understanding of the human from the other's point of view? Indeed, we might further ask, shouldn't development policy be decided democratically by each affected country or, at least, by equal participation of all countries?

One additional set of questions presents itself: Inasmuch as the list appears to presuppose a rich philosophical theory concerning the human and concerning the good, is it plausible to suppose that agreement on the contents of such an articulated and controversial philosophical perspective is required in order to guide public policy? Is this a case of philosophical hubris? And, if we decide that we do need global agreement on universal principles or guidelines, shouldn't they be kept somewhat less voluminous, not necessarily minimal, of course, but perhaps more open and clear? In her later version especially, Nussbaum emphasizes that the list she offers is open and flexible, but in fact it seems quite determinate and drawn from a fundamentally classical philosophical perspective.

Nussbaum is well aware of most of these and other criticisms of her view and attempts to meet them in various ways. It is helpful now to briefly examine the transformations in the view that she introduces, especially in her later book, to see whether they go far enough or whether, as I suggest, a newer conception of universality is necessary. We can leave aside the transformations in the older essentialism that are introduced by Nussbaum's interpretation of the universal characteristics in terms of a positive freedom conception of capabilities to function, an interpretation that in her case is specifically derived from Sen's work. I believe this is a salutary move, and I share the view that a conception of positive freedom is required. My own elaboration of this, here and in my previous work, has been in terms of a conception of the development of capacities as self-development or self-transformation over time,[16] and I would additionally propose that this version of positive freedom is inherently more open to emergent capacities and functionings than the "capabilities" approach that Nussbaum and Sen present.

More to the point here are the other qualifications that Nussbaum introduces (some presented in the earlier article and some in the revised version in her book). Importantly, she states that "universal ideas of the human do arise within history and from human experience, and they can ground themselves in experience."[17] This is certainly a significant point, but what is its cash value in her account? This move toward historicity and experience primarily permits the specification or interpretation from diverse cultural perspectives of each of the items on Nussbaum's list. But, at least in the earlier version, she does not hold that the choice of *which* items should make up the list is itself historically or culturally emergent. Thus she writes, "The list claims to have identified in a very general way components that are fundamental to any human life. But it allows in its very design for the possibility of multiple specifications of each of the components."[18] There is the idea that we have a common conversation concerning the *interpretation* of these basic capabilities. The second threshold list – of good functioning – is more open; it is subject to plural and local specification. But, at least in the original presentation, Nussbaum seems to resist the idea that there can be multiple fundamental conceptions of human functioning that emerge and change historically, culturally, and socially, recognizing only variability in the interpretation of these essential functionings.

It seems problematic to me, however, to propose that we can have a conversation on the interpretation of the essential properties but not on *which* properties are essential. Why can't these too be understood as varying historically? If, as Nussbaum seems to be suggesting, we suppose that there is already consensus on the list itself, then this observation might be in bad faith, inasmuch as it turns out that the consensus is for clearly Western, late-twentieth-century views that we prefer. If the claim is, even more stringently, that there needs to be worldwide consensus

---

[16] See Carol C. Gould, *Marx's Social Ontology: Individuality and Community in Marx's Theory of Social Reality* (Cambridge, MA: The MIT Press, 1978), especially Chapter 2, and *Rethinking Democracy: Freedom and Social Cooperation in Politics, Economy, and Society* (Cambridge: Cambridge University Press, 1988), especially Chapter 1.

[17] Nussbaum, "Human Capabilities," 69.

[18] Ibid., 93.

on a philosophical theory (and not just a contemporary outlook more loosely), then this is prima facie implausible. How will we get people worldwide to agree to a detailed and contestable philosophical position? If, on the other hand, Nussbaum means only to rule out subjecting the choice of fundamental properties to consensus (or to be the object of a "common conversation"), which is the most plausible interpretation of her claims, then we may still wonder whether this is really an alternative type of essentialism at all. Such an approach would seem to reintroduce a perspective that is ahistorical at its core, retaining openness to the interpretation only of the details of the theory in each cultural and historical context.

In the revised version of her views, Nussbaum proposes only one list, that of "human functional capabilities" that are required for a "good human life."[19] It no longer includes separateness or strong separateness. And significantly, it is now claimed that the procedure through which the account of the human is derived "is the attempt to summarize empirical findings of a broad and ongoing cross-cultural inquiry" and as such is open-ended and "can always be contested and remade."[20] This revision certainly represents a plausible direction for theory, but it is not clear to me, for the reasons given earlier, that such a cross-cultural and empirical approach would issue in an "account of the central human capacities and functions...which can be given in a fully universal manner, at least at a high level of generality."[21]

Finally, to the important objection that conceptions of universally human properties exclude the powerless, Nussbaum rightly points to the role that the conception of the human has played in countering prejudice and exclusion in the long term. Thus, in response to the claim that the basic human capacity to develop various capabilities to function has frequently been denied to women, she says, "[I]f we examine the history of these denials we see, I believe, the great power of the conception of the human as a source of moral claims."[22] Indeed, such universal norms do play an important role in revealing when an injustice has been done, simply by showing that some human being has not been treated equally. We can know *that* a violation of universality has occurred, but we will not know *why* or on what grounds.[23] Knowing the sources of a case of

---

[19] Nussbaum, *Sex and Social Justice*, 41–42.
[20] Ibid., 40.
[21] Ibid., 8.
[22] Nussbaum, "Human Capabilities," 98.
[23] See the discussion in Gould, "The Woman Question," especially 29–30.

injustice, in terms of the specific context of oppression that gives rise to it, is required if one is concerned not only with rectifying the specific case but also with eliminating the conditions that give rise to the injustice in the first place. Thus abstract norms permit us to deal with the effects of injustice, but not with its causes. An alternative conception of universality, in one of its aspects, may be superior in this regard.

Concrete Universality and Human Rights

If we want to avoid cultural relativism but still wish to give due weight to the claims and strengths of other cultures, should we replace the conception of abstract universality and the norms based on it with another conception of universality? The answer, I think, is yes and no. I believe that two moves are needed: first, the introduction of a conception of concrete universality, both as a characterization and as a norm; and second, a more refined and less philosophically demanding conception of an abstractly universal norm, such that it can be more fully cross-cultural and less biased. Ideally, we would also be able to show the relation of these two conceptions – namely, the abstract and the concrete – to each other and establish their mutual coherence. In this small frame, I wish to set out the parameters and basic characteristics of each of these in order to suggest possible directions for understanding this alternative conception.

Let me start with the more unusual notion of concrete universality. I want to depart from one aspect of the characterization that I gave of this in my article "The Woman Question," where it is understood to arise from the totality of interrelations within a society. The conception of concrete universality in Hegel's use, and to some degree Marx's as well, regards society as made up of internal relations among individuals who are mutually interconstituting. However, if this were extended beyond a given society to a global context of interrelating individuals and societies, it would seem to pose a requirement for some sort of unity, which is unimaginable and thus quite empty. Furthermore, in Marx if not in Hegel, there is little discussion of the universal norm or norms that might emerge from this description of society as a totality of interrelations, so the import of this interactive understanding of individuals, however attractive it may be, remains unclear in the value context. Certainly, there is the important recognition that the interrelations among individuals or groups often have been characterized not by equality among participants but instead by one-sided relations of domination, superiority, or oppression, and this necessitates a social critique of the conditions that contribute to this one-sidedness. I would like to retain this emphasis in the conception proposed here.

This new view conceives of society as constructed by individuals in concrete and differentiated social relations, but there is no presumption of totality – only *networks of relationships* and what I would call *networks of engagement*, themselves interconnecting. (We can think of the Internet – less commercialized, of course – as an analogy here.) In an increasingly globalized context of interacting people and cultures, we might suppose that diverse cultural groups contribute to an increasing interdependence, within shared and overlapping contexts at a given historical period. I call this interdependence *cosmopolitan association* or *intersociation*. In one sense, this globalization can be seen as a sort of universalization, inasmuch as it is marked by increasing interconnections at a distance, certainly from economic and environmental standpoints, and to some extent from social or personal ones as well.[24] The idea of a shared world comes to have a global interpretation, where previously it may have had more local ones.[25] In this way, perhaps, the notion of one world may have some place, not in a Hegelian sense of totality, of course, but rather as a potential framework or horizon for interaction.

In this context of globalization, individuals also become more universalized and less localized, as Marx already observed,[26] in the distinctive sense of becoming many-sided, subject to culturally and socially diverse influences, and open to a wide variety of interactions in many spheres. This does not, however, necessitate a wholly cosmopolitan conception of the individual, as purely a world citizen, for we can suppose that this person remains rooted in one or two cultures and societies but is newly receptive to many of them and their influence.

From an analytical standpoint, a conception of concrete universality that emphasizes networks of social relationships and engagements, where these may involve relations of domination or oppression, is an important supplement to any abstract characterization we may be able to give of all human beings. It suggests not that "affiliation" (to use Nussbaum's word) is simply one among many other human traits but rather that social interaction frames all of them in profound ways. Even basic bodily needs and functions take on their shape and significance within social, historical,

[24] See Andrew Collier, "Marxism and Universalism: Group Interests or a Shared World?" in *International Justice and the Third World*, eds. R. Attfield and B. Wilkins (London: Routledge, 1992), 87.

[25] Ibid., 84–88.

[26] Marx, *Grundrisse*, 409–410.

and cultural frameworks. Examples might be found in the mundane uses "I need a slice of pizza" or "I need a Ben & Jerry's ice cream cone"; or again, in the more general fact that my body is experienced by me in part as others perceive it; or yet again, in the experience of hugging my child, in which I become part of him for the moment; and in many other cases. This view has by now become almost a truism in social philosophy, but it requires that we characterize the human not only as a singularity but also as a social being. This involves the recognition that characteristics are not only interpreted but also constructed through the concrete interactions of particular caring and choosing individuals, who are often concerned for each other and make choices together with others with whom they are engaged in common projects and interdependent networks (economic, technological, social, cultural, or personal).

I have proposed that the characterization of this sort of interdependence requires a distinctive social ontology, in which the basic entities that make up society are understood as individuals-in-relations or social individuals, in place of the externally related individuals characteristic of traditional liberal theory. The specific interrelations of these individuals or groups, whether they are relations of oppression or of reciprocity, play a central role in our understanding of who they are and of the conditions for their activity, as do the opportunities that they have for participation in and control over common or joint activities.

What would this interactive account signify for the norm of universality? Should it too be thought of as relationally constructed through the concrete interactions, contributions, and communications of historically situated individuals who would approach it from different cultural perspectives? And what would this mean?

For our purposes in this chapter, conceiving of universal norms, values, or obligations as *intersociative norms* emerging from such an interaction of cultures – or, better, of people in diverse cultures – has much appeal. If such a conception is true, it would allow us to claim that in bringing to bear a universal norm, we are respecting these cultures and not merely privileging our own; yet it also would not see the norms as simply relative to a given cultural context. One version of this view sees the values as emerging from a consensus or conversation posited to be fully open (not one limited to current Western-influenced views). However, most theorists are understandably reluctant to posit this sort of actual consensus, since without built-in liberal constraints, the results would probably not be acceptable; yet with these constraints, it would seem that no genuine consensus could be achieved.

If we can give some purchase to the view that norms emerge from interactive multicultural contexts or from communication across cultures, at least to a degree, then this would go part of the way toward specifying the conception of concrete universality. Let us consider the crucial concept of human rights themselves, which are central to our discussion here and so are particularly significant. Contrary to the idea that it is simply a Western conception, the contemporary notion of human rights is distinctively *pluricultural.*[27] And this is so even leaving aside the as yet not fully developed claims to the effect that human rights, either as a general conception or in regard to some specific rights, can be found in the Koran or in Chinese Confucianism, or other texts, although some of these claims undoubtedly have merit, even if they mainly arise retrospectively, as a reconstruction of possible origins after the fact.[28] More to the point, it can be noted that the content of the United Nations list of human rights (in the Universal Declaration of Human Rights and related documents) in fact reflects the conceptions of developing countries as much as those of North America and Western Europe in its extensive list of rights tied to basic needs, such as means of subsistence, health care, and employment, as well as certain group rights, such as that concerning development. The coalition of Eastern Europe – with its Marxist views at the time – and the Third World countries ensured the adoption of documents that did not much privilege Western liberal conceptions of the priority of liberty and security of the person, or private property and democratic forms of political participation.

But what of the concept of human rights itself? This seems much less multicultural in origin, obviously deriving from the modern Western rights tradition. Yet if we wanted to see a cross-cultural aspect here, we could stress both the political interpretation of such human rights – where they more loosely concern the claims that people and societies can make on each other as well as the protection they give for oppressed individuals worldwide – and the fact that from their own diverse perspectives, a wide variety of countries did sign on to them (although admittedly not necessarily as natural expressions of their own cultural perspectives). However, it might be more straightforward to grant that the concept itself is in fact Western in origin, although it now appeals to people in various cultures, perhaps because of so-called modernization in these cultures or

---

[27] I discuss this term in Chapter 5, along with "multicultural" and "intercultural."

[28] See Jack Donnelly, *Universal Human Rights in Theory and Practice* (Ithaca, NY: Cornell University Press, 1989), Chapter 3.

because it provides a critical edge to those seeking progressive changes there.[29] After all, as Benhabib and others correctly point out, we must not underestimate the importance of evolution or debate within cultures worldwide, partly in reaction to external influences.[30] Yet, despite the Western framework of rights discourse itself, which conceives of rights as inhering in individuals the aspect of rights that I have stressed here, that they are claims we make on each other as inherently social individuals, is a more communitarian notion that goes beyond the liberal tradition in Western thought and certainly has resonances, if not also roots, in other cultural traditions.

The Genesis of Intersociative Norms

Does it make sense, then, to speak of values or norms generally – and not only the specifically universal ones – as emerging from concrete interactions or communications among individuals or among cultures? Leaving aside the "ought" from "is" issue, since my emphasis is on the social interactive context for norms, and without attempting to introduce a new theory of value here, we can identify several aspects to such value emergence. There are three to note here: (1) values generated in relationships of care, concern, empathy, and solidarity; (2) those posited through common choices or co-agency, whether based on common goals and projects or on shared needs or interests; and (3) norms generated through consensus or a common conversation. Although talk, or more elegantly, communication, permeates the first two that is, care and choices, I believe these are not reducible to communicative discourse, but rather are practical, lived features of our interaction itself.

Care and concern, introduced in Chapter 1, as well as empathy for others, have been widely discussed by feminist philosophers and some others in the philosophical tradition. Such caring or empathic relationships – often but not always personal – give rise to particular values that people or sometimes things may have for us, as well as (on reflection) to the value of care itself. These caring relationships, or those expressing concern or empathy for others, permeate ordinary life, from love and family, to neighborhood, work, voluntary groups, clubs, and associations of all sorts, but they are also extensible to possible others at some remove

---

[29] See Seyla Benhabib, "Cultural Complexity, Moral Interdependence, and the Global Dialogical Community," in *Women, Culture, and Development*, 235–255.

[30] Ibid.

from us. In this context, others may be present as potential objects of our care, concern, or empathic understanding, as beings like ourselves, with needs and interests, or as individuals who stand in mutual emotional relations with us.

A social correlate to this sort of empathic relation to individual others has traditionally been considered under the heading of *solidarity*, and it is perhaps time to bring this conception back into discussions of political philosophy. Feeling solidarity with others normally applies between people in different social groups and is a sort of standing with others based on an empathic understanding of their concrete social situation. Through much of the twentieth century its connotation was tied to labor movement contexts or to socialism, but there is no inherent reason to limit solidarity narrowly to such contexts, and, indeed, it has recently been used to refer to international solidarity of various sorts, such as in the anti-apartheid movement. Solidarity may also involve the performance of an action that expresses a sympathetic understanding at a distance of the situation of oppressed others. It is in any case a feeling of affiliation with them and their cause. We can also distinguish between solidarity with others on the grounds of sharing their particular interest and a more general human solidarity that can be shared with everyone. I return later to this universalistic import.

A second key practical source of value is co-agency in the determination of common goals, that is, common choices. Things are endowed with value not only through our individual efforts to pursue them but also through processes of jointly choosing ends. These common goals are best understood as ingredient in our jointly pursued activities or shared engagements – for example, at the workplace, or in leisure, or in explicitly cooperative ventures of an economic or political sort – rather than necessarily as a subject of deliberation, which often comes after the fact. Shared ends or goals are posited as values for us in our experience. Others, including those from distant cultures, may present themselves here as potential co-actors or co-creators in common projects. This is not to say, however, that they bring the same interests and background to these projects; we may instead appreciate the different interests and points of view that these others bring to these activities.

Shared goals ingredient in common activities may not always represent equal input from all participants but instead may initially reflect particular interests or needs, particularly where oppressive relations hold sway, and may in this way start as one-sided. Yet it is also clear that critical reflection can play an important role in revealing the perspectival, or even in some cases prejudiced, nature of these values. And this emphasis on critique of one-sided needs and interests, both as social critique in terms of the social conditions and institutions that may contribute to them and as self-criticism by individuals or groups, is an advantage, I think, of the concrete understanding of value creation proposed here.[31]

Efforts to achieve consensus on generalizable interests or norms, as Habermas, for example, has discussed it,[32] may indeed be helpful in this process of critique, although it is questionable whether these conversational efforts will lead to universal agreement, even ideally. Such consensus or communication about values does, however, represent a third important source of the genesis of value in practical contexts. We are always talking about what is important, personally and politically, and this discussion often leads to provisional agreements about values and norms. Of course, this communication is frequently about our concerns and our common projects (aspects 1 and 2 enumerated earlier), but it can also introduce values of its own, whether rationally considered or less so. Here, the other may appear to us as a possible interlocutor in the dialogue.

Each of these three practical contexts of the genesis of norms implies a conception of universality. Yet it does so in all three cases as some sort of limit concept or imaginary projection to which we can approximate. In the first case – that of care, concern, or empathy for particular others, or solidarity with another group – ties to all others or solidaristic relations with them appear either as a limit notion or by analogy to the empathy or concern we feel for those with whom we directly interact or for whom we specifically care. Certainly, contemporary communications technologies make it possible for us to experience the suffering of famine victims in the Sudan, for example, as powerfully as the suffering of some in the local neighborhood (and sometimes more so). More philosophically, we can say that although there are practical limits to our caring and concern for others, there is no inherent boundary to its extensibility to particular others or groups worldwide.

We can also learn to reason in an imaginative way (and this is the kind of reasoning that Hannah Arendt thought Kant described in his Third Critique) from our understanding of the feelings and needs of those about whom we are immediately concerned to the feelings and needs of everyone, such that we can bring these others close to us in imagination

---

[31] See Gould, "The Woman Question," especially 25–30.
[32] See the discussion of Habermas in Chapter 1.

and understand matters from their perspective. Developing this line of thought might provide us with a concern-based justification of universal obligations, or at least of potential universal ties. In Chapter 12 of this book I return to the import of this sort of empathic thinking.

A similar sort of extension might be made for the second and third aspects of the practical contexts of value creation. Setting common goals, which we take to be values for us, can involve increasingly large contexts of cooperative activity. It is involved in the small, such as groups of friends deciding to do something together, to intermediate cases such as goal setting for a firm, to the very large: planning by national governments and indeed by international organizations, whether economic or political. Alternatively, the extension of common goals to more universalistic contexts can proceed by way of an interaction of diverse individual or cultural projects, in which their reach and interpretation are made more inclusive. A sort of universalizing of co-agency is thus imaginable, although it is not clear how much of a role it has at the global level beyond the concept of a horizon or limit. Certainly, where common goals are oriented to meeting needs, an extension to the needs of all (perhaps coming to our awareness through a confrontation with the needs of others), as well as measures to meet these more extensive needs, is clearly useful. Furthermore, worldwide cooperation at a general level is increasingly relevant in ecological and economic contexts, as previously noted. Beyond this, a process of universalization at the level of reflection and critique can provide a helpful corrective to the potentially one-sided concern that groups tend to have in the satisfaction of their own needs and interests and the distortion in their outlook that this may entail.

In the third case as well, that of consensus and communication as a source of norms, universalization is often thought to play a role both in ensuring that everyone may enter into the dialogue and in the idea that norms to be adopted should be agreeable to all affected by them. This essentially democratic idea may indeed be ingredient in the speech situation, as I think it also is more generally in the structure of interaction, to the extent that anyone with a reasonable consideration can raise it (we might add that if they have unreasonable considerations, those may be relevant too). This opens up the possibility of cross-cultural and intercultural dialogue, if we are careful not to make the constraints on the communication too one-sidedly liberal.

In all three of these practical contexts for normative activity, then, we can observe that a norm or value of universality of a concrete sort plays a role. These normative interpretations add to the descriptive sense of concrete universality introduced earlier, where people are understood as tied together through their interactions and as transforming themselves through their relations with others. Furthermore, an emergent universalization in practice can be seen in processes of cultural interchange and growing interdependence across cultures. Yet this account still leaves open a number of questions concerning these various senses of universality: For example, is universal relatedness good in itself or good because of its contribution to freedom? To the degree that it entails increasing cooperation among cultures, it might be thought to be valuable as such. Yet it also derives value from its contribution to the self-development of individuals (as expanding the options for choice or possibilities for growth of capacities), and perhaps too, as J. S. Mill would have it, from its contribution to sounder ideas. Furthermore, although universal norms or values are posited in our experience, their status beyond a horizon or imaginary limit in the three cases studied is not yet clear, nor is the relation of the conceptions of universality to each other. Moreover, it remains a question whether we can speak of universality in these normative senses as itself changing historically and socially, although the descriptive sense of it clearly does.

Another important set of issues concerns the feasibility or plausibility of the universalistic extension in each of the three aspects of value just described. Especially in the case of empathy or the extension of care or solidarity in more universalistic ways, we observe what seem to be limits on this extension in the many cases of individual and group hatred that reflect the very absence of such empathic understanding, especially with those demarcated as different or, worse, as deficient or insignificant. Although it is plausible to suppose that no barrier exists in principle to the universalization of empathy or feelings of solidarity, practice reveals what may seem to be insuperable barriers and limits to the requisite extension.

Yet, as the argument in this work suggests, this problem calls for a twofold response. At the level of practice, addressing this situation requires new types of education and media, as well as the development of political and economic institutions that enable people to have more control over the conditions of their lives. In Part III, especially, I develop the view that democratic participation in decisions is needed not only in traditional communities but also in the newer transborder networks of association, giving rise to a conception of intersociative democracy, which has to be based on more equal access to the means for satisfying economic, social, and cultural needs. At the level of norms, as proposed here, the problematic current situation requires cultivating not only respect for universal human rights but also sensibilities of empathy and transborder solidarity. When applied across borders, these sensibilities support the need for such intersociative democracies to be open to the impact of their own decisions on nonmembers and on those situated at a distance.

It is interesting to observe that the value of feelings of empathy and solidarity have been articulated by a wide variety of cultural traditions, in a way probably more widespread than rights discourse itself. For example, one thinks of the importance of empathy or sympathy in the work of the followers of Confucius – for example, in the Book of Mencius.[33] Thus, it is plausible to suppose that the cultivation of empathy and solidarity can gain support from a diversity of approaches, although it must be granted that its universal extension remains problematic in practice for all of these traditions.

Universality and Normative Critique

Yet perhaps the most difficult set of questions for the normative understanding of universality proposed in this chapter is different: Even if we can show that important universal norms, such as human rights, are indeed cross-cultural in that they draw on the contributions of many cultures, or else that they have arisen through a universalizing consensus, this would not establish any independent normative status for them; they would still be culturally relative, albeit now relative to the totality of cultures that contributed to them. Although our account has suggested the importance of self-criticism and social critique with respect to the genesis of such norms (to make sure they are not one-sided or ideologically distorted), it has not indicated how these norms can be used critically with respect to cultural practices in one or another culture. In a related way, even if we emphasize the role of intercultural interaction in the genesis of norms, this still does not show how we can criticize oppressive practices within any given culture, except from the standpoint of others or even of all the others.

These considerations show the need for a moment of abstract universality and, in particular, a conception of universal human rights that can be used normatively to criticize cultural practices that violate them, such as those centering on the oppression of women that I noted at outset of

---

[33] "The Book of Mencius," in *A Source Book in Chinese Philosophy*, translated and compiled by Wing-Tsit Chan (Princeton, NJ: Princeton University Press, 1972).

this chapter. Such rights could then be understood as setting constraints on cultural practices, whether in our own society or elsewhere. As rights pertaining to all humans as such, the abstractly universal norm of human rights makes a claim to be based on a universal feature or features of human beings themselves. But as we have seen from the critique of Nussbaum's earlier conception, we need to avoid an overly rich and highly determinate list of such features if we are to avoid falling into the trap of the essentialism of a fixed human nature or into the error of projecting our own contemporary liberal culture into a general account of the human. How can we do this? We need a conception of human beings that supports their equality and the idea that each should recognize all the others as bearers of human rights.

As I suggested earlier in this work, following the lines introduced in *Rethinking Democracy*, I would propose that the basis of a principle of equal and universal human rights can be found in the transformative power of human agents itself – that is, their very capacity for social and historical transformation, or what I have called their equal agency. Given the pervasive phenomenon of such change and development by differentiated and related individuals through time, as in fact is pointed to by the descriptive concept of concrete universality, we can see that the capacity or power for such transformation and self-transformation is characteristic of social individuals in all cultures. It is, we might say, ingredient in their activity, as an activity of growth and development through time. I have argued that this capacity of humans as agents, which both is constructive and operates socially, can be referred to in terms of the idea of freedom, but in a sense beyond the traditional liberal conception of simple free choice, taken apart from such contexts of social transformation and the self-development of people through time.[34] (Free choice is in a sense a specification of this capacity.) As characteristic of each human being as an agent, this power requires recognition by all the others. This recognition is at the same time the acknowledgment of the equality of others with me in respect to having this capacity and, in this sense, of their equal freedom or equal transformative power.

As I argued in *Rethinking Democracy*, this bare capacity or agency, which I there characterized as a capacity for self-development but which I am here describing a little more broadly, presupposes access to social and material conditions for it to become concretely realized. If all people equally possess this capacity and if it requires conditions, then recognizing

---

[34] See also Carol C. Gould, *Marx's Social Ontology*, especially Chapter 2.

them as human entails recognizing their (prima facie) equal rights, or equally valid claims to these conditions. As suggested previously, these rights include negative ones of freedom from interference and from oppression and also positive or enabling material and social conditions, including means of subsistence, health care, as well as social recognition of various sorts, access to education, training, culture, and so on. And one of the important social conditions is in fact the right to democratic participation in common activities. The variety of these prerequisites is specified in human rights, including basic ones that concern access to the means necessary for any action whatever, and nonbasic ones, indicating those necessary for the fuller development of people.

In emphasizing the conditions for people's development of their capacities and the realization of their projects, the account given here comes fairly close to other views within the positive freedom tradition, such as that of Sen and to some degree Nussbaum. In my view, this tradition emerges from Marx's theory and is later elaborated in Macpherson's critique of the purely negative liberty conception of freedom, as the absence of interference with each person's choices, and goes on to put emphasis on what people need to make their freedom or agency effective. The version I give is not primarily an account of the good life (like Nussbaum's) nor primarily an account of justice but rather attempts to integrate certain elements derived from both theories of value and of justice. It presents a conception of agency and of freedom as a value that goes beyond free choice to emphasize the concrete transformation of material and social conditions in varying historical contexts, and it emphasizes equal access to these conditions for the emergence and self-development of people's goals and capacities over time. It thus argues for social and political protection of liberty and democracy in a more extended sense, and for equal access to the conditions of subsistence, health, and education. The account that can be given of these conditions, and to an extent even what these prerequisites are, are seen as emerging from a historical and multicultural process of interaction and discussion among individuals and cultures, one that is increasingly universalized, in part because of the growing social relatedness that this process has produced. However, inasmuch as these are prerequisites for the development of agency or of human capacities, which vary among individuals, it follows that although there is a prima facie requirement for equal access to conditions, the actual ones needed will in fact vary among individuals as well as among cultures.

The conception of equal agency as a moment of universality that I have proposed seems to me less culturally relative than Nussbaum's proposal, especially in her earlier formulation, since my conception avoids the interpretation of strong separateness that informs her view there. It does aim to provide something of an independent ground for human rights in suggesting that there is a characteristic of human beings that people recognize and ought to recognize in other people and that this entails a conception of the valid claims that each human being can make on all the others. In focusing on the power of social and personal transformation itself, or agency, as characteristic of humans, it presents a general characterization, which might be thought to be an essential trait. But I would argue that this is distinguished from traditional essentialist views, including that of Nussbaum, in avoiding any idea of fixed human characteristics or traits that could compose a list of any sort. It is largely the fixedness of the characteristics that renders essentialism problematic. On the view presented here, it is the power of change and self-change itself, without a content, that is seized on as a sufficient basis for the recognition of the equality and universality that are needed for an effective human rights principle. This conception of human rights can then provide a crucial ground for criticizing and challenging practices in any culture that violate them. This sort of universalistic conception is indispensable, I think, if we are to avoid cultural relativism.

We can see that this sense of universality is dependent in some ways on the other sense discussed, namely, concrete universality. This is so both because the actual conception of human rights can be supposed to have emerged from the contributions of various cultural perspectives, as noted earlier, but more so because of the way it is founded in the constructive and interactive power of differentiated individuals in society. I have suggested that it is these individuals acting in relation to each other over time – and, indeed, in increasingly universalistic relations with each other – that supports the recognition of people as having this power or agency. We can in turn abstract the latter from these practical contexts of activity and use it as a basis for a critical principle, inasmuch as it comes to be embodied in the norm of universal human rights. The conception of concrete universality can thus be said to contain as crucial elements the abstract norms of equal freedom or of human rights, inasmuch as the emergent relations and interactions that it refers to are based on the agency of social individuals who have equally valid claims to the recognition of this agency and therefore have equal rights in this sense.

Only by taking such a new double-sided approach to universality can we avoid falling into the opposite traps of cultural relativism on the one hand and essentialism on the other. The conception of universality set forth here provides, I think, important and much needed support for a nonrelativist conception of human rights, which can set limits to what is normatively acceptable in any culture, but which can nonetheless see universality, and to some extent these rights themselves, as constructed from the contributions of different cultural perspectives. Only such a conception of rights can do the necessary critical work of arguing against existent repressive cultural practices as much as against violations of traditionally protected liberties or the lack of provision of adequate means of subsistence.

PART II

DEMOCRACY AND RIGHTS, PERSONALIZED AND PLURALIZED

3

Embodied Politics

In the introduction, I suggest that one important sense in which democracy and human rights need to be globalized is in fact to reinterpret them as applying to a variety of contexts outside the strictly political and to understand them in terms of more diversified cultural frameworks. Along these lines, in Chapter 1, I introduce the idea of bringing democracy closer to home in the consideration of care; and, in Chapter 2, I propose that human rights and other universalist norms need to be pluralized by taking into account the variety of cultures and historical formations, but in a way that preserves their critical edge.

In this second part of this work, I turn more fully to the task of personalizing and pluralizing the conceptions of democracy and human rights. In particular, I explore here some of the relations of democracy and politics more generally to the idea of embodiment; then I go on in Chapter 4 to consider interrelations between democracy, race, and racism. In Chapter 5, I take up the idea of cultural identity, analyze it from the perspective of social ontology, and consider its import for democratic decisions and for the difficult question of the recognition of group rights. Subsequently, in Chapter 6, I turn to the issue of women's human rights and consider the transformations in human rights that this personalization requires.

Our question here, then, is the important, although often neglected, one of the significance of the body for politics. What is the relevance, if any, of our having bodies or being embodied for our membership in communities, for conceptions of justice and rights, or for the role of government and questions of representation? Recognizing that we are embodied persons, as feminist philosophers have stressed, what import

77

does this have for the understanding of the proper scope and character of the political? Does it, for example, have implications for the structure and procedures of democratic institutions or for public policy?

To lay the ground for answering these questions, I here critically review several historical and current approaches to the body and its relation to the political, and then I consider possible new directions for developing what I call an embodied politics. Specifically, I first take up a number of leading feminist approaches to the body and embodiment and suggest that most of these, despite the soundness of their analysis and critique, do not yet work out the implications of this embodiment for communal and political life. Second, I consider certain accounts in the history of political theory of the role of the body in politics and uses of the body as a metaphor in this context – in particular, the older idea of the "body politic," together with some proposals by Nietzsche and by Claude Lefort, which also turn out to be problematic. I then briefly touch on the two dominant contemporary political philosophies that I considered previously – those of Rawls and Habermas – and propose that they are excessively cognitivist and nonembodied in their approach to politics and community. Then, in the final and constructive section of the chapter, I delineate a conception of embodied politics, which, although it builds on existing conceptions of the role of material needs and of recognition of individual and communal identities, goes beyond them to an emphasis on social needs and embodied interpersonal relationships in familial and communal contexts.

Feminist Approaches to the Body

Several French feminist theorists – notably Luce Irigaray, Hélène Cixous, and Julia Kristeva – have focused on the female body and female sexuality as sources for a radical reconception of women's identity and of gender hierarchy. Taking off from a Lacanian psychoanalytic framework, these theorists have, in different ways, criticized the characterization of woman as Other with respect to the male subject as dominant, where woman's body is constituted as the object of male desire. They have sought to describe an originative feminine way of being, understood in terms of a distinctive sexuality or erotic life, emphasizing "writing the body," that is, the discursive reimagining of the feminine, or "jouissance," the fluidity of female being and the multiplicity of her sex organs, or else identification with the mother and the presymbolic aspects of motherhood. These approaches reintroduce the phenomenon of sexual difference, identifying it now affirmatively, as an expression of female sexuality, rather than negatively, as "non-male" or "other," and thus in a way that radically departs from the traditional phallocratic or male-dominant gender distinction. As critics have pointed out, this seems to verge on a female essentialism, especially when it gives central significance to features of women's sexual physiology, as in Irigaray's "two lips" or Kristeva's account of birth and mothering as fundamental to the reclaiming of feminine identity. However, there is at the same time a constructivist aspect in some of these views that seems to qualify or even cast doubt on this essentialism. This constructivism can be found in the emphasis on the transformative role of the *écriture féminine*, of the symbolic revisioning of the body, and the corollary critique of the traditional "phallocentric" cultural and historic shaping of the female body, through which it is subordinated and made submissive.

Do these views have political import, that is, implications for the organization of society or the transformation of political life? Plainly, these theorists are centrally concerned with questions of the subordination of women in male-dominant or phallocratic societies, and especially with the symbolic or discursive forms of gender coding and cultural control of female sexuality. This is political insofar as it aims to subvert these linguistic and cultural practices and to replace them with open and polymorphic feminine ways of being. Thus, some of these views, especially Irigaray's, are said to have a utopian element in their anticipation of such a creative "postphallocratic" sexual and cultural life.[1]

However suggestive this vision may be, its concrete import for the relations of people within a political community, although sometimes touched on, remains largely unarticulated and rather unclear. What does it entail for gender relations, but even more, for the whole range of political and social questions beyond this, such as ways of meeting material needs; conceptions of freedom, justice, and rights; social interaction within a community and recognition of differences; and issues of membership and citizenship? Granted that these approaches are neither intended nor required to have elaborated political programs, these French feminist theories of the rethought body nonetheless provide few proposals as to how to address such questions.

---

[1] See Nancy Fraser, "Introduction," in *Revaluing French Feminism*, eds. N. Fraser and S. L. Bartky (Bloomington: Indiana University Press, 1992), 11. Cf. also Arleen Dallery, "The Politics of Writing (the) Body: Écriture Féminine," in *Gender/Body/Knowledge*, eds. A. M. Jaggar and S. R. Bordo (New Brunswick, NJ: Rutgers University Press, 1989), 59–65.

A related feminist approach to the body takes off from Foucault's analysis of it as a site of shaping or inscription by regulatory institutions of culture and politics. Whereas Foucault pointed to institutions such as prisons, schools, the military, and the medical profession, one strand of feminist analysis emphasizes the noninstitutional forms of such disciplinary, regulatory, or regimenting practices in the production of "femininity" and the female body. Thus, Sandra Bartky speaks of the "disciplinary practices that produce a body which in gesture and appearance is recognizably feminine,"[2] such as diet regimens and body-shaping exercises, make-up and skincare, as well as deferential modes of bodily comportment in walking, sitting, and so on. She writes that by contrast to the institutional forms of power and discipline that Foucault describes, "[t]he disciplinary power that is increasingly charged with the production of a properly embodied femininity is dispersed and anonymous. . . . [It] is peculiarly modern: it does not rely upon violent or public sanctions. . . . For all that, its invasion of the body is well-nigh total. . . . The disciplinary techniques through which the 'docile bodies' of women are constructed aim at a regulation that is perpetual and exhaustive. . . ."[3]

This is a useful critique of the sources and methods of the oppression and control of women, which, while it builds on Foucault's analysis, goes beyond it in specifying new forms of the operation of power. Still, the alternative to such imposed and self-surveilling femininity is not yet clear in this account. Does it point to the need for androgyny or instead gender neutrality, or perhaps to new forms of femininity free from this coercion? Or, more relevant to our purposes here, beyond the question of gender in society, what implications does this Foucauldian and specifically feminist critique have for a new conception of politics more generally?

We can note in passing another strand of feminist analysis that emphasizes more overt forms of social control over women's bodies, by way of control over the diverse reproductive technologies involved in contraception, abortion, and assisted fertilization.[4] Here, the concern is over the delimitation of women's autonomy and the restriction of their right to privacy and their control over their own bodies.

---

[2] Sandra Bartky, "Foucault, Femininity and the Modernization of Patriarchal Power," in *Women and Values*, ed. Marilyn Pearsall (Belmont, CA: Wadsworth, 1993), 152.

[3] Ibid., 162.

[4] See, for example, Barbara Katz Rothman, *Recreating Motherhood* (New York: W. W. Norton, 1989), James Knight and Joan Callahan, *Preventing Birth* (Salt Lake City: University of Utah Press, 1989), and Zillah Eisenstein, *The Female Body and the Law* (Berkeley: University of California Press, 1988).

A seemingly more radical feminist approach to the body, which also shows the imprint of Foucault's thought, combined with themes from French feminism and deconstruction, is found in Judith Butler's views. She sees not only gender but also sex itself as constructed or as the product of significations. In this view, there is no neutral body prior to construction, which then is "inscribed" or formed by the discourses or the practices of phallocracy. Instead, "body" itself is constituted in the political process of its identification as sexed and gendered. Such a view helpfully points to the social constructedness of these categories and the contingency of identities; yet how does it account for the limits to such a radical construction of the body – for example, death, illness, basic needs, and, in general, "facticity" (however culturally interpreted or variable these may be)?

More problematic, perhaps, it isn't evident how this version of constructivism can lead to the openness to alternatives and the possibilities of transformation that Butler seeks. For when these constructions are seen simply as the products of a history of significations and where subjects themselves are regarded as constituted as sites of such significations, it becomes unclear what possible source there could be for the agency that puts such constructions in question and changes them. Previously, Butler seemed to want to eschew such a conception of agency or of the subject.[5] More recently, she concedes a role to the subject as "the permanent possibility of a certain resignifying process."[6] But at the same time, she wants to retain a view of the subject as completely a product of (or constituted by) previous significations, apparently for fear of ending up with the old Cartesian substantial subject. However, the subject cannot be at the same time completely constructed and also capable of changing itself, since change presupposes agency or a power of acting that transcends the given situation. This need not, however, entail a substantial and preformed self, a confusion that has led several philosophers to a radical structuralist position in which there are no subjects whatever. On the view I have developed, one can recognize the role of social relations as constituting persons but still see these persons as agents who can choose these relations or change them, at least to some degree.[7]

5 See Judith Butler, *Gender Trouble* (New York: Routledge, 1990), 142–145.
6 Judith Butler, "Contingent Foundations: Feminism and the Question of Postmodernism," in *Feminists Theorize the Political*, eds. J. Butler and J. W. Scott (New York: Routledge, 1992), 13.
7 Carol C. Gould, *Rethinking Democracy: Freedom and Social Cooperation in Politics, Economy, and Society* (Cambridge: Cambridge University Press, 1988), Chapters 1 and 3.

In the case of Butler, there is an intriguing suggestion of a connection between her feminist critique and politics. Specifically, she claims that this feminist constructivism supports radical democracy,[8] presumably entailing fully participatory processes of political decision making among equals. This democracy, she suggests, is the political corollary of the openness and contestability of identities, sexual and other. This is strikingly reminiscent of Claude Lefort's characterization of democracy as an "empty space" in which every issue is always open to being put in question.[9] There are at least two problems here, however. First, it isn't clear how we can get to democracy from Butler's version of constructivism, since the justification of democracy itself would require the normative recognition of the freedom and equality of individuals as agents (who therefore have a right to participate equally in decisions). Without this, construction could just as easily lead to alternative political forms, as in, for example, Nietzsche. Second, despite the initial attractiveness of the particular conception of radical democracy proposed, in which nothing and no one is excluded, this will not work for real democratic communities, which have to respect certain rights as being off the agenda and which need to use some criteria for membership, that is, for answering the question of who will participate. But these requirements are necessarily both normative and not completely inclusive.

Another important feminist approach to the body comes out of Anglo-American feminist philosophy. This is the well-established critique of traditional conceptions of rationality, understood as universal, nonsituated, and separated from the body and the emotions. Reason on this view is neutral, transcending particularity or interest, and identified as a male characteristic, whereas the body is the locus of error, illusion, and temptation, and the obstacle to truth, and quintessentially female. This conception of disembodied rationality has its obvious classical sources in Platonistic–Cartesian philosophies. Critiques of this view have been presented by many feminist philosophers – among others, Genevieve Lloyd[10] and Susan Bordo.[11] In this context, the body has been reconceived and revalued as an essential aspect of epistemic activity as well

---

[8] Butler, "Contingent Foundations," 16.

[9] Claude Lefort, *Democracy and Political Theory* (Minneapolis: University of Minnesota Press, 1988), 17.

[10] Genevieve Lloyd, *The Man of Reason: Male and Female in Western Philosophy* (Minneapolis: University of Minnesota Press, 1985).

[11] Susan Bordo, "Feminism, Post-Modernism, and Gender-Skepticism," in *Feminism/Postmodernism*, ed. L. J. Nicholson (New York: Routledge, 1990), 133–156.

as of moral practice. This emphasis brings to the fore such previously ignored or denigrated features as desire, the emotions, and aesthetic responsiveness as themselves constitutive of a more richly conceived rationality.

The political implications of this critique of disembodied rationality have been elaborated by such theorists as Iris Young, in terms of the limitations of the ideal of impartiality in theories of justice and the law and the blindness to differences of the norm of universality in conceptions of civic life and citizenship.[12] The alternative that Young develops emphasizes the representation of oppressed social groups – African-Americans, women, Native-Americans, the elderly – within the political process as a way of taking differences into account.[13] As to the role of the body or of bodily characteristics in the identification of such groups, a difficulty to avoid is the ascription of group-identifying characteristics to people simply by relying on the "objectivity" of bodily features, such as sexual physiology or skin color. Even when one avoids a reductive pluralistic essentialism, in which social groups are identified as "natural kinds," and instead takes these groups to be socially constructed, an ascriptive construction by others of the members of the group still tends to objectivize group identity and does not give scope to processes of self-construction and self-interpretation of oneself as a member of a group.[14] Granted that one has to take account of "thrownness" into situations – that people initially find themselves placed in historical, social, and cultural contexts – a theory that values freedom needs to leave open the possibilities of voluntary group identification, including choice, change, and mixtures of group affiliations, as well as the opportunity for the active and creative appropriation of cultural heritages and traditions. These features also play an important role in the next two chapters, which discuss racism and cultural identity.

A different feminist approach, with decided implications for politics, centers its theory on the female experience of mothering and the related practices of caring and nurturing. Here, I am not thinking of the psychoanalytic or semiotic framework of Kristeva and other French theorists, but rather of the large body of feminist work on care and mothering and especially on its consequences for the conceptions and practices of

---

[12] Iris Marion Young, *Justice and the Politics of Difference* (Princeton, NJ: Princeton University Press, 1990), 96–121.

[13] Ibid., especially 42–48 and 183–191.

[14] Cf. Iris Young's discussion of this issue in *Justice and the Politics of Difference*, 42–48.

politics as developed by such theorists as Sara Ruddick,[15] Virginia Held,[16] Joan Tronto,[17] and Jane Mansbridge[18] as well as in my own work,[19] referred to in Chapter 1. Diana Meyers's writing on the role of empathy in the law[20] could also be included in this group. The political content of this care/mothering emphasis has been variously understood to include a concern with world peace, with welfare and the protection of the vulnerable in society, with attention to the individuated needs of specific persons and empathic understanding of their situation, and with concern for the common good.

On the face of it, this care/mothering approach would seem to be closely related to notions of the female body and to the traditional historical or cultural association between giving birth and providing nurturance. Yet most of the theorists who draw consequences for the political domain tend to interpret "mothering" as open to males to participate in, as parenting, and thus to disengage it from any essential relation to the female body, although not necessarily from the body and bodily affect in general. Another element of embodiment that works through these theories is a notion of openness, sensibility, or responsiveness and sympathy, or what we might call *affective resonance* with the other. These characteristics have often been identified with the feminine. But they have also historically played a role in several general ethical theories and occasionally in social and political theory as well, in the form of such conceptions as "fellow-feeling" or "Verstehen."

Reflecting on these approaches to mothering and care suggests two tasks for a distinctively feminist conception of politics. The first, as noted, would be to work out in what sense the body or embodiment plays a role in politics and its transformation, and the second is to elaborate

---

[15] Sara Ruddick, *Maternal Thinking: Toward a Politics of Peace* (Boston: Beacon Press, 1989).

[16] Virginia Held, "Feminism and Moral Theory," in *Women and Moral Theory*, eds. E. F. Kittay and D. T. Meyers (Totowa, NJ: Rowman & Littlefield, 1987), 111–128; "Non-Contractual Society," in *Science, Morality and Feminist Theory*, eds. M. Hanen and K. Nielsen (Calgary, Canada: University of Calgary Press, 1987), 111–137; and *Feminist Morality* (Chicago: University of Chicago Press, 1993).

[17] Joan Tronto, *Moral Boundaries: A Political Argument for an Ethic of Care* (New York: Routledge, 1993).

[18] Jane Mansbridge, "Feminism and Democratic Community," in *Democratic Community: NOMOS XXV*, eds. J. W. Chapman and I. Shapiro (New York: New York University Press, 1993).

[19] Carol C. Gould, "Feminism and Democratic Community Revisited," in *Democratic Community: NOMOS XXXV*.

[20] See, for example, Diana Tietjens Meyers, "Social Exclusion, Moral Reflection, and Rights," in *Law and Philosophy*, Vol. 12, no. 2 (May 1993): 217–232.

the features of a caring politics beyond the more general formulations that have been presented in the history of political theory. The extent to which this would have to entail a new model of politics is brought home to us by Carole Pateman, who in a series of works has argued that the traditional liberal model of the social contract is fatally flawed as a model of democracy by its presupposition of what she calls the sexual contract.[21] This latter contract is, on her view, a tacit agreement among men for the continued control and subordination of women and, in particular, of women's bodies. The operative concept of women's body in this context is the sexual body to be used and controlled by men. As such, women are assigned to the private sphere, where their role is predominantly sexual and only secondarily familial or maternal. The public sphere – the civil realm of the social contract – is, by contrast, the domain of individuals who are not explicitly differentiated by gender and who are formally characterized as universal and free beings, but who in fact are exclusively masculine. Pateman believes that we need to abandon the model of a contract because it is necessarily tied to the notion of property in the person, which has as one of its root forms the sexual possession of women by men.

Despite the trenchancy of several features of Pateman's critique, the feminist alternative that she goes on to describe may in effect entail a problematic essentialism. She criticizes the ideals of gender neutrality and of the participation of women in the public sphere on the same basis as men, since these serve only to mask the continuation of male domination in politics. She proposes instead that women and men should participate in this domain as feminine and masculine. She writes, "Women can attain the formal standing of civil individuals but as embodied feminine beings we can never be 'individuals' in the same sense as men. To take embodied identity seriously demands the abandonment of the masculine, unitary individual to open up space for two figures; one masculine, one feminine."[22] While it is important to emphasize the role of embodiment and of the recognition of differences in politics, we can question whether such a quasi-essentialist and dualist ontology of separate and distinct masculine and feminine identities is the appropriate direction.

The final feminist approach to be briefly considered in this context is that of socialist feminism. Here, embodiment is highlighted under the

---

[21] Carole Pateman, *The Sexual Contract* (Stanford, CA: Stanford University Press, 1988); and *The Disorder of Women* (Stanford, CA: Stanford University Press, 1989).

[22] Ibid., 224.

aspect of the centrality of bodily needs and the practical activities of production and reproduction. While such feminist approaches stress the role of the system of patriarchy in addition to that of class domination in understanding oppression, they retain a Marxist emphasis on the material conditions of life. Crucial to their account is the analysis of the double burden of women's work: as wage labor and as unpaid domestic labor. The woman, as housewife and mother in a capitalist form of society, has the function of the reproduction of labor power, not only in having and raising children as future workers but also in sustaining the daily reproduction of the labor power of her husband (and of herself if she works). Socialist feminists have pointed to the ways in which patriarchal modes have facilitated economic exploitation and, conversely, how the drive of capitalist economy for greater profits has strengthened the special forms of oppression of women that patriarchy represents. In contrast to earlier forms of Marxist feminism, socialist feminists have argued that explanations of women's oppression in terms of patriarchy are not reducible to class analysis.

For our purposes, the emphasis on the body in socialist feminist approaches is an emphasis on the historically and socially situated being with needs, both material and social – in short, a body constructed in and through certain forms of social relations and not simply a physical organism. More recent versions have focused on the special forms of oppression that characterize the economically most deprived segment of the population of advanced industrial countries, namely, impoverished women and children who are dependent on welfare and lack the opportunities for jobs. The term "feminization of poverty" vividly describes this phenomenon.

The theoretical approach provided by Marxist or socialist feminism is impressive in its recognition that politics is necessarily connected with the meeting of material needs and thus with the body. What has been problematic in some versions of this view has been the tendency to reduce the political to a reflection of economic or material interests, what has been called "economism." Furthermore, feminist considerations of the oppression and exploitation of women have often taken second place in these analyses to considerations of the economic functions of work and the family under capitalism. Thus, the addition of this perspective of women's body as working body or as embodying and meeting material and social needs provides a useful supplement to the earlier emphasis on women's sexual body, but neither of these yet arrives at a notion of embodied politics that would take the feminist critique into account.

Views of Embodiment in Political Philosophy

Whereas the various feminist approaches to the body do not yet sufficiently interpret its significance for political contexts, conversely the leading traditional approaches to the role of the body in politics tend to be distinctively nonfeminist, if not antifeminist. We can leave aside the historically ubiquitous sexist view of the body in philosophy and political theory that excludes women from politics on the grounds that they are bodily, sensuous, and emotional creatures who lack the requisite rationality for political judgment and participation in decision making. Such views have been well criticized by feminist philosophers and by now require no further discussion. However, there are several other nonfeminist if not antifeminist positions that interpret the body's significance for politics in an affirmative way. I focus on two of them here and then take note of others in passing.

The first such view is the conception, found especially in early modern political theory, of the "body politic," where the body serves as a metaphor or a model of the political community or the state. This has a minimal and a more elaborated interpretation. The first is the simple analogy of a political body – a legislature, citizens, inhabitants of a state – as a unified collection of individuals under common law or with a common purpose. The second interpretation takes the political community to be a kind of organism having a head, extremities, and various organs or parts that function for the sake of the whole. In this organic model, the relation of the parts is usually interpreted hierarchically, where authority flows from the head or the soul to the lower organs.[23] The "head" was often taken to be the sovereign as a monarch who had power and authority over his subjects. Or, in Hobbes, where the sovereign was understood as mutually constituted by contract and invested with this authority, it was seen as "an artificial soul, as giving life and motion to the whole body."[24]

Typically (with Hobbes the exception), the body politic was exclusively and rigorously male. Here, in contrast with the exclusion of women on the grounds of their "bodiliness," only men count as members of the body politic, or as embodied subjects. However, these individuals are most often seen as subject to the authority of the sovereign because the sovereign represents the spiritual power or is legitimated by a superior

---

[23] Cf. John O'Neill, *Five Bodies* (Ithaca, NY: Cornell University Press, 1985), 74–76.
[24] Thomas Hobbes, *Leviathan* (New York: Collier, 1962), 19.

reason. In this way, this view exemplifies the separation between spirit and the flesh, between mind and body, and between reason and mere sensibility, a separation that has been the object of feminist criticism.

Perhaps the bluntest account of the role of the body in politics is the one that associates bodily strength, force, and the ability to command with political power and excellence, and the authority to lead. This view may have had its origins in the tradition of warrior kings or of military conquerors as the "natural" leaders of men. An early expression of a view of this sort, offered by Thrasymachus in Plato's *Republic*, is that justice is what is in the interest of the stronger or, as it came to be expressed proverbially, that "might makes right."

A more modern approach to bodily strength and force as the basis for political rule is theorized in Nietzsche's account of the *Übermensch*, that vigorous and dominating male who expresses the will to power in noble action and in occasional outbursts of anger and violence. Thus, for example, Nietzsche writes admiringly, "The chivalrous and aristocratic valuations presuppose a strong physique, blooming, even exuberant health, together with all the conditions that guarantee its preservation: combat, adventure, the chase, the dance, war games, etc."[25] Or again, "Among the noble, mental acuteness . . . is much less important than is the perfect functioning of the ruling, unconscious instincts or even a certain temerity to follow sudden impulses, court danger, or indulge spurts of violent rage, love, worship, gratitude, or vengeance."[26]

By contrast to the primacy of the male body interpreted in this "macho" way, Nietzsche characterizes women as the antithesis to this robust embodiment. He says,

Finally: woman! One half of mankind is weak, typically sick, changeable, inconstant – woman needs strength in order to cleave to it; she needs a religion of weakness that glorifies being weak, loving, and being humble as divine: or better, she makes the strong weak – she rules when she succeeds in overcoming the strong. Woman has always conspired with the types of decadence, the priests, against the "powerful," the "strong," the men –.[27]

The political consequences of this view of a superior race of men are vividly suggested in Nietzsche's aphoristic style. He extols tyrannical rule, the exploitation and use of the weak, the rejection of conscience and

[25] Friedrich Nietzsche, *The Genealogy of Morals*, first essay, VII (Garden City, NY: Doubleday, 1956), 167.
[26] Ibid., X, 172–173.
[27] Friedrich Nietzsche, *The Will to Power* (New York: Vintage, 1968), #864, 460.

guilt, and the indulgence of the whims of power. The hero is set off against the mass, strength of will against degenerate weakness, and all in the name of the priority of the body over the soul and of action over thought. Thus, in *The Will to Power*, Nietzsche writes, "'Tyrannization' is the quality of great men: they make lesser men stupid."[28] And again, "The Revolution made Napoleon possible: that is its justification."[29] Or yet again, in the might makes right tradition, he writes, "We do not believe in any right that is not supported by the power of enforcement. We feel all rights to be conquests."[30] As to the relation of the ruler to the ruled, Nietzsche muses (in the fragment titled "The Body as a Political Structure"), "Inference concerning the evolution of mankind: perfecting consists in the production of the most powerful individuals, who will use the great mass of people as their tools (and indeed the most intelligent and most pliable tools)."[31]

Nietzsche's views here in some ways anticipate the fascistic glorification of the body as brute force and of authoritarian control by the heroic leaders over the mass. However, he might not have recognized the degree of mechanization and ritualization that the new "master race" introduced in making the mass an obedient instrument of its despotism. Walter Benjamin reflects on this phenomenon in the final passages of his "The Work of Art in the Age of Mechanical Reproduction." He attempts to show how fascism aestheticizes this politics of violence and provides a framework for its expression. He writes,

Fascism attempts to organize the newly created proletarian masses without affecting the property structure which the masses strive to eliminate. Fascism sees its salvation in giving the masses not their right, but instead, a chance to express themselves. The logical result of fascism is the introduction of aesthetics into political life. . . . All efforts to render politics aesthetic culminate in one thing: war.[32]

Benjamin goes on to quote the fascist Futurist sculptor Marinetti's eulogy to what he called an "aesthetics of war," including Marinetti's assertion that "[w]ar is beautiful because it initiates the dreamt-of metalization

---

[28] Ibid., #875, 468.
[29] Ibid., #877, 469.
[30] Ibid., #120, 74.
[31] Ibid., #660, 349.
[32] Walter Benjamin, "The Work of Art in the Age of Mechanical Reproduction," reprinted in *Marxism and Art*, eds. Berel Lang and Forrest Williams (New York: David McKay Co., 1972), 299.

of the human body."[33] (All this almost a half-century before *Robocop* and cyborgs!) The glorification of the warrior-body and of the heroics of domination and destruction, and of course the regimented rituals of a militarized fascist state, represent a politics of the male body radically at odds with the images and roles of the female body considered earlier. Yet here is an account of the body that is explicitly political and constructed in part to suit the demands of a specific politics of a male-dominant totalitarianism.

More positive conceptions of the role of the body in political life can be found in other political philosophies. There are the theories, cited earlier, that emphasize bodily needs, taken as material or economic and not simply as physiological, and that see them as fundamental to questions of politics. I refer here primarily to the variety of Marxist theories and secondarily perhaps to strongly welfarist theories, which are oriented to overcoming poverty and the achievement of well-being. To the degree that these approaches emphasize practices of production and the social and class relations in which they are embedded, they may also indicate that the body is not that of an isolated, individual organism but rather is a social body, in some sense transformed through social relations.

Another political approach in which a conception of the body plays a role, although not in terms of needs or material practices, is that of Claude Lefort. He proposes that a significant break occurs between the political space of sovereignty and that of democratic polities. According to Lefort, in the earlier case of monarchy, the body of the ruler filled the space of sovereignty, whereas in democracy, this space is "an empty place," open to contestation by the variety of competing or plural interests. There is literally, in his view, no body that occupies this democratic space, as a matter of principle. As Lefort writes,

The democratic revolution . . . burst out when the body of the king was destroyed, when the body politic was decapitated and when, at the same time, the corporeality of the social was dissolved. . . . The modern democratic revolution is best recognized in this mutation: there is no power linked to a body. Power appears as an empty place and those who exercise it as mere mortals who occupy it only temporarily or who could install themselves in it only by force or cunning.[34]

Lefort goes on to argue that under conditions of conflict and social disintegration, democratic societies may yield to a desire to "weld power

---

[33] Marinetti, as cited in Walter Benjamin, "The Work of Art in the Age of Mechanical Reproduction."

[34] Claude Lefort, *The Political Forms of Modern Society* (Cambridge: Polity Press, 1986), 303.

and society back together again, to efface all signs of social division, to banish the indetermination that haunts the democratic experience."[35] The totalitarian apparatus is set up just for this purpose, drawing on a democratic source but transforming it into a unitary notion of what he describes as the "People-as-One." The formerly empty space of democracy comes then to be filled with the political body of totalitarianism, in which the omniscient, militant leader, "the Egocrat," presents himself as standing for the whole. According to Lefort, "[He] offers his own body – individual, mortal, endowed with all the virtues – whether he's called Stalin or Mao or Fidel. A mortal body which is perceived as invulnerable, which condenses in itself all strengths, all talents, and defies the laws of nature by his super-male energy."[36]

Lefort usefully suggests that democratic society separates the power of the state from identification with a given, concrete body and that this power is in principle open to contestation. Yet Lefort's concept of the body seems to be limited to the particular personal identity of a sovereign. Inasmuch as individuals in democratic society are not bodies in this sense, they are, for Lefort, "disembodied." There is what he calls a "disincorporation of the individual."[37] But this view of democracy seems problematic in that it excludes the concrete embodied persons who in reality participate in the political processes of democracy. In Lefort's view, the "ungraspability" of democratic society, because of the lack of any definite identity of the sovereign ("the people"), leads to what he calls "a multi-layered discourse that tries to grasp [this identity]. . . . The attempt to sacralize institutions through discourse is directly related to the loss of the substance of society, to the disintegration of the body."[38] This implies, however, that democratic society is constituted of anonymous individuals (involved in a plurality of groups), where their concrete identity and their bodily existence seem to be replaced by this "multi-layered discourse." The realm of the political is thus transmogrified into the realm of discourse. There's no body in sight, only words. Clearly, there is some truth in the view that the political domain is a realm of discourse and that needs, desires, and many other aspects of bodily existence enter into politics in the communication among individuals. But these bodily facts cannot be reduced to such discursive interaction.

[35] Ibid., 305.
[36] Ibid., 300.
[37] Ibid., 303.
[38] Ibid., 304.

   This focus on discourse in politics has been central in recent political philosophy, prominently in the work of Habermas and, in the form of consensus theory, in the work of Rawls. I cite these here not as additional examples of theories of embodiment in politics but rather to suggest that these two dominant contemporary theories appear to leave such considerations in the background. In this way, their views seem excessively cognitivist, and the absence of a developed conception of embodiment may in fact impact their accounts of community and of politics.

   We can discern a certain cognitivism in Rawls's focus on shared conceptions, whether as a shared conception of justice in his account of the political or as a shared conception of the good in his account of community. Thus, as he writes, "By definition, let's think of a community as a special kind of association, one united by a comprehensive doctrine, for example, a church."[39] Or again, in distinguishing a democratic society from a community, Rawls characterizes a community as "a society governed by a shared comprehensive religious, philosophical, or moral doctrine."[40] Democratic societies, by contrast, have no such shared conception of a comprehensive doctrine. Rather, their basic structure "is regulated by a political conception of justice," formed through an overlapping consensus.[41]

   While such conceptions clearly play a role, and perhaps a major role, in constituting society or community as a structure that binds people together, Rawls's characterization here seems to leave out of account the activities or practices in which people jointly engage to meet their needs and to create their social world. If a political society or a community is *defined* by the shared conceptions of its members, little room is left for what lies outside of and beyond these conceptual understandings, such as bodily needs and desires; the social and material dependency of persons on others for their lives and nurturance, security, or education; and common action and social practices.[42]

---

[39] John Rawls, *Political Liberalism* (New York: Columbia University Press, 1993), 40, fn. 43.
[40] Ibid., 42.
[41] Ibid., 44.
[42] Rawls does acknowledge this in a sort of backhanded way. Concerning the "first principle of justice" – the "equal basic rights and liberties" principle – Rawls writes,

> [A]s one might expect, important aspects of this principle are left out in the brief statement as given. In particular, the first principle covering the equal rights and liberties may easily be preceded by a lexically prior principle requiring that citizens' basic needs be met, at least insofar as their being met is necessary for citizens to understand and to be able fruitfully to exercise these rights and liberties. Certainly any such principle must

In some ways, a similar critique can be made of Habermas's approach. In particular, Habermas, like Rawls, presents a model of coming to agreement or arriving at consensus on norms or principles of justice by means of rational and discursive procedures. For Habermas, the central feature of such a discourse is that it aims at universalizability, or at the articulation of a generalizable interest that goes beyond the particular interests of individuals. The precondition for arriving at such an ideal agreement is the ability and responsibility of each participant in the discourse to take the perspective of the other. Along these lines, Habermas, like Rawls, has been criticized for translating substantive moral norms into matters of procedural decision, and thus for formalism in the Kantian tradition. But more to our point here might be a certain cognitivism evident in the weight that Habermas gives to rational discourse as constitutive of the public domain. In focusing on the shared understandings of members of the discursive community, this approach defocuses the range of nondiscursive actions and practices of embodied persons, which also make up their political life. Furthermore, inasmuch as the aim of this discursive activity is to achieve consensus or to arrive at a generalizable interest, the account tends to diminish the importance of the recognition of differences and hence of the individuality of the members of the political community.[43] Since this individuality is closely linked to embodiment, this emphasis on discursive agreement and the overcoming of differences would seem to yield a somewhat disembodied political community.

However, Habermas does address embodiment in the form of a concern with needs and with the problem of the application of universal

be assumed in applying the first principle. But I do not pursue these and other matters here (*Political Liberalism*, 7).

In another place, he writes, similarly, that "beyond" the guarantees of liberty of conscience and freedom of thought, association, movement, and so on, "measures are required to assure that the basic needs of all citizens can be met so that they can take part in political and social life" (*Political Liberalism*, 166). These "basic needs" do not enter here as "principles" in the theory; rather, they are introduced as "assumed," as "lexically prior" to the first principle. The meeting of basic needs would seem to bespeak a concern with embodiment, with the facts of the needs of concrete persons in their interactions, not simply in terms of their shared conceptions but in terms of their bodily practices, affect, physical and social needs, interdependences, and so on. For Rawls, however, meeting these needs is considered here only in passing, as prerequisite for the functioning of a democratic society.

43 Cf. Carol C. Gould, "On the Conception of the Common Interest," in *Hermeneutics and Critical Theory in Ethics and Politics*, ed. M. Kelly (Cambridge, MA: The MIT Press, 1990), 253–273 (especially 264–267).

norms and principles to concrete cases. He has characterized the kinds of relations that are marked by empathy and concern for particular others as solidarity and has argued that discourse theory is able to bring together coherently the concern for a universal and abstract principle of justice with the concrete concerns of solidarity.[44] However, these suggestions in his theory remain relatively undeveloped, particularly as they may introduce a conception of embodiment or of the relation of the body to politics. Furthermore, at times Habermas has stated that issues of practical, concrete, or social responsibility in politics and public life – the sort of issues that would involve the interests of the body, its well-being, its survival – cannot be addressed within philosophy itself and that these matters typical of embodied politics fall outside a discursive theory of moral and political norms. Instead, he proposes that they are more the concern of the historical and social sciences.[45] Although he holds that these concrete matters of moral and political decision and action are central responsibilities of philosophers as of others, he does not see that they fall within the purview of a philosophical theory of politics.

Embodiment, Agency, and Community

What, then, are the outlines of a conception of embodied politics that takes feminist theory into account – including both its critique and its positive reinterpretation of the body – but that extends it more fully to the social and political domain, while also drawing perhaps on some insights from the nonfeminist approaches? We can discern in the preceding critique certain desiderata that emerge for an adequate view of the role of the body in politics: that it should be not only feminist but also nonessentialist – that is, that it should conceive the body as socially constructed yet open to self-interpretation and change. This recognition of embodiment in politics signifies not so much the introduction of an entirely new set of categories but the transformation of many of the traditional ones, a shift in their meanings – for example, of need, power, interests, practices, and so on. Here, I focus on needs, with the suggestion that similar analyses remain to be given for these other categories. In

---

[44] See Jürgen Habermas, "Justice and Solidarity," in *Hermeneutics and Critical Theory in Ethics and Politics*, 32–51 (especially 47ff.).

[45] Jürgen Habermas, *Moral Consciousness and Communicative Action* (Cambridge, MA: The MIT Press, 1990), 211.

addition, certain new concepts have to be introduced in this exploration of embodied politics.

We can begin by marking out three aspects of need that relate to political and social life, which in turn involve different sorts of embodiment. These are (1) material and sensuous needs, (2) the need for recognition, and (3) the need for relationships. Whereas the first two have been rather fully discussed in political philosophy, the third has not. It turns out that each of these is mediated by the body in a different way.

First, material needs point to the fundamental bodily requirements for food, clothing, shelter, and so on, which are satisfied by the creation of objects through work. In Marx's classical account of this process, as "the production of the means of existence," this is analyzed as an activity of "objectification," in which people transform the natural world through work in accordance with their purposes so that it can be appropriated for their use. This is a process of embodiment in two senses: The object produced is an embodiment or an externalization of the capacities and intentions of the agent-producer; and people embody their desires and needs in the objects that their activity produces, in that these objects are shaped in accordance with the end of meeting such needs or satisfying such desires.[46]

Among the needs satisfied by the creation of objects are not only the material needs but also sensuous needs, and in particular, those that are satisfied by aesthetic objects or by the creation of art. Here, embodiment or objectification serves as a means of gratifying the senses and as a means of spontaneous creative expression. One may thus speak of the "aesthetic body" and its needs here.

A second basic need is the need for recognition, which has increasingly been taken into account in political philosophy. This need in turn has two aspects: recognition of the self as an autonomous individual (for example, as described by Hegel in terms of a struggle for recognition that eventuates in mutual recognition among persons) and recognition of oneself as belonging to a community (as discussed, for example, by

---

[46] Some of the objects produced in order to satisfy material needs are tools or artifacts used for the production of other things. These are also embodiments of the agent's purposes. In a certain sense, the tool is an extension or expansion of the body in terms of the range and power of its capacities. See Marx W. Wartofsky, "Piaget's Genetic Epistemology and the Marxist Theory of Knowledge," *Revue Internationale de Philosophie* (Special double issue on Piaget, ed. Leo Apostel), no. 142–43, 1982 (published 1983): 470–507, and "Epistemology Historicized," in *Naturalistic Epistemology*, Boston Studies and the Philosophy of Science, Vol. 100, eds. Abner Shimony and Debra Nails (Dordrecht and Boston: D. Reidel, 1987), 357–377.

Taylor and Kymlicka[47]). Thus both of these aspects of recognition involve identity – individual and group identity. The process of recognition is necessarily one of social interaction, since it entails being recognized by others or recognizing others. It can be seen that embodiment mediates this interaction in two ways. The bodily element here can be one's own body as the form through which one's identity manifests itself to others (and reflexively to oneself); or it can take the form of created objects, through which agents can represent their capacities to others and in this way come to be recognized as who they are.

In connection with the second aspect of recognition, namely, group identity, it may be useful to distinguish between bodily characteristics and embodied characteristics. This corresponds to the distinction between the ascription by others of physical characteristics to persons as a basis for categorizing them into groups, and their own interpretation of themselves as members of groups – that is, their self-ascription of bodily characteristics. To speak of these characteristics as embodied suggests that they are integrally tied to agency. More generally, we can speak of an "agential body." In this conception, agency is not something added to body as an extrinsic and contingent property that a body may or may not possess; nor is body conceived as a separable entity, such as a physical body in space-time. Rather, the bodies we are referring to are distinctively human, where agency or the capacity to choose makes them the kind of bodies they are, and where bodies are expressive of agency.

One implication of this notion of embodiment for group identity in political contexts is that it introduces a more open and fluid conception of a group in place of the traditional categorical ascription of fixed physical characteristics as defining groups. In this way, this approach follows the work of many feminist theorists and theorists of group identity, in their critique of essentialist accounts of gender and race. Since embodiment implies that group membership is determined by a process of social self-ascription by agents, ideally at least it is a matter of some choice or interpretation as to what bodily characteristics will be taken to define a group and what significance these characteristics have. In Chapter 4 I consider the implications of this constructivist approach for understanding race and racism. None of this is to deny, however, that it may be valuable to retain traditional ascriptive group identities for the purpose of rectifying

---

[47] See Charles Taylor, *Multiculturalism*, ed. Amy Gutmann (Princeton, NJ: Princeton University Press, 1994); and Will Kymlicka, *Multicultural Citizenship* (Oxford: Oxford University Press, 1995).

the consequences of previous oppression, inasmuch as these presuppose such an ascriptive process. Thus women and African-Americans, among others, have a right to receive just treatment and in some cases compensation to remedy past discrimination based on bodily characteristics, and for such purposes it is important to acknowledge these groups in their traditional ascriptions.

In addition to the two types of needs thus far described, namely, material needs and the need for recognition, there is a third sense of need that has not been widely noted. This is what I call the need for relationships or for connectedness. This does not only apply to communal belonging. I have in mind also more interpersonal relationships, including relations to individual others to whom one is attached, as well as family relationships. This connectedness, which has been stressed in some recent feminism, can be distinguished from the kind of interaction involved in the need for recognition discussed earlier. In recognition, what is involved is a largely cognitive relationship in which there is a conscious and explicit acknowledgment of another's identity as well as concomitant respect for it. In the case I am talking about now, what the person needs is *to be in the relationship*, not only to be recognized by another as being who they are. Being in the relationship is its own end. Such relationships might include the range of interpersonal ones such as friendship, companionship, love, nurturance, and family; associational ones such as clubs and interest groups; and also a range of communal relations, such as membership in a cultural group or local community, as well as citizenship. Whereas the need for recognition requires relations with others as instrumental to this end, in this third case, the relationships themselves satisfy the need and are not instrumental to some other end such as recognition. Even when the relationship also serves other ends – for example, as being in the family may satisfy economic needs or participating in cultural activities may be aimed at perpetuating the culture – nonetheless there is often an autonomous need for being in the relationship itself, for its own sake.

In the diversity of these relationships, the satisfaction of this third sort of need is mediated by the body, as were the first two. This is obvious in that these are relationships among embodied persons, and this is so even if these persons are not immediately or physically present to each other. The body that is required in the light of this neediness is what I would call *the relational body*. That is, the body itself is not simply a physical object to which are added relations of an external sort, but rather it is in part defined by this need and shaped by the relations that satisfy it. The body

is relational in that through it people manifest themselves to each other
and establish their relations.

The concept of need as used here is not to be taken reductively in a
biologistic interpretation, nor is it to be taken as connoting metaphysical
necessity. There is no reason that the notion of need has to be restricted
to the necessities of organic or physical life. In fact, in our ordinary use
of the term "needs," we do not restrict it in this way but rather use it
more flexibly, relative to purposes or norms. "Need" implies lack and
an awareness of lack, where something can be lacking only if there is
some norm or end with respect to which such a lack is defined. The
norms we are speaking of in this case are not biological but rather arise
out of the conditions of human practices and social life, and they are
necessary only relative to human ends and to a social ontology. Thus
the identification and interpretation of needs have a socially constructed
aspect and also involve a personal ascription of these needs to oneself.
Additionally, beyond these factors of construction and self-ascription, we
might note the set of higher-order conscious needs that goes beyond
any limitation to the biological. Thus we have needs for culture, art, love,
respect, and so on, which are no less serious for their not being reductively
organic or metaphysical. Moreover, we can observe that the concept of
need as used here is relational, tying the individual to nature and to other
persons.

The three types of needs that I have discussed, which entail different
modes of embodiment, have specific import for a political society. Some
of these implications are obvious, particularly in regard to the first two
types of needs. Material needs require organized forms of political and
economic life to deliver the goods needed for their satisfaction (economic
production, systems of distribution, markets, regulatory practices, and so
on), as well as systems of education, welfare, and health care, and provisions for the security of persons and of their property. Likewise, sensuous
needs are addressed politically in the concern for quality of life and a de-
cent environment, as well as support for the arts and a concern with the
aesthetic aspects of the public domain, such as architectural planning, opportunities for recreation, and so on. The need for recognition is served
by the wide range of political and legal rights and liberties that secure
the freedom and equality of persons and protect their dignity, including
protection against discrimination and oppression. And the recognition
of group and national identity is expressed in the status and rights of
citizenship, in rights of democratic participation, and in the equitable
representation of group interests, while recognition of cultural or ethnic

identity may proceed through various individual rights (such as freedom of conscience or freedom of religion) or may call for the introduction of certain group rights, an issue I address in Chapter 5.

But what does the third need, namely, the need for relationships, require? Presumably, that political society provide the conditions for the free development of these relationships. Somewhat paradoxically, one of the principal prerequisites for the flourishing of interpersonal relations is for the state *not* to interfere but to secure a domain of privacy within which people can freely choose how and to whom to relate. The correlate to the noninterference in private relationships is freedom of association at the social and political level, namely, the right to join groups, associations, and communities as one chooses and without penalty. Needless to say, freedom from interference concerning private relations does not preclude legal prohibitions on abuses within such relationships, for example, prohibitions against child abuse, marital rape, woman battering, and so on.

Positively, too, each form of relationship – from personal to associational and communal – has conditions that a political society can provide or facilitate. Although perhaps obvious, these are often overlooked in practice. For the family, these include provisions of parental leave to permit nurturance, and of childcare to facilitate the continuation of family relations and to contribute to the child's development. The more general features of welfare and child support, as well as health care and education, as discussed earlier under the first need, are also important in this context. Economic and social factors clearly contribute as well to other interpersonal relations, such as friendship, companionship, and even love. These relations, as well as the associational ones – affiliations, clubs, interest groups, professional societies – are also facilitated by background conditions such as means of communication. Beyond this, at the level of cultural groups and communities, satisfying the need for relationships might require some support for such groups and their activities by the public or by the government, but this is a difficult issue in terms of fairness of allocation and practicality.

The question arises, however, as to whether the conception of needs and of embodiment more generally has implications for a political society that go beyond such policies and programs. Starting from the individual who is the subject of this embodied politics, we have claimed that this person is not adequately described as the abstract self-interested individual of classical liberal theory, nor as a purely political citizen of a state, nor as a producer of economic values. Rather, as characterized earlier, the subject of embodied politics is an agent, whose body is an expression of this agency or capacity for free activity and not simply the passive bearer of attributes. Thus, this body does not have a mind but is minded; it is an integrated mind/body. This agent is what I called an individual-in-relations, whose activity is often shared and interactive; and as proposed earlier, whose body can be characterized as relational, shown in the body's receptivity to others. Thus we are not talking about an agent who "has" a body through which this agency is expressed, nor a body that "has" agency as one of its attributes, but rather of the whole person. This is what I would characterize as a *whole person view* of the subject of embodied politics.

An emphasis on the recognition and relationships of whole persons leads, I think, to a conception of *inclusive communities* as frameworks for political life. As used here, inclusiveness connotes openness to and acceptance of the whole person on the part of others, where persons are taken in their embodied and diverse complexity. There is no exclusive concern then with cognitivity, or with any given criteria of ethnicity or objective bodily characteristics. Nor is there a requirement for agreement on some comprehensive doctrine – moral, religious, or philosophical – for there to be a community. This is therefore a community of differentiated whole persons. In this way, this view differs from Rawls's notion of community and from his conception of political society, since here an inclusive community also serves as the basis for a political society. Of course, this inclusiveness does not entail the absence of borders or one single worldwide community. This issue of the scope of political communities remains a real one; and we need also to accommodate the possibility of overlapping communities. I pursue these questions at some length in Part III of this book.

The idea of communal embodiment suggests further that the expression of the communal relations among whole persons may relevantly take the form of rituals and practices. Participation in these rituals and practices may symbolize membership in this community and may express this belonging in concrete and bodily ways. Included here are forms of music, dance, the arts, poetry, and celebratory practices that join mind and body, affect and thought, and that express solidarity with others. Yet these rituals and practices have to be open, inclusive, nonexploitative, and freely chosen. By participating in these expressive practices, the agents do not lose themselves or their identities but rather show their ties with others.

This reflection on the expressive and affective features of communal relations may give rise to a conception of *embodied community* or perhaps even of a *communal body*. We would then be pointing not only to these communicative and sensuous practices but also to the material life shared in by members of the community who reside and work together. Here, their mutual participation represents an organized and symbolically mediated relation not only to each other but also to nature. However, to speak in this way is somewhat hazardous from my point of view, since it may call to mind the old "body politic," with its associated connotations of holism and organicism, as well as hierarchy and patriarchy. The communal body in the sense used here is not a single or unitary body in which individuals are subordinated. Rather, it refers to nothing but the relations among embodied persons who are materially and affectively interdependent, and, as we have already noted, such relations are becoming increasingly global in scope, a point to be developed further in subsequent chapters.

Two additional substantive features of an embodied politics can be noted here in conclusion: participation and receptivity. Both have significant roots in feminist philosophy. First, although participation in political decision making aims at an extrinsic good, namely, self-governance, the activity in itself has a certain potential to satisfy the need for relationships as an aspect of embodied politics. In contrast with often faceless forms of bureaucratic and administrative politics, participation involves networks of engagement with other concrete individuals. We can say that the political is personal in this context. Such relations of engagement are easier in contexts of face-to-face interactions (e.g., in committees, small groups, or the occasional town meeting, or in interactions among individuals in governmental or deliberative bodies); but such relations may also occur in more mediated forms between constituents and their representatives or other elected officials. Less ideally, the de facto emphasis on political personalities and the nitty-gritty concern with relationships of status, power, and reciprocal obligations can also be seen as ubiquitous and unavoidable from this perspective of embodied politics.

The second feature that characterizes persons in embodied political relations is receptivity, where this refers to responsiveness to others in terms of their individual differences and needs (as discussed in Chapter 1) as well as to their cultural differences. It is an "attunement" to the whole person as this concrete embodied individual, where the understanding of others is individuated rather than in terms of types or general categories. This characteristic is familiar to us in personal terms as sensitivity to, and as empathy with, particular others. In its import for politics, receptivity would not imply an absence of general principles or laws, which would render it inapplicable in a domain where fair treatment of large groups of people is central. Instead, it would entail a competence in the application of laws and principles to particular cases that is sensitive to differences in people's needs and interests. In this sense, it requires the casuistic art of interpreting the general for particular cases, and it endorses a flexibility in dealing with special or exceptional circumstances.

Beyond the administration of law, receptivity also manifests itself in policy making that anticipates the need for differential applications of policies to individuals in order to achieve equal treatment. One standard case, of course, has been the treatment of the disabled, whether by remediation or in other ways. But such receptivity can be applied more widely not simply by a cognitive or cerebral comprehension of differentiated needs but as a matter of support for the concerns and needs of others and what I have previously called solidarity with them. Receptivity could also be as expressed in openness to and support for the variety of cultural and other group differences and for their interaction, within a given society and also extending beyond its borders. In this sense, the inclusive democratic communities described earlier would be intercultural. This theme is pursued further in Chapters 4 and 5.

4

Racism and Democracy

In light of the previous analysis of embodied politics, I would like now to consider the role that the idea of the social construction of race can play in democratic theory as well as take up certain hard questions that bear on the persistence of racism within democratic societies. I begin with the conceptual connection between the requirement of democracy and the critique of racism. I then turn to the issue of whether racial identity can be interpreted in cultural terms, taking up Anthony Appiah's argument on this point. Concerning the norms of democracy, I want to argue for a reinterpretation that draws on a conception of what I have called in Chapter 2 concrete universality. In this connection, while appreciating Charles Mills's trenchant critique of the "racial contract," I suggest that his appeal to an ideal social contract, with its set of natural and human rights, does not yet provide an adequate normative basis for a fully non-racist democracy. Instead, we need a conception of inclusive, intercultural democratic communities, on a certain interpretation. In terms of this approach to group differences, I then briefly consider the potential impact of economic democracy for reducing racial divisiveness. As background for taking up these difficult questions, however, it is helpful at the outset to briefly review the present situation regarding racism and theories of democracy.

Racism and Existing Democratic Frameworks

Why does racism, as well as the idea of race itself, play almost no role in most democratic theories? As Frank Cunningham has noted,[1] this is the case even for C. B. Macpherson and, we might add, for some recent theories, too, such as that of Thomas Christiano.[2] In the long view of democratic theory, one answer is obvious: It is for the same reason that feminist theory has only recently come to influence democratic theory – namely, the latter's tendency to disregard difference (except as individually different opinions or conflicting interest groups), and the liberal conviction that democracy is primarily a matter of ensuring equal rights to vote and majority rule. Additionally, from within this traditional understanding, democratic citizenship itself, with its requirement of equal treatment, should simply disregard an individual's race. In this approach, while racism is ruled out at the formal level, not much more can be said about it.

In fact, as has been argued by Bernard Boxill and others, the central democratic procedure of majority vote tends to render minority groups invisible.[3] Because of this, formal democracy, especially the procedure of majority vote, not only disregards underlying racism but also exacerbates it in practice, because votes can give enormous power to an absolute majority of one race or culture over cultural minorities, as Boxill points out;[4] it thereby may permit a tyranny of the majority over these minority groups.

Not only has most democratic theory had little to say about racism, but also democracies have coexisted in practice with racism for many centuries, as Charles Mills and others have recently stressed.[5] Beyond insisting on equal voting rights, then, democracy, as a formal and procedural system, offers little basis for the critique of racism. This neglect by democratic theorists and the tolerance of democracies for racism suggest on the face of it that there is something wrong with the traditional understanding of democracy. I argue here that the inadequacy goes beyond the often-observed formality of democracy and

---

[1] Frank Cunningham, "Democratic Theory and Racist Ontology," in *Social Identities*, Vol. 4, no. 4 (December 2000): 463–482.

[2] C. B. Macpherson, *Democratic Theory: Essays in Retrieval* (Oxford: Oxford University Press, 1973); Thomas Christiano, *The Rule of the Many* (Boulder, CO: Westview Press, 1996). There are important exceptions, such as Thomas Simon, *Democracy and Social Injustice* (Lanham, MD: Rowman & Littlefield, 1995).

[3] Bernard Boxill, "Majoritarian Democracy and Cultural Minorities," in *Multiculturalism and American Democracy*, eds. Arthur M. Melzer et al. (Lawrence: University Press of Kansas, 1998), 112–119.

[4] Ibid., 112–113.

[5] See Charles Mills, *The Racial Contract* (Ithaca, NY: Cornell University Press, 1997), especially Chapter 1.

its disregard of social and economic inequalities outside the political sphere.

Before proceeding, we should note that racism has in fact been addressed in the United States in certain delimited democratic contexts: first, in the issue of the representation of blacks in Congress, in terms of the legitimacy of creating black majority districts,[6] and I return to this issue later in this chapter. Second, there has been the federal role in instituting affirmative action programs, as required by concepts of justice. To the degree that such programs have been seen as appropriate political decisions by democratic governments, affirmative action provides another tie between democracy and racism. Mention might also be made of the idea that achieving black community control of local governments would increase opportunities for political participation. In general, though, in dealing with racism, the emphasis – even on the left in the United States – has been on overcoming discrimination through affirmative action and achieving greater economic equality; this in turn has been seen as the way to ensure increased political participation. While this is clearly of great importance, there is need for further reflection on the connection between racism and democracy itself.

To sum up the existing situation: From the standpoint of basic norms for political philosophy – namely, the key values of freedom, justice, community, and democracy – we can say that race and racism have been tied primarily to justice (as equality – political, social, and economic) as well as to freedom (from discrimination or oppression or stereotypes), and in this connection race and racism have been tied to the conception of the social construction of racial characteristics. Increasingly, in recent years, the overcoming of racism has been connected to an understanding of community as inclusiveness, where "inclusive community" refers to one that not only tolerates but also encourages differences and supports diverse cultural and ethnic groups by assigning them rights and by enlarging the scope of interpersonal interaction, both within racial groups and among them.

Yet the missing term in these accounts often has been that of democracy.[7] And while the elimination of injustice (freedom from discrimination or oppression – racial and otherwise) and "leveling the playing

---

[6] The writings of Lani Guinier are especially central here. See her *The Tyranny of the Majority* (New York: The Free Press, 1994).

[7] A notable exception is Iris Marion Young, *Inclusion and Democracy* (Oxford: Oxford University Press, 2000).

field" surely are presuppositions of full democracy as Thomas Simon shows,[8] this cannot exhaust the account of the relations between the key terms "racism" and "democracy"; nor does the issue – albeit a crucial one – of achieving genuine representation of African-Americans, whether through black majority districts or proportional representation. In what follows, then, I take up some of the other connections that racism (and race more generally) has to democracy.

Conceptual Connections

The first point to note – of great importance, if perhaps obvious – is the intrinsic and deep connection between the critique of racism (and sexism) and the requirement for democracy. The idea of equal positive freedom – or more generally a conception of equal agency, which is at the normative core of democracy as analyzed here – provides a basis for both the critique of discrimination and the justification of democratic participation. In the first case, equal positive freedom, as prima facie equal rights to the conditions for individuals' self-development, entails (negative) freedom from discrimination and domination – both institutional and personal – inasmuch as these limit or curtail such flourishing, as well as the (positive) availability of social and economic conditions for this self-development. Hence it excludes both racism and sexism and entails an affirmative requirement for reciprocal recognition, as well as some equalization of social and economic resources. At the same time, this very principle of equal positive freedom serves as the justification for equal rights of democratic participation in all contexts of what I have called common activity. As I presented the argument earlier: Since participation in such common or joint activities is among the conditions for self-development, and since in order to be an expression of agency these activities need to be under the control of those engaged in them, it follows that individuals have equal rights to codetermine these activities or to participate in decision making concerning them.

As suggested in Chapter 1, then, democratic decision making emerges as the institutional analogue to relations of reciprocity in face-to-face interactions. In particular, the connection is to that type of reciprocity that can be called social reciprocity, or reciprocity of respect, rather than to lesser forms such as instrumental reciprocity – colloquially, the reciprocity of "tit for tat," or return for benefit given. The conceptual connection

---

[8] Thomas Simon, *Democracy and Social Injustice*, especially Chapter 5.

between the critique of racism and the requirement of democracy is as follows then, mediated through the principle of equal positive freedom: The critique of systemic discrimination entails an emphasis on equal access to conditions of self-development, which also implies the requirement for equal rights of participation in decision making concerning common activities.

On this view, the conception of self-development – presented originally by Marx and Mill and subsequently by Macpherson and others, and which in turn is seen to support the requirement for democratic participation – is not so much to be opposed to consumerism and acquisitiveness, as it primarily was for Macpherson,[9] although it does indeed contrast with that. Instead, the main opposition is with the control by some over the conditions needed by others for their self-development – that is, domination, or in lesser modes, discrimination – one of whose manifestations (although a unique one in various ways) is racism. Equal agency, in the richer sense of the equal right of individuals to be free from domination and free to develop their capacities, gives rise both to an egalitarian critique of racism and other forms of oppression, and to the conception of widely equal rights of participation in democratic decision making. Of course, the question of the scope of such decision making, and the correct delimitation of those who have rights to participate in varying contexts, remains a difficult and important question for democratic theory, a question that is not yet addressed by noting this conceptual connection.

Yet I have already noted a troubling set of difficulties that arises here: Despite these deep and inherent conceptual connections, in practice there is rather often a sharp disconnection between the critique of racism and the support for democracy. Numerous self-proclaimed democrats have in fact been racists, and some of those critical of racism have favored authoritarian rather than democratic forms of government as essential for achieving their goals. In addition, and this often has been noted, there is frequently no tie between the critique of racism and that of sexism, despite the intrinsic theoretical connection between them. In short, some of those most critical of one occasionally turn a blind eye to the other.

It is only partially adequate, I think, to point by way of explanation to misinformed theories that fail to notice the conceptual connection

---

9 C. B. Macpherson, *Democratic Theory: Essays in Retrieval* (Oxford: Oxford University Press, 1973). It should be noted, though, that Macpherson also understands it as "counter-extractive liberty."

between these themes. Again, it is only partially adequate to point to empirical explanations, in terms of the various social background circumstances of the different groups of people involved and differences in their "cultures," or again, to the general fact that people tend to be concerned with their own narrowly defined interests rather than the interests of others. One could suggest, of course, that many do realize that these concepts are related but simply fail to measure up to their own rational standards. But this is surely not always the case and would itself not fully account for the discrepancies. Chapter 2 introduces an additional conceptual factor that I later reflect on – namely, the weakness of these abstractly universal norms themselves, when taken alone, a weakness that is pointed to by this divergence of theory and practice. Yet it is by now a truism that the bare critique of racism and sexism and the correlative appeal to justice or freedom are inadequate for genuine social change. And this too is only one factor in explaining the puzzling separation between racism and sexism and, more to our purposes here, between the critique of racism and the requirement for democratization.

Democracy and Socially Constructed Characteristics: Racial Versus Cultural Identities

Before we return to this issue in the next section of this chapter, it is useful to consider the outlines of one social constructivist approach to race and racism. It is not an indifferent matter for democratic theory as to whether racial characteristics are inherent or constructed, but the connection between such a constructivist interpretation and democracy needs to be clarified. There are by now several versions of this constructivism.[10] Thus it has been widely argued – and correctly, I think – that the account of race and of group differences more generally needs to conceive them as socially constructed – as initially ascriptive, but changeable, characteristics. Of course, the issue of social construction is in part a factual or empirical one and needs to be independently argued for. The claim simply is that such a view is harmonious with a democratic one. In contrast, a biological or essentialist analysis that regards races as fundamentally different – or, worse, asserts the superiority of one to another – at best sits uneasily with democracy, even in its most formal senses, and certainly lends no weight to a fuller, more participatory sense of democracy. The critique of racism

---

[10] See Leonard Harris, ed., *Racism* (Atlantic Highlands, NJ: Humanities Press, 1999), especially Part II.

also follows more easily from a social constructivist view, although such an approach of course requires independent arguments in its support.

There are numerous versions of such constructivism, and these have been well argued for. On one such social constructivist view that I prefer, one can argue that the basis for membership in a racial group may initially be a matter of objective circumstances, of being put in a particular situation of oppression not by choice. To this degree, it is what has been called an "ascriptive identity," that is, what members of the group are taken to be by others and in particular by the dominant group. Yet this does not commit us to an essentialist account of group differences, closely akin to an abstract universality in which all the individuals of the different group are the same. Instead, what constitutes a relevant difference in social and political terms with regard to race and gender is not one's genetic sex determination or one's skin pigment but rather what has been made of these by social and historical construal, largely by discrimination and oppression. On this view, it is not being black or female that constitutes the group difference but rather being subject to oppression as a black or as a female. This works the other way as well: The positive features of gender, race, or ethnic identity are also historical accomplishments. This is not to say that individuals can always throw off a characteristic or change its significance by themselves. To do so may well require joint action over a period of time.

The goal in this type of social constructivism, then, is to move to self-ascription. On such an approach, skin color as a criterion of group identity understood as a matter of self-interpretation changes the character or meaning of that bodily characteristic and hence of the group in political terms. On this view, which bodily characteristics will be taken to define a group and what significance these characteristics will have is, at least in part, a matter of choice, often of a collective sort. Along these lines, the affirmation of blackness in previous decades as a positive feature of cultural and political group identity transformed a stigmatizing characteristic into one that served as a basis for pride and solidarity. This replaced an earlier reaction to racism that had attempted to eliminate the color line, so to speak, by a wholly color-blind assimilationism, in which group identity based on skin color was rejected. However, both the assimilationist and the affirmationist responses to racism were in part still defined reactively, in opposition to this earlier categorization. More recently, there have been efforts to establish a more fluid group identity associated with the phenomenon of mixed race – that is, those who have only one African-American parent or only some African-American ancestors.[11] The question arises, however, whether it might not be possible to shift the focus of group identity even more radically toward an open and fully constructivist model. Here, there would be the freedom to shape one's group identity with others and to develop multiple group identities, where the criterial features – bodily or otherwise – are open to continuous interpretation and choice.

A proposal along these constructivist lines can be found in Anthony Appiah's work. Appiah's discomfort with any given identities (and his analysis of theories of race from a scientific standpoint) leads him to propose the elimination of the category of race itself and its replacement with a conception of racial identities. These identities are understood as based on a "toolkit" of options given by one's social and historical context but open to self-identification.[12]

Appiah further argues that such a concept of "racial identity" is superior to using the concept of culture, which would ultimately assimilate racial identities to cultural identities. His argument seems to be that the use of the concept of culture would commit us to a single or common culture for all African-Americans, something that is clearly lacking, and would prevent us from acknowledging that cultures are frequently shared between African-Americans and other (hyphenated) Americans. Clearly some reification would be entailed in attributing a common culture to all members of each of these groups. However, this notion of one single culture for all members of a group does not seem to me to be implied in the concept of culture. By contrast, cultures are increasingly plural among various "ethnic" and "racial" groups and are also shared in diverse ways across groups.

Indeed, the concept of culture has the advantage of being more open and more fully free than the alternatives of "race," "ethnicity," and "nationality" (as discussed further in Chapter 5). This voluntarism is misunderstood, however, if it is taken as the creation of a single individual, another charge that Appiah makes against the concept of culture here. Rather, cultural creation is most often social, joint creation and may proceed through the creation of artifacts and through new discursive interpretations. To accept the relevance of cultural creation and co-creation,

---

[11] See Naomi Zack, *Race and Mixed Race* (Philadelphia: Temple University Press, 1993).

[12] K. Anthony Appiah, "Race, Culture, Identity: Misunderstood Connections," Part II: "Synthesis: For Racial Identities," in *Color Conscious: The Political Morality of Race*, eds. K. Anthony Appiah and Amy Gutmann (Princeton, NJ: Princeton University Press, 1996), 74–105.

and the emergence of new mores and traditions, does not therefore commit us to the idea that an individual constructs his or her own culture in isolation.

However, it can rightly be objected that oppressed groups are in fact identified by discriminatory, exclusionary, or exploitative treatment. They constitute groups within a given society that are excluded from the equal rights and benefits of other members of that society; they are subjected to discriminatory or exploitative treatment severely affecting the freedom or well-being (or both) of the members. An oppressed group is excluded in some systematic and effective way from whatever norms of equality may prevail in the society at large. Here, the basis for membership in a group is not common purposes or shared understandings, but rather the objective circumstance of being put in a particular situation of oppression not by choice; and of ascriptive identity, where, as noted, this refers to the ways in which members of the group are taken by others and in particular by the dominant group.

Thus, in considering the issue of racial identity versus cultural identity, we can say that the concept of racial identities has the distinct advantage of recognizing the current reality of race and its pervasiveness in Western societies[13] (and in other societies, although in different ways). As Mills puts it, race (and, we might add, racial identity as well), although socially constructed, is yet real.[14] Racial identities are clearly central for empirical study and historical and social understanding. Despite their wholly arbitrary basis, they cannot be simply willed away. From the standpoint of social critique, race and racial identity remain crucial categories.

Yet, from a forward-looking normative perspective, the concept of racial identity also brings with it the distinct disadvantage of reifying race and perhaps tacitly lending support to those who take a biological or essentialist approach to race. "Race," although different in some ways from "ethnicity," shares with this latter concept an unfortunate indissoluble tie to blood, birth, and descent, and this seems ultimately incompatible with a concept of the free transformation of people in directions that they individually or jointly choose or strive for. While culture has normative

---

[13] See Charles Mills, "'But What Are You Really?': The Metaphysics of Race," in *Blackness Visible: Essays on Philosophy and Race* (Ithaca, NY: Cornell University Press, 1998), 41–66.

[14] Ibid., 48. Cf. the analogous approach to women I propose in "The Woman Question: Philosophy of Liberation and the Liberation of Philosophy," in *Women and Philosophy: Toward a Theory of Liberation*, eds. Carol C. Gould and Marx Wartofsky (New York: G. P. Putnam's, 1976), 5–44, and elaborated in Chapter 2 in this book.

weight as a set of shared practices and resources for action (individual
and social), I don't yet see that a similar case can be made for race or
racial identity, except to the degree that people in fact value it. But unless
one argues that blood or descent is inherently valuable (and what would
be the argument for that?), what is valuable from a forward-looking perspective in these other concepts is already included in the concept of
cultural identities.

This is not to deny the importance of recognizing racism, or oppression on the grounds of race, for purposes of compensatory and distributive justice, as I have noted previously. Oppressed groups have rights to
compensation for unequal treatment in the past and to efforts aimed at
providing what has been characterized as a level playing field for present
members with respect to the rest of society. Here we can observe in passing that a set of group rights – whether in the form of affirmative action,
compensatory treatment, the removal of special barriers to participation
in political and economic life, and of course desegregation – is justified by reference to the same principle of prima facie equal rights to
the conditions of self-development discussed earlier. Yet on the view presented here, these group rights are in fact understood as deriving from
the rights of individual members of the oppressed groups, in a way to be
considered further in Chapter 5, which discusses group rights and social
ontology.

The history of racism and oppression is obviously relevant to the cultural identities of African-Americans, Native-Americans, and other oppressed minority groups (and, we might add, also to the oppressor cultural groups) as obstacles that have been or are yet to be struggled against
and overcome. These cultural identities, more than racial identities, seem
to me susceptible of the multiplicity, as well as the interactive qualities
with other cultures, that Appiah seeks. To speak of African-American
cultural identities as group characteristics, then, is to recognize the identification that many make with a set of (changing and changeable) cultural identities, and to preserve the reality of diverse historical heritages,
while avoiding the reifications and ascriptivism that are inevitably tied
to the concept of race or even to "racial identities." At the same time,
it avoids the simplistic and wrong assimilationism of the pure universalism of being "American." However, the latter, too, is not a neutral assig-
nation involving only the commitment to a set of principles (although
these commitments are important) but is also a diversified cultural identity, which includes numerous traditions and practices, historical and
changing.

Intercultural Democratic Communities

Based on this analysis of socially constructed racial and cultural identities, we can return to the original set of issues and ask: If democracy, with its equal rights, is antithetical to racism, why does racism persist within it? Abstracting from the empirical causal factors and focusing on this only from the side of the concept of democracy here, we can answer that it is due in part to existing limitations in the understanding of democracy. I want to disagree, then, with Charles Mills's normative approach, while appreciating his powerful critique of racism as a system of accumulated entrenched privilege or differential racial privilege that is institutionalized and global (or nearly so). Mills suggests that the normative requirement in dealing with this system of white supremacy is to base democratic political organization on a true understanding of social contract and natural or human rights[15] and to bring these Enlightenment ideals to full realization. But I think that more is required, and specifically a rethinking of democracy along several dimensions.

The problems with contemporary liberal democracies have already been well analyzed in terms of their formality and proceduralism, and their disregard of social and economic inequalities that set limits to participation. I would add, too, the factor of their delimitation to the political realm alone. At the basis of this traditional understanding of democracy is a conception of what I have called abstractly universal norms of negative freedom and formal equality, with a social ontology of individuals whose relations to each other are external.[16] An alternative view would adopt these very norms while reinterpreting them, and would also reconceive democracy in relation to the notion of concrete universality introduced earlier, understood as having both empirical and normative aspects.

Descriptively, concrete universality not only adds to the social ontology an understanding of the individuals as internally related to each other, but also sees societies as constituted and interconstituted through these multifaceted relations. While abjuring the holistic interpretations of this universality originally delineated by Hegel, this point of view finds a certain utility in an emphasis on interconstituting relations, including here

---

[15] Charles Mills, *The Racial Contract,* 129.

[16] See Carol C. Gould, *Rethinking Democracy: Freedom and Social Cooperation in Politics, Economy, and Society* (Cambridge: Cambridge University Press, 1988), Chapters 1–3, and *Marx's Social Ontology: Individuality and Community in Marx's Theory of Social Reality* (Cambridge, MA: The MIT Press, 1978), especially Chapters 1 and 2; and Chapter 1 of this book.

racial relations, and places new weight on the possibilities for intercultural creation (intra- and interracial) that this may open.[17] The latter may even extend to the co-constitution of concepts, procedures, and institutions themselves based on understandings from multiple cultural or racial perspectives.

Within a given society, a concrete universalist approach regards the interconstitution of social relations, including racial interactions, as taking place among individuals and groups who differentiate themselves and are recognized by others through relations that are initially often oppositional or oppressive but perhaps increasingly reciprocal over time. From the normative side as well, the distinctiveness of such a concrete universalist approach consists in its requirement that abstract moral, political, and legal norms, although of great importance, need to be put in the context of actual social conditions to understand critically why they have not been realized. It proposes too that social cooperation and a variety of other social values be integrated with the abstract individual ones that are already well established.

When conceived in relation to the idea of multiple and interactive cultural identities that I posed as the prospective counterpart to historically developed racial identities, what then does such a conception of concrete universality entail? The answer is threefold, I think: Democracy needs to be understood as multi- or pluricultural in a specific sense, it has to be connected to citizenship on a certain interpretation, and it requires a substantive interpretation in terms of democratic communities. These admittedly quite demanding requirements can be summed up in the idea of *inclusive intercultural democracy*. It seems to me that democratic theory can make a contribution to countering racism when it is reconceived in these ways, yielding certain suggestions for practical change. The additional impact of economic democratization for counteracting racism is considered in the concluding section of this chapter.

The inclusiveness required by this new conception arises in part from the connection of democracy to citizenship. Thus it has increasingly been recognized that the issue of who counts as a member of a political community is as central to political theory as the issue of the degree of participation in the governance of the resulting polity. The inclusiveness required here consists in the idea that all those resident in a given territory need to be recognized as citizens, with rights of democratic participation. Racist

---

[17] This interpretation would, of course, contrast with Hegel's rather Eurocentric cultural perspective.

exclusions or denigrations are eliminated on this view. Certainly, full civil, social, and economic rights for immigrants are implied, while for illegal immigrants a range of hard issues would center on whether one could show them to be residents within the polity. Yet the question of fully open borders is not yet addressed by such an account, and it seems evident that the inclusiveness of a democratic community does not necessarily require that there exist no borders or that it be extended worldwide. The issue of the scope of political communities and of borders remains a real one; and we need also to accommodate the possibility of overlapping communities. In Part III of this book, I return to these issues of scope and transborder communities. For now, we can observe that the inclusive democratic community called for would also be multi- and intercultural, the topic of Chapter 5. It will be seen that this does not require mere toleration for diverse cultures but rather efforts, including at the public level, to support their self-interpreted distinctiveness and their interaction with other cultures.

Economic Democracy and Racial Divisiveness

Perhaps the most unexplored interrelation between democracy and racism concerns the ways in which economic democracy, and specifically employee participation in management, might constitute a factor in countering racism. In theory at least, having common economic interests in a shared project rather than opposed ones should contribute to the development of modes of cooperation and reciprocity. It would also seem, on the face of it, that in democratically managed firms, opportunities for face-to-face interaction in decision making could engender new, more empathic understandings among coworkers. Aside from the conceptual interconnections here, it is of course an empirical question as to whether such a benefit is observed, and it would be of interest to see whether concrete studies support this supposition of a beneficial effect of economic democracy in this sense for the elimination of racism. However, even if empirical support for the connection is not yet in evidence, it remains possible that changes in existing management structures might yet have such an effect.

A cautionary note in the appeal to economic democracy here is provided by the somewhat analogous critique that has been offered concerning reducing women's issues to economic ones – in this case, that there is an autonomy to racism (or sexism) that transcends merely economic factors and makes use of them. Thus it is clear that a commitment to equality in social relations and the elimination of racial discrimination remains central, including the development of communication and other tools to overcome nefarious distinctions and the exertion of power by some over others. Yet, as suggested, if democracy is interpreted in a fuller sense not only as majority vote but also as involving opportunities for widespread participation in spheres beyond the political, the hypothesis here is that it might well contribute to the melioration of this discrimination. Whereas it is usually claimed that the elimination of discrimination is a condition for democratic participation, here the reverse is also held to apply. In this process, the "democratic personality," with its qualities of agency, receptivity, flexibility, and openness to differences, would play a role,[18] as would the greater degree of economic egalitarianism potentially entailed by certain systems of economic democratization.

Additionally, the fact that majority rule does not necessarily protect minorities even when they are represented, as Guinier and others have pointed out,[19] points to the need for this conception of democracy to be interpreted along deliberative and discussion-based lines. In this way, developing common interests and building shared concerns in various contexts of social life take center stage, and democracy beyond the political takes on new significance. In such an approach, which is clearly in need of considerably more theoretical attention, participation in democratic decision making in a variety of associations, including the relatively nonvoluntary but central context of firms and workplaces, can contribute to changing participants' understandings and expectations of each other's differences. Joint participation in decision making fosters reciprocity.

There is, however, no way around actual participation. Guinier and Phillips want to move representation toward "presence,"[20] in the sense of the representation by people who share the experiences of oppressed or excluded groups. This is clearly an important part of the democratic theory of representation. But the argument here suggests that we cannot wholly bypass actual participation, and this is best achievable (sometimes only achievable) in smaller-scale and lower-level multiple contexts of economic firms and various sorts of social associations. In these contexts, difference can be expressed directly by individuals or groups, and concretely recognized; it can be presented rather than simply talked about,

---

[18] Gould, *Rethinking Democracy*, Chapter 11.

[19] See Guinier, *The Tyranny of the Majority*, especially Chapters 3 and 4.

[20] Anne Phillips, *Engendering Democracy* (University Park: Pennsylvania State University, 1991), Chapter 3.

and more effective action can perhaps be taken on behalf of the different needs and interests. Yet it must be acknowledged that the presentation of difference may sometimes be (certainly, has often been) antagonistic or even hostile instead of being mutually supportive. The conviction of both participationist and deliberative democrats is, however, that somewhat more positive and individuated forms of recognition will emerge through democratic interaction processes. Here, the positive freedom tradition would additionally note that a condition for this transformation would be an institutional structure providing for more equal access to economic resources among the participants, and, as Mills puts it in radical – although well-founded – terms, the elimination of the economic system of white supremacy.[21]

In conclusion, it may be useful to observe that although recognition of differences – of individuals and cultural groups – and support for these differences is crucial, perhaps the pendulum has swung a little too far toward difference in democratic theory. There is a need to discern shared commonalities and experiences, and set common goals, in addition to drawing on others' different cultural experiences, appropriating them in new ways. Here, it is not the imposition of common goals but the mutual determination and choosing of them through deliberation that may in turn help to diminish racial divisiveness. In a variety of ways, then, democratic participation in a wide array of contexts presents itself as a significant part of an approach to dealing with racism.

[21] Mills, *The Racial Contract.*

5

Cultural Identity, Group Rights, and Social Ontology

In Chapter 4, I introduced an interpretation of cultural identities, and with it a conception of intercultural societies, to suggest the importance of the diversity and interaction of cultures. Yet we can also observe that the increasing globalization and universalization of culture worldwide have paradoxically been matched by increasing cultural particularism and separatism. These two conflicting trends are reflected in cosmopolitanism or the homogenization of cultures, on the one hand, and in claims to cultural autonomy or to ethnic and nationalist chauvinisms, on the other. At the same time that sixteen-year-olds all over the world are drinking their Cokes while listening to MTV and wearing their Levis (many sizes too large), their parents and siblings are often reviving ancient ethnic feuds, rediscovering their distinctive cultural identities, and attempting to exclude alien others from their midst. Against the background of an increasing awareness of the value of cultural difference, but also in the context of the alternative claims of equal and universal freedom and global interconnectedness, the question of group rights has reemerged with particular force in recent decades and has been developed in newly sophisticated ways in social and political philosophy. What are group rights? Do we need to recognize them as a condition for preserving and enhancing cultural diversity? Are they fundamental rights, or do they instead derive from individual rights? And indeed, what do we mean when we speak of a "group" in this connection?

In my discussion here, I draw upon the social ontology introduced earlier and use it as a framework for considering what constitutes a group and what normative claim there can be for group rights. The main focus of this chapter is on the rights of cultural minorities in liberal democratic societies and the problems that arise when a democratic majority takes its dominant culture and language to be obligatory and adopts assimilationist or integrationist policies that deny rights of cultural self-expression and development to such minority ethnic groups. I also briefly consider the somewhat different question of the rights of oppressed groups within a larger polity, where such groups are identified by discriminatory, exclusionary, or exploitative treatment, as discussed in Chapter 4. I leave aside here the related questions of the rights of relatively smaller groups such as corporations, professions, and so on, as well as of such larger collectivities as polities, whether at the local or the national level, where issues analogous to those of group rights might also arise. The discussion of multiculturalism, particularly when put into the recent context of globalization, does, however, suggest a way of approaching the concepts of nation and state conjoined in the idea of a nation-state, and I turn to this in the final section of this chapter.

This consideration of cultural groups and of their rights is intended to contribute to the project of pluralizing democracy and rights, which constitutes one aspect of their globalization, replacing less interactive abstract individualist approaches to the polity. The recognition of the diversity of such groups and of the significance of their cultural development suggests a new emphasis on such rights and also raises some difficult questions for democratic theory, especially regarding the role of minority groups in decision making.

Groups as Constituted Entities

In the discussion that has developed on group rights, there has been no little confusion about what the term "group" should be taken to refer to. It is commonly agreed that it is not simply an accidental aggregation of individuals, nor even one where the individuals share some common characteristic. This is far too abstract for a social group of the sort intended. It is also commonly agreed that it is not a reified entity, a collectivity that exists over and above its individual members, on the model of a Platonic class or Durkheimian structure. Instead, a number of theorists have characterized a group as made up of individuals who stand in certain relations to each other – for example, as sharing a common purpose or having a common intentionality, or acting together, or at least having a common interest.

As noted earlier, I developed a view along these lines in previous work, including the book *Marx's Social Ontology: Individuality and Community in*

Marx's Theory of Social Reality (1978),[1] a 1979 paper to the Metaphysical Society titled "Ontological Foundations of Democracy," and, subsequently, in my book *Rethinking Democracy* (1988).[2] In this social ontology, I characterize a social group as an entity constituted by individuals-in-relations, eschewing both the aggregative and the holistic readings. Furthermore, I argue that while individuals as agents are ontologically prior to the groups that they constitute, they stand in internal relations to each other such that they become the individuals they are in and through such social relations and can therefore be described as social individuals. Internal relations are relations among entities that are at least in part constitutive of the identity of these entities; a change in these relations would therefore effect a change in the character of the entity itself. In external relations, by contrast, the identity of individuals is independent of these relations. Thus, where such internal relations are social relations among persons – for example, in those between teacher and students or between parents and children – the characters of the individuals are transformed by the interactions between them. The ontological priority of the individuals is retained, however, by virtue of their agency, as a capacity to change these relations and to choose new ones (either by themselves or, most often, together with others).

The sociality of individuals consists not only in their interactions, which may take reciprocal or nonreciprocal forms, but also in what I have called common or joint activity. When many individuals act together with a shared purpose, there is not simply an aggregation of individual activities, which may be accidentally coordinated. Indeed, such activity cannot be understood in terms of the actions or intentions of individual agents alone, but only by reference to the shared aim itself and the joint action required to realize it. Furthermore, participation in such activity is one of the main conditions for individual self-development. In this framework, then, groups are defined by such joint activity or common purposes, whether explicitly recognized or not. On my view, groups are constituted entities – that is, they come into being by virtue of actual relations among

[1] Carol C. Gould, *Marx's Social Ontology: Individuality and Community in Marx's Theory of Social Reality* (Cambridge, MA: The MIT Press, 1978), 31–39.

[2] Carol C. Gould, "Ontological Foundations of Democracy," paper presented to the Metaphysical Society of America, 1979; *Rethinking Democracy: Freedom and Social Cooperation in Politics, Economy, and Society* (Cambridge: Cambridge University Press, 1988), especially Chapter 2, and "Beyond Causality in the Social Sciences: Reciprocity as a Model for Nonexploitative Social Relations," in *Epistemology, Methodology and the Social Sciences: Boston Studies for the Philosophy of Science*, eds. R. S. Cohen and M. W. Wartofsky (Dordrecht: D. Reidel, 1983), 53–88.

their constituent individual members but are not reducible to the individuals distributively, taken apart from these relations. We can observe that constituted entities are not any the less real for being constituted; but they do not exist independently as Platonic universals. Rather, they exist only in and through the individuals related to each other in the group and cease to exist when these relations no longer hold.

Norms and Ontology

The normative question of whether there are group rights is distinct from, although related to, the ontological question of what constitutes a group. My view here differs in this respect from that of Allen Buchanan, who argues in his book *Secession* that although there are group rights, the question of ontology is irrelevant. He claims that liberalism is committed to individual moral rights but is not limited to an individualist ontology that would preclude an emphasis on the sociality of individuals. He holds that liberalism's individualism is moral and not ontological.[3] Whatever one thinks of this particular claim about liberalism, I do not accept Buchanan's sharp fact-value or ontological–moral distinction with regard to social facts and would instead suggest that the social ontology of both individuals and groups makes a difference to the normative arguments about group rights.[4] To take the extreme cases, it would obviously make a significant difference if one argued that only individuals exist and that their relations to others are simply external relations that have no effect on who they fundamentally are; or by contrast, that the identity of individuals derives entirely from their group membership and that they have no independent existence apart from this. It would be odd to attribute moral values or rights to groups in the first case, where only individuals are held to exist; or to deny such group rights in the second, where individual identity is seen as deriving from group membership. Indeed, I would suggest that the social ontology itself is already in a way normative – for example, that the very characterization of individuals as agents or persons with cultural identities supports an argument for certain rights as valid claims of such individuals. Conversely, the values and rights recognized depend in part on how one characterizes the existence of individuals, social relations, and groups. This does not render such

---

3 Allen Buchanan, *Secession* (Boulder, CO: Westview Press, 1991), 8, 79–80.
4 We might observe that Buchanan himself appeals to numerous arguments that are social ontological in this sense. See, for example, *Secession*, 39, 77.

an ontological account "metaphysical" in the sense pertaining to "being as such," since it remains a regional ontology concerned exclusively with concrete human beings in their social interrelations and practices.

How to Derive Group Rights from Individual Rights

We begin from the principle of justice as equal positive freedom, which (as I suggested earlier) is the normative conception that goes along with such a social ontology of individuals-in-relations and constituted social groups. This principle entails a (prima facie) equal right of individuals to the conditions of their self-development or to the exercise of their freedom over time. Since participation in joint activity is one of the main conditions for such self-transformation, it follows that individuals as agents have prima facie equally valid claims or rights to opportunities for participation in such activity. Among the modes of activity involving a shared understanding of common interests and a mutual recognition as participants in it are work, political life, culture, and also various forms of voluntary association and face-to-face interactions. If we focus on culture here it is because it is a pervasive source of social identity, providing a context for thought and action that involves language, values, modes of behavior, education, socialization, practices, traditions, and shared history. Cultural life, in these terms, essentially involves common or joint activity with others, as members of the cultural group. Such activity is taken generically here to include not only taking part in explicit and organized or institutionally defined practices, such as the celebration of holidays or historic events, but also the more tacit forms of activities expressing shared beliefs or values, such as modes of social behavior, styles of dress or speech, and so on. It is evident from this pervasiveness of culture, then, that an individual's participation in some mode of cultural life as a form of common activity is a condition for self-development. It therefore follows that if individuals have equal rights to the conditions of their self-development, they have equal rights to have the opportunity to participate in a culture. We can say that there is an equal right of access to the conditions of cultural self-development.

This remains a relatively transparent right, tacitly assumed, as long as there is no special problem concerning access to or participation in one's culture. Thus for dominant cultures what may be at issue is equal educational opportunity or cultural literacy or the availability of cultural resources in a fair distribution. However, for minority cultures what is at stake is precisely the question of their continued existence or the denial of the conditions of access to or participation in the life of that culture. This may result from lack of means for learning the language or the history and traditions of a minority culture; or it may mean deliberate discriminatory repression of the minority culture. In such a case, the provision of the equal rights to the conditions of cultural development may justify a claim for group rights.

A number of very sharp issues concerning the rights of cultural minorities have thus become the focus of the current discussion on group rights. The normative framework proposed here can therefore be characterized as a theory of *cultural justice*, where this concerns the rights of groups to the expression and development of their own cultures when they exist within a different dominant culture, and, more generally, it concerns the rights of individuals to cultural self-development.

The other focus of this recent discussion is on the rights of oppressed groups that are not characterizable as – or not *simply* characterizable as – cultural minorities – for example, women or African-Americans in the U.S. context. There is, of course, some overlap, since some oppressed groups are at the same time clearly identifiable as cultural minorities – for example, Native-Americans and to some degree African-Americans. Moreover, oppressed groups may develop shared modes of understanding and action that may be characterized as cultural. So, for example, some have attempted to talk in this way of "women's culture" or again of "a culture of poverty," but clearly some reification is entailed in attributing such a common culture to all members of these groups. (The same may well be true of more standardly identified cultural groups.) In talking about groups and their rights, then, one has to be sensitive to the degree of diversity even within the framework of a common culture and where the term "culture" is used by metaphorical extension.

But what exactly is a group right as against the rights that individual members of a culture have to their own cultural expression and development? And how could such group rights be derived from the cultural rights of individuals? Part of the confusion in talking about group rights derives from an ontological error, specifically, to consciously or unconsciously reify the conception of a group as something independent of or abstractable from its constitution by individuals, in the specific relations that characterize them as members of that group. Such a group as an abstract entity cannot have rights. Even if one were to identify a culture with such institutional or social facts as language or a system of values, or structures of belief, these entities would themselves be constituted by the actions, beliefs, and linguistic practices of individuals-in-relations. On

the other hand, individual members of a culture, whether majority or minority, cannot develop their cultural activity except with respect to the
existence of a culture to which they belong, namely, to a relatively persist-
ing and emergent form of cultural life, which they in turn appropriate in
the course of their interaction with others.

Group rights therefore pertain to groups as constituted entities and
thus are rights derived from the rights of the constituent individuals who
are members of the group and who have these group rights insofar as
they are members of the group and not apart from these relations to each
other. The group rights that a cultural minority can bear are therefore
rights to the cultural conditions for the self-development or transformative activity of its members. Since it is not the group that has the equal
right to cultural development but rather the individual members of the
culture, these group rights are derivative from and instrumental to the
equal rights to self-development of the members. They are not rights of
the group sui generis. Yet group rights are not reducible to or identifiable
with the distributive rights of each individual to the conditions for his or
her own cultural development, but rather are rights of the constituency
of the culture in the literal sense of those who constitute the group collectively. As a necessary condition for the exercise of the individual's rights,
the group can make a valid claim against the majority culture to provide
the individuals with these conditions. Thus, a minority culture that may
use a language other than the dominant language of the majority would
have a group right to provide the means for the perpetuation of that
linguistic community through its educational system and other means.
This does not entail, however, that the cultural minority could insist that
all of its members were required to be educated only in that language,
but rather that the choice to be educated in this way would be available
to its members.

This addresses a special problem concerning group rights of minority
cultures, namely, the preservation of the human rights of members of
the culture and their freedom of choice to remain members or to leave
the group or indeed to combine their cultural identity in the group with
other cultural identities or affiliations. I will have more to say on this later.

Another condition for cultural participation of members of a minority
culture could be the freedom to observe certain cultural traditions or
practices, whether religious or secular – for example, the celebration
of certain festivals or commemorations, or observation of dietary rituals.
Here, again, the right of the group would consist in its access to the means
to provide for these practices and not to be interfered with in them by the

dominant culture or the powers of the state. Yet here too an important constraint is noted later, namely, that the practices of a minority culture cannot be such as to violate the human rights of its members. In other words, the special group rights must be compatible with the universalistic human rights to which the dominant culture is presumably committed. Where this is not the case and the dominant culture is itself repressive and in violation of the human rights of its members, the minority culture is not thereby absolved from this constraint.

The approach I present is related in certain respects to the views of such theorists of group rights as Will Kymlicka, Charles Taylor, Michael Hartney, Michael McDonald, Allen Buchanan, and Vernon Van Dyke. A full account of the similarities and differences between the view presented here and these others would require a more extended discussion than I can give in this chapter. Suffice it to note a similarity with Kymlicka, Buchanan, and to some degree Taylor, in the general strategy of regarding culture as a condition for the agency of individuals or their development.[5] In addition, like Taylor and McDonald (and Van Dyke earlier), I would argue that there is a need to go beyond traditional liberal individualism in recognizing the claims of cultural groups or communities.[6] However, I am wary, as is Hartney,[7] of a tendency among such theorists toward a collectivist interpretation of groups or an assignment of independent value (such as survival) to the group as such.

A difference between the view developed here and most of these others concerns their characterization of what constitutes a culture or a cultural group. In general, they operate with a strong, even overarching conception of culture, as not only "encompassing" (in Raz and Margalit's term[8]), but also as national and territorially based, or in Kymlicka's phrase, as a "societal culture."[9] The idea here seems to be something like that of a

---

[5] See Will Kymlicka, *Multicultural Citizenship* (Oxford: Oxford University Press, 1995), 76, 82–93; Buchanan, *Secession*, 53–54; and Charles Taylor, *Multiculturalism* (Princeton, NJ: Princeton University Press, 1994), 61.

[6] Taylor, *Multiculturalism*, 56–61; Michael McDonald, "Should Communities Have Rights? Reflections on Liberal Individualism," *Canadian Journal of Law and Jurisprudence*, Vol. IV, no. 2 (July 1991): 217–237, especially 237; and Vernon Van Dyke, "Collective Entities and Moral Rights: Problems in Liberal-Democratic Thought," *The Journal of Politics*, Vol. 44 (1982): 21–40.

[7] Michael Hartney, "Some Confusions Concerning Collective Rights," in *The Rights of Minority Cultures*, ed. W. Kymlicka (Oxford: Oxford University Press, 1995), 202–227.

[8] Avishai Margalit and Joseph Raz, "National Self-Determination," *The Journal of Philosophy*, Vol. LXXXVII, no. 9 (Sept. 1990): 448.

[9] Kymlicka, *Multicultural Citizenship*, 18, 75–80.

national minority with group claims against the majority nation-state in which it finds itself or as a national culture with a full range of social and political institutions. In this way, culture is thought of in terms of such group rights as property right, political sovereignty or self-determination, and secession. While the question of the group rights of national minorities or societal cultures is clearly an important one, there is a wide range of highly significant culturally defined groups that lie outside this strong definition of cultural identity. It is this range that is my main focus here, in contemporary multicultural societies and given the phenomenon of multiple cultural identifications.[10] This sort of cultural networking is evidently of growing importance in the context of contemporary globalization.

There is one other important and systematic difference between these other views and the one developed here. Although the philosophical discussion in these theorists is often sophisticated and the concrete examples very rich, it seems to me that there is as yet insufficient attention to the social ontology of cultural groups and therefore to the relevance of such an ontological analysis for the normative question of rights. I think it could be shown that each of these theorists does in fact operate, at least implicitly, with an ontology of individuals and groups. Nearly all of them advance a criticism of the one-sided alternatives of ontological individualism and holism or collectivism. Yet several of them go on to explicitly reject the relevance of any ontological analysis, either because of the unacceptability of these dichotomous alternatives for the case of cultural rights (e.g., Kymlicka[11]) or because of the belief that moral or normative values such as justice or rights are independent of the "factual" characterization of entities such as individuals or groups (e.g., Buchanan, and Hartney[12]). I have criticized this latter approach in my earlier discussion of Buchanan. As to the former view, which correctly perceives the inadequacy of the presumed ontological alternatives in this case, one can respond that there is in fact an acceptable mediated ontology that is relevant to the issue of cultural rights, an ontology that moreover avoids the criticisms that can be leveled at the one-sided views. This position,

---

[10] Although some of these theorists do consider this wider range of cultural groups – for example, Kymlicka in his discussion of "polyethnic" and immigrant groups (*Multicultural Citizenship*, 30–31, 78, 96–98, 176ff.) – this does not appear to fundamentally affect the theoretical frameworks proposed, which center on a national conception of culture.

[11] Kymlicka, *Multicultural Citizenship*, 34–35, 46–47.

[12] Buchanan, *Secession*, 79–80; Hartney, "Some Confusions Concerning Collective Rights," 208.

while it draws on the strengths of both the individualist and the communitarian emphases, integrates them in an ontology of social individuals. Such a social ontology in turn supports a notion of group rights that neither reifies the group as a rights-bearer nor reduces these rights to the distributive rights of individuals.

In fact, one can propose that such a mediated view is essential even to Kymlicka's own version of liberalism, in which he wants to combine an emphasis on the capacity of agents to autonomously revise their goals with the availability of a cultural and group-based storehouse of practices and traditions that provide meaningful options for individuals' choices.[13] As to whether such a revised position is to be called liberalism or not is a matter of how one wants to use this term; his version clearly differs from classic liberal views, which eschew group or communal identities in favor of rationally chosen cooperation among separate individuals. Yet I would suggest that a combined view of the sort Kymlicka favors cannot be viable if it simply takes group identifications as holistically determinative of the character and interests of individuals who are brought up and socialized within it, for it would then be impossible to see how such individuals thereby come to construct and revise their own plans of action. These group identifications thus cannot be simply social givens imposed on individuals. Instead, one would need an account of them as socially constructed by prior agential and socially related individuals in a way that leaves them open to further individual and social appropriation and transformation. My suggestion here is that a social ontology of individuals-in-relations is central in such an account. It proposes that cultural significance cannot be taken as a fixed framework for socialization that fully shapes individuals, nor can individuals be taken as purely individual choosers who somehow, as adults, come to be able to set goals and revise plans. The focus, instead, has to be on interactive contexts of cultural creation that are appropriated and transformed by individuals, most often in networks with others. Further elaboration of such a model is clearly necessary and is a task that would have to draw on both empirical sociology and social philosophy.

Oppressed Groups and Group Rights

Before proceeding with the discussion of group rights and possible constraints on them, we can note that there is a parallel construction for

[13] Kymlicka, *Multicultural Citizenship*, 82–84.

the derivation of group rights from rights of individuals in the case of oppressed groups. As I noted earlier, an oppressed group is characterized as
a group within a given society that is excluded from the equal rights and
benefits of other members of that society or is subjected to discriminatory
or exploitative treatment severely affecting the freedom or well-being of
its members. The special rights of an oppressed group would bear on the
rectification and compensation for unequal treatment in the past and
would aim at establishing a more equal starting position for its members
with respect to the rest of society. So in this case, group rights – to desegregation, affirmative action, compensation, reparations, and so on –
would be justified by reference to the same principle of prima facie equal
rights to the conditions of self-development and hence in terms of the
rights of individual members of the oppressed groups.

Here, as argued in Chapter 4, the basis for membership in a group is
not a matter of social identification nor common purpose nor shared understanding, although these elements of solidarity among the oppressed
may develop as a common consciousness of their relevantly similar situation. Rather, it is a matter of objective circumstances of being put in
a particular situation of oppression not by choice; thus it is a matter of
an identity ascribed to group members by others, and specifically, by the
dominant group. While such oppressed groups can also be regarded as
constituted entities in the sense that the groups do not exist apart from
the individuals in relations of oppression, nonetheless such groups are
not defined by shared purposes of their choosing or the sort of intentionality often characteristic of cultural groups.

Constraints on Group Rights for Cultural Minorities

An interesting and common problem arises with respect to group rights
for some cultural minorities: When the practices of a cultural minority,
which are to be supported by group rights, themselves violate the human
rights of individual members of the culture, does the autonomy of the
cultural group permit the violation of human rights? I would argue that
any of the rights of a minority cultural group would have to be compatible
with the human rights, for otherwise the justification of the group rights
on the basis that they provide conditions for the equal freedom of self-
development of the individuals who are members of that group would
be undermined. Since the human rights are the fundamental conditions
for the exercise of agency and hence are given priority in the application

of the principle of equal positive freedom, they cannot be abrogated by group rights applied or interpreted in such a way as to violate them.

This has particularly important bearing for the difficult question of the pervasive oppression of women within many cultural minorities (and majorities as well!). Thus, for example, traditional practices of female genital cutting are still condoned within certain cultural groups. The claim has been made that the autonomy of a culture demands noninterference or nonintervention even with such practices. On the view here, however, cultural group rights would not justify such practices inasmuch as such practices entail a violation of human rights, especially those concerning bodily integrity and health. Furthermore, insofar as women's equality is formally protected by human rights, it can be appealed to as a ground for eliminating other cultural practices that oppress women. The question of how to conceive of women's human rights is our topic of concern in Chapter 6.

Other constraints on cultural group rights that need consideration, although I cannot analyze them here, include the issue of the democratization of decision making within a cultural minority where autocratic or other antidemocratic practices may prevail. A related issue is that of who is authentically representative of the cultural minority and can speak for it. Another important constraint on the scope of group rights concerns what can be called "minorities within the minority." Especially in territorial situations where a minority culture holds sway over a geographical region, inevitably there will be minorities living within this minority cultural framework. Clearly, the rights of these subminorities to their own cultural expression need to be respected, and these minorities within the minority should not suffer the same suppression or discrimination that the minority culture has itself suffered. This norm of the protection of minorities within what were previously oppressed cultures or nationalities has been widely and wildly violated in recent history and at present. I would also hazard the suggestion that the issue of such subminorities has not received enough attention from political philosophers.[14]

A practical question emerges from this issue of minorities within a minority. How large must a cultural group be before it is legitimated in its demands for cultural autonomy and recognition of group rights? Will we be led on a slippery slope here to the absurd condition that any group of

[14] An exception is the essay by Leslie Green, "Internal Minorities and their Rights," in *The Rights of Minority Culture*, ed. W. Kymlicka (New York: Oxford University Press, 1995), 256–272.

two or three can call itself a cultural group and demand special rights for the preservation and the practice of its "culture"? Clearly, some measure of good judgment is required here, especially in a historical period in which long-suppressed minorities of ethnic, religious, or linguistic sorts have emerged to make claims not only for recognition and cultural self-determination but also for secession and national identity.

From Separatism to Interculturalism

Perhaps the most salient development in the recent period has been a move away from monocultural identity associated with the traditional nation-state to multi- or intercultural identities in which there is an interaction and an admixture of two or more cultures. This is to be distinguished from mere assimilationism, in which an older or parent culture yields to a dominant culture that essentially replaces it or corrupts it. Especially in large cities and in the context of major waves of immigration, populations have become culturally heterogeneous. Likewise, with the development of the world market and the globalization not only of the economy but also of communications and the media, an increasing cosmopolitanism has emerged. There are two aspects to this: The first is a rapidly changing world culture, especially as a youth culture transcending national, ethnic, and geographic barriers; and the second is the interaction among existing cultures and pluralization of cultural identities.

This phenomenon has been identified as multiculturalism, but this term has been used in importantly ambiguous ways, meaning different things to different people; and by now it has some unfortunate connotations. Still, the term has usefully served to highlight the multiplicity and increasing interconnection of cultures. Other ways to refer to this include "pluriculturalism" or "social pluralism," but I prefer to speak of *interculturalism* to point to the interactive and more global aspects of this development. "Multiculturalism" has two uses that can be distinguished here: In one, it designates an aggregate or collection of different and relatively separate cultures, together with an awareness within an older dominant culture of these differences and of the contributions of the cultures of oppressed groups – paradigmatically, the recognition of the contributions of African-American, Latino, and other minority cultures in the United States – or an awareness of non-Western cultures beyond the dominant Eurocentric canon. In this aggregative sense, too, it has unfortunately sometimes come to be used in a denigrating and racist way to refer to generalized, unspecified racial demands by African-Americans and other racial minorities on white people.

The term "multiculturalism" has also been used, in a second sense, to designate a newer interactive model of culture, where cultural identity itself is open to plural definition and where there may be cultural creation through the appropriation of diverse cultural influences. Here, the concept becomes more one of being multicultured or multiply-cultured (and analogously, perhaps, multiracial), a connotation retained in the idea of interculturalism. A noteworthy and often-cited example of this interactive cultural creation is American jazz. There also have been more recent forms of this – for example, in graffiti art, in the influence of various sorts of ethnic dance on the forms of modern dance, in hip-hop music, and more generally in the phenomenon of "fusion" styles of art, music, and even cuisine. Yet this does not necessarily entail a homogenization of cultural strains, and it is also a continuation of the historically common phenomenon of cultural diffusion. But we can say that such multi- or intercultural creation has become a more intensely dynamic phenomenon than it was in the past, due in part to the powerful contemporary technologies of global communication.

On the normative side, from the standpoint of a single individual, these developments contribute to the possibilities of cultural choice and change and accord with the social constructivist conception of racial or cultural identity presented earlier. Customary views of cultural, ethnic, or political identity have most often seen this identity as simply given, as a matter of birth into a culture, ethnic group, or community; or else these views have considered this identity to be ascriptive, determined by what salient or authoritative others take one to be. I have argued instead that cultural identity and group membership need to be defined in such a way that they are open to choice and to the possibility of multiple cultural identifications. This would add an important element of self-definition and the appropriation of diverse cultures to the more passive traditional characterization of cultures as matters of birth or ascription.

These normative considerations as well as the fact of increasing interculturalism raise a host of practical and interesting questions concerning cultural group rights. Since determining whether groups have rights and what rights they have also depends on the answer to the question of what makes an individual a member of a group, interculturalism significantly complicates the identification of a given cultural group as well as the question of which group rights any given individual can lay claim to. This complexity would be especially difficult if we wish to move to a plural

cultural policy within the public sphere in which there would be public
support for cultural groups as a matter of group rights.

Culture and State: Alternative Models

We can clarify the relations between cultural differences and the public
sphere by considering some models of the state in regard to culture as
well as ethnicity and nationality. In particular, we can distinguish five
alternatives:

1. The purely political or abstractly universal model of the state, which
    is defined entirely independently of any condition of or relation
    to ethnicity, nationality, or culture. In such a neutral state, cul-
    tural or ethnic differences may exist, but they are irrelevant to the
    definition of the state as a polity and are assigned to the private
    sphere. Matters of ethnicity or culture are benignly ignored, and
    citizenship is defined without any reference to them.
2. The multicultural state, in which a diversity of cultures exists and is
    recognized in various ways by the state. These cultural differences
    are not only tolerated but also supported by the state, although they
    are not requirements for citizenship, which is defined apart from
    them. Such cultural affiliations do not bear any essential relation to
    ethnicity or nationality in the strong sense of characteristics given
    by kinship or country of origin.
3. The monocultural integrationist state, in which there is a dominant
    statewide (and in that sense national) culture, in which all citizens
    are required to participate, but which is open to anyone regardless
    of particular ethnic, national, or cultural affiliations. In this case,
    the different cultural, ethnic, or national identities are tolerated as
    pertaining to matters of private preference, but integration within
    the state requires the adoption of its official or national culture.
    This is therefore distinguished both from the neutral state, dis-
    cussed in the first model, and from forced assimilationism or the
    eradication of minority cultures or ethnicities, which is discussed
    in the fifth model.
4. The binational or multinational state, which combines two or more
    well-defined nationalities within a single political entity. Here there
    is formal recognition of ethnic or national affiliation, and specific
    rights are given to each of the constitutive nationalities with respect
    to certain areas of state law and policy. This case also involves the

formal recognition of two or more official languages. In this model, the nationalities could be of relatively equal size, or one might constitute a majority and the other (or others) a national minority (or minorities). However, ethnic or national identity need not be made a condition for citizenship in this model.

5. The nationalist state, which, in its strongest version, makes a particular ethnicity or nationality a condition for citizenship and thus for full political rights. Such a state is exclusively national in that it makes no provision for the equal treatment of minority ethnic, national, or cultural groups and regards members of them at best as resident aliens or denies them rights to reside there altogether.

The uneasy relation between the state as a political entity and considerations of ethnicity, nationality, and culture manifests itself in each of the five models, which exhibit responses to this tension ranging from the most universalist to the most particularist. When considered from the standpoint of cultural minorities within the state, the fifth model is clearly normatively unacceptable, and so in most formulations is the fourth. The crude, exclusive nationalism of the fifth by definition leaves no scope for equal rights for members of cultural or ethnic minorities within it. Any democratic theory would normatively require some basic set of equal rights – individual and political – which the fifth model denies in principle. The best that one could have on this model would be democracy for the right kind of people, but even this is highly unlikely given the authoritarian bent of most highly nationalistic regimes. The fourth model is more complicated inasmuch as it provides for representation and cultural self-determination for a set of different cultural groups. Nevertheless, there will certainly be minority cultures within a binational or multinational state that are not included among these nationalities, ethnicities, or recognized minority cultures. Therefore, despite the attempt to represent cultural variety in the context of political equality, some will inevitably be excluded and thus will be discriminated against, in terms of the expression of their culture, even if they possess equal rights as individuals.

The third model, of monocultural integrationism, despite its toleration of minority nationalities and cultures outside the political domain, still has a coercive dimension, in its imposition of the official national culture as a requirement for citizenship. This national culture also tends to be the culture of the majority, so that even with fully democratic procedures of majority rule, minority cultures could have their interests subordinated by the votes of a permanent majority. Interestingly, the first model of the neutral state is open to a similar problem in practice, with respect to the dominance of permanent cultural majorities. Although in this case there is no explicit imposition of acceptance of the dominant culture, democratic majorities may still deny equal treatment to cultural, ethnic, or national minorities by discriminatory allocation of resources or the adoption of policies that privilege members of the cultural majority in public life.

In terms of the protection of rights of cultural minorities, the second model, namely that of multicultural democracy or cultural pluralism, which is now in its nascent form, is normatively the most attractive. While it shares with the first the priority of a framework of equal individual and political rights, it promises to offer greater protection for minority cultures by explicitly building in support for a diversity of cultural expression and development. This model also differs from the others in providing for the facilitation and encouragement of interrelations among different cultures, thus making possible a richer cultural environment for citizens; to this degree, it can be denominated a model of intercultural democracy. The cultural pluralism of this model implies that the political community not only tolerates diverse cultural groups but also finds ways of supporting them that are compatible with basic principles of equal treatment. It would need to eliminate the favoritism of civic life toward one leading set of cultural characteristics – that of the majority – and permit the development of new forms of such civic life reflective of the polity's fuller cultural variety. Some degree of public support of diverse cultures and for their interaction is possible, with the proviso that individuals must be understood to be capable of belonging to more than one culture. And particularly where there is a dominant majority and a clearly articulated set of minority cultures, I have suggested that certain group rights for these cultural minorities may also need to be protected.[15] Such an intercultural democracy thus goes beyond the model of a neutral and universalist public sphere, where all particularity is supposedly relegated to a private domain in which particular cultural identities are allowed to flourish. Rather, this view suggests that some cultural diversification can actually be supported within the public sphere itself, compatible with fairness and human rights, and where there is an ongoing and open dialogue about emergent civic traditions. But it must be admitted that the question of how public support for cultural groups could

---

[15] For some of the difficulties here, see *The Rights of Minority Cultures.*

be allocated without being unfair to some individuals remains a difficult problem.

Nation-States and Culture in the Context of Globalization

In the concluding section of this chapter, I briefly take note of the import of the preceding analysis of cultural identity and groups for the ideas of nation-state and citizenship, considered especially in terms of globalization. This development poses an obvious challenge to the sovereignty of nation-states insofar as it is contemplated to cede major aspects of their present autonomous authority to supranational bodies or associations of which they are members. I return to this issue in Chapter 7. Here, we focus on the globalization of culture, which, to the degree that it has entailed a certain homogenization – particularly through the proliferation of Western and especially American cultural modes, such as in music, film, and dress – has also tended to evoke a reaction in defense of traditional national cultural identities. In a related way, the increased cosmopolitanism resulting from the interchange of cultures – especially among young people and among active participants in transnational discourses (whether explicitly cultural, or else scientific, technological, or managerial) – has been coupled with reassertions (sometimes repressive) of local ethnic, nationalist, or religious particularisms. On the positive side, it also has provided wider access to a diversity of non-Western cultures. In addition, globally interdependent economies have contributed to the establishment of immigrant minority cultures or nationalities in the midst of the dominant national cultures, especially in view of the needs of the labor market for global corporations. Just as such corporations and capital flows have ignored national boundaries, so too, although in less fluid ways, has the labor force begun to distribute itself in transnational ways. The extensive presence within the national economies of new immigrant groups has brought into focus questions about the relation of citizenship in a state to cultural, national, and ethnic identity.

What then becomes of the concept of the nation-state with respect to its traditional features of sovereignty, the identity of state and nationality, and the concept of self-determination? Without attempting any full discussion of these questions here, I would like to make a few comments on the concepts of the nation-state and of citizenship, in this new context.

We can observe that the term "nation-state" already bears within it an ambiguity. It appears to combine in some essential connection the elements of nationality in a sense that connotes ethnic or cultural identity with the notion of a polity or political entity within the boundaries of a certain territory. In short, the concept of the nation-state places both national culture and political authority within the same borders. It even seems to suggest that citizenship in a state is coterminal with national or ethnic identity. While there is a certain ambiguity between the meanings of the terms "nation" and "nationality," nonetheless most nations have made the claim to be based on nationality or ethnicity, usually identified as well with a language and a culture. (I return later to a somewhat different use of the term "nation," one that is not essentially tied to the notions of nationality and ethnicity.)

The assimilation of state and nation is problematic on several counts. In the first place, it is in no way entailed by the definition or the functions of a state that its members have to be of a particular nationality. The exercise of political authority, participation in political processes and in the duties of citizenship, the defense and security functions of the state, its role in economic life – none of these depends on the nationality or ethnic characteristics of its citizens. Furthermore, the association of state and nationality is a historically contingent fact where it exists, and, in the case of the major modern states, it is largely a fiction or a political myth that these states are or were homogeneous in nationality. In addition, where state and nation are identified with each other, it has often given rise to the subordination and even forced assimilation of minority ethnic or cultural groups, whether these are historically resident in the state (or even native to it) or are the result of recent immigration.

These considerations raise the issue of citizenship, or who counts as a member of the political community. In the context of this discussion, the two alternative conceptions of citizenship can be characterized roughly as *universalistic* or *particularistic*. Both are defined with respect to membership in a given state and do not currently extend to supranational entities, so that the term "universalistic" here does not connote anything like world citizenship. What is universal about the first conception is that the status of citizenship is open to all those members of the population who undertake to fulfill the obligations and duties of citizenship and are competent to exercise its functions. In practice, of course, such purely political citizenship is linked with additional conditions and constraints. This universal conception of citizens defines them independently of any requirements of ethnicity, nationality, or religion. By contrast, the particularistic conception of citizenship identifies characteristics of ethnicity or nationality as qualifications for membership in the state. These characteristics usually connote conditions deriving from kinship or birth and hence as "given" or in some vague sense as "natural." The term "cultural" is more complex because it is sometimes used in a similar way to these others but also connotes an intentionalistic identification with certain modes of life or practices, along the lines discussed in this chapter and Chapter 4. In the latter sense, cultural identity is not necessarily given but may be chosen or in any case may be acquired or ascribed independently of kinship or birth.

I have proposed the separation of the concept of state from that of nation, where *nation* is understood as bound to particular nationalities or ethnicities. I favor instead the notion of culture, inasmuch as it connotes a phenomenon in which historical traditions and practices, as well as relations with others within the culture, are subject to appropriation and transformation in a way that is not connoted by the more objectivistic and "natural" concepts of ethnicity and nationality. However, there is another use of the terms "nation" and "national" that is not bound to nationality or ethnicity in this way. In reflecting on the complex entity that we can call *political community*, we observe that there is not only the state with its government, citizens, rights, and laws, but also the community that constitutes it and whose members recognize themselves as belonging to it. This community can be referred to as a nation. It usually also entails a recognition by its members of a common history, and an inherited set of traditions, as well as a common economic and social life. Moreover, the members of a nation most often live together within a common territory that is identified with the boundaries of the state. As understood here, then, the nation is a different aspect of the same entity as the state, namely, that aspect that designates the community of which the state constitutes the political organization and the legal framework for the rights and duties of citizens.

We can finally note that the ambiguity in the use of the terms "nation" and "national" discussed earlier carries over to the frequently used concept of the self-determination of nations. That is, it is unclear whether the claimed right of self-determination of nations resides with nationalities or ethnic groups on the one hand or with the political community (that is, the state and its community) on the other. My discussion here suggests that the ambiguity should be resolved in favor of the latter, so that national self-determination, where this is held to pertain to rights to independent political statehood and to nonintervention, is not to be understood as a right of nationalities or ethnic groups as such, but rather of political communities.[16] Having said this, however, we need to introduce a

---

[16] See also Omar Dahbour, "Self-Determination in Political Philosophy and International Law," *History of European Ideas*, Vol. 16, nos. 4–6 (1993): 879–884.

qualification in applied contexts. Although it remains the case normatively that nationalities have no inherent claim to rights of self-determination (contrary to the views of Raz and Margalit[17]), in the near term and under specific conditions one can argue that a severely oppressed nationality would have a valid claim to self-determination as a state, provided that it respected the equal rights of minority cultures within such a new state. We can say that this would be justified if statehood were the only viable way to protect its members from severe oppression or the danger of annihilation. However, a further treatment of this complex issue lies beyond the scope of the present discussion, with its focus on what I have called interculturalism, and the pluralization of democracy and rights implied in it.

[17] Joseph Raz and Avishai Margalit, "National Self-Determination," *The Journal of Philosophy*, Vol. 87, no. 9 (Sept. 1990): 439–461.

6

Conceptualizing Women's Human Rights

In this part of the book, I have taken up the project of globalizing democracy and human rights in the important, although limited, sense of conceiving them to apply both more personally and in more plural ways than is customary. The idea of a more embodied politics, the critical analysis of race and racism and their import for democracy, and the analysis of cultural identities and group rights are all aspects of the broad reconceptualization that I believe is required. In this chapter, I turn finally to the issue of interpreting human rights to make them more relevant to women's experience.

There has already been considerable progress in reformulating human rights along these lines. At both the theoretical level and in more concrete efforts through the Convention on the Elimination of All Forms of Discrimination against Women (CEDAW) and the work of women's nongovernmental organizations (NGOs), as well as in certain legislative and judicial interpretations in various countries, human rights have increasingly been extended to rectifying discrimination against women and promoting women's health and education needs, and have begun to be put to use to address gender-specific violence against women. Of course, in practice, this effort has only scratched the surface of the very deep structural inequalities and endemic violence often faced by women because of the profound social effects of historically sedimented systems of patriarchal oppression. On the theoretical side, human rights have been criticized as addressed primarily to the state actions that are feared primarily by men (e.g., torture, wrongful imprisonment, etc.) rather than to the wrongs women suffer, which often have their locus in the home and the so-called private sphere.[1] Yet human rights have also been increasingly reinterpreted in ways that show them to be applicable to nonstate actors (such as nongovernmental organizations, corporations, and even individuals) and in particular to the requirements of preventing harms to women outside the more public sphere of government and the economy, as well as within it.[2]

Needless to say, much more remains to be done at both the practical and the theoretical level if human rights are to really be women's rights as well as men's. In this chapter, I deal with some of the still unclear and controversial theoretical issues that arise concerning the extension of human rights to women. But I do not focus primarily on the interpretation of the existing list of human rights to apply to women's experience. Others have done this and done it quite well. For example, there is Martha Nussbaum's effort to show the applicability of a long list of human rights to eliminate harms against women[3] in addition to the work collected in *Human Rights of Women* and in *Women's Rights, Human Rights*,[4] as well as the more practical efforts of human rights activists in connection with world conferences and the United Nations and in more regional contexts. Rather, my focus is on some difficult issues concerning how to conceive of women's human rights, within the overall framework of democracy and human rights presented in this work, and I draw on both feminist theory and political philosophy to try to make a certain amount of progress about these questions, keeping in mind that they have practical import as well.

---

[1] See, for example, Hilary Charlesworth, "What are 'Women's International Human Rights'?" and Celina Romany, "State Responsibility Goes Private: A Feminist Critique of the Public/Private Distinction in International Human Rights Law," in *Human Rights of Women*, ed. Rebecca J. Cook (Philadelphia: University of Pennsylvania Press, 1994), 58–115; and Donna Sullivan, "The Public/Private Distinction in International Human Rights Law," in *Women's Rights, Human Rights*, eds. Julie Peters and Andrea Wolper (New York: Routledge, 1995), 126–134.

[2] See, for example, Rhonda Copelon, "Intimate Terror: Understanding Domestic Violence as Torture," and Rebecca J. Cook, "State Accountability Under the Convention on the Elimination of All Forms of Discrimination Against Women," in *Human Rights of Women*, 116–152 and 228–256; Charlotte Bunch, "Transforming Human Rights from a Feminist Perspective," and Rebecca J. Cook, "International Human Rights and Women's Reproductive Health," in *Women's Rights, Human Rights*, 11–17 and 256–275.

[3] Martha Nussbaum, "Religion and Women's Human Rights," in *Sex and Social Justice* (New York: Oxford University Press, 1999), 81–117.

[4] See note 2.

Outstanding Theoretical Questions Concerning Women's Rights

The issues can be summarized as follows:

1. What sort of reconstruction of human rights is required if we take seriously women's historic preoccupation with care and with relations and responsibilities toward others, rather than simply focusing on the traditional emphasis on individual rights-claims and correlative duties? Do human rights in their dominant individualist interpretation, based largely on men's experiences in politics and economic life, in fact conflict with these feminist/feminine emphases on care and the relatedness and responsibilities toward those close to us?

2. How should we understand the public–private distinction that historically underlies human rights discourse if these rights are to be effective in addressing such wrongs to women as domestic abuse, wife battering, and even wife murder? The problematic status of privacy is also of interest here: We can be critical of it as a domain in which such gender-specific violence can continue and yet wish to preserve some sense of it, perhaps in a more relational interpretation than it currently has. The traditional understanding of the public sphere as the state, excluding other institutions such as corporations and voluntary associations, and the private sphere understood as independent of power relations in economic and social life, also merits scrutiny in this connection.

3. Whereas the issue of public and private has been interpreted primarily as applying to the domain of civil and political rights,[5] there is also the crucial question of the interconnections between women's rights and social and economic rights, including especially subsistence, health, the right to work, and education. The connections between these and the elimination of harms and even violence toward women need more examination.

4. A long-standing problem, particularly from the standpoint of liberal political and legal theory, concerns how any so-called special or differentiated rights for women can square with the idea of rights for all human beings and the requirement for equal treatment

---

[5] See, for example, the discussion in Henry Steiner and Philip Alston, *International Human Rights in Context*, second edition (Oxford: Oxford University Press, 2000), 158–224.

under the law. Do the recognition of rights concerning pregnancy or maternity or, more generally, any special mention of harms to women – for example, of a sexual nature – somehow violate the requirements of universality and equality?

5. Another issue concerns how to achieve intercultural agreement on women's human rights, given the divergent cultural claims concerning how much inequality for women can be tolerated on grounds of tradition, custom, and religion and, more generally, the question of how the plurality of cultural approaches impacts human rights and their interpretation. This issue is discussed in Chapter 2 in regard to cultural relativism versus the universalism of human rights. As I suggested there, its feminist import needs further development if we are to avoid these extremes and also avoid essentializing women's experience or reifying the concept of culture.

6. Finally, there is the question of the impact of globalization and also regionalization on women's human rights. Beyond the traditional emphasis on holding states responsible for human rights violations and the more recent effort to have them monitor wrongs by nonstate actors including not only corporations but also private individuals (e.g., men's actions toward women in the home), there is the further question of whether women's human rights would be better implemented if nation-states were deconstructed or diminished in power, or at least if new, more global institutions of justice and even of government came to have more power than they now do.

Clearly, this is too large a list of topics to discuss adequately here. And even though it would be of value, I think, simply to clarify these problems more fully, I do not want to remain at the level of merely programmatic analysis, even if that were to have a heuristic value. Also, I am in agreement with the overall thrust of the theoretical work on women's human rights thus far and do not want to engage in any polemic with it or advocate an entirely new direction. Therefore, I focus here on a number of the most problematic and unresolved issues where I feel considerably more attention is required if progress on women's human rights is to be deep and not only to remain a matter of extending existing rights to women. In part because it deals with a process still very much under way, I must put aside issue 6, concerning globalization, despite its interest and importance, although the more general role of human rights in the context of globalization is treated in the next part of the book. It can be noted here that there is a divergence among feminist human rights analysts about the role of the nation-state, with some arguing for its continued centrality,[6] and others for a more internationalist perspective.[7] Of the other five issues, which I abbreviate as (1) rights and care, (2) the private–public distinction, (3) women's social and economic rights, (4) the status of differentiated rights for women, and (5) traditional cultures versus women's equality in a human rights framework, I focus primarily on the first two, with some attention to the other three.[8] Still, I believe that it is useful to consider the various outstanding problems together because they are interrelated and because to a degree they can all be approached from a perspective that emphasizes the importance of both human rights and concrete social relationships.

Care and Human Rights

Turning first, then, to the issue of rights and care, discussed in Chapters 1 and 2, we can observe that this primarily ethical concept, which feminist theorists have drawn from women's experiences of nurturance and supportiveness, has already had some impact on political philosophy in connection with democratic community, where, as we have seen, it involves introducing concern for others more explicitly into the political domain.[9] It has also been tied to international affairs by, for example, Fiona Robinson in her book *Globalizing Care.*[10] But this care discussion has as yet had almost no impact on conceptualizing human rights. In fact, most commentators who discuss care regard it as either standing in opposition to rights discourse (e.g., in the original work of Gilligan concerning two alternative modes of moral development[11] and those influenced by her analysis) or as a necessary supplement to a rights perspective, but still

---

[6] See, for example, Cook, "State Accountability under CEDAW."

[7] See especially Karen Knop, "Why Rethinking the Sovereign State is Important for Women's International Human Rights Law," in *Human Rights of Women*, 153–164.

[8] On issue 5, concerning culture, see also Chapters 2 and 4.

[9] See, for example, Sara Ruddick, *Maternal Thinking* (Boston: Beacon Press, 1989), Joan Tronto, *Moral Boundaries: A Political Argument for an Ethic of Case* (New York: Routledge, 1993), Virginia Held, *Feminist Morality* (Chicago: University of Chicago Press, 1993), and Jane Mansbridge, "Feminism and Democratic Community," and Carol C. Gould, "Feminism and Democratic Community Revisited," in *Democratic Community*, eds. John W. Chapman and Ian Shapiro (New York: New York University Press, 1993), 339–413.

[10] Fiona Robinson, *Globalizing Care* (Boulder, CO: Westview Press, 1999).

[11] Carol Gilligan, "Moral Orientation and Moral Development," in *Women and Moral Theory*, eds. Eva F. Kittay and Diana T. Meyers (Totowa, NJ: Rowman & Littlefield, 1987), 19–33.

of a completely different order. The reason for this stance, as suggested in the earlier chapters, is that care is thought to be tied to relations with a particularistic set of those close to one, whereas rights – and particularly human rights – are thought to have a more universalistic scope.

Yet I believe that the connection between rights and care is deeper than heretofore supposed. To see this, we have to look at the nature of human rights themselves and consider whether they are correctly characterized as individualistic, as in their standard interpretation. I have argued that this interpretation is partly incorrect and that to take human rights as simply an enunciation of an Enlightenment universalism of such an abstractly individualistic sort is in error. This is so partly in view of the fact that rights always hold as claims on others, or on society as a whole, to do or refrain from doing something. Clearly, without the intersubjective ties among people presupposed here, the very concept of a right as such a claim on others would make no sense. Although Robinson Crusoe probably did have human rights – inasmuch as he was a proper Englishman, with the upbringing that entailed, who simply found himself marooned on an island – we could not say the same for a truly isolated individual, who lacked any culture or social context. Indeed, it is hard even to conceive of such an individual. It is of course true that in recognizing a human being as a bearer of human rights, we are in fact recognizing someone as a person with freedom and dignity, and this is an abstractly universal moment that holds for every human being regardless of his or her concrete differentiation (although it is not entirely a Kantian moment, we might add, because Kant restricted rights-bearers to rational beings, rather than human beings). It must be granted too that the recognition we accord to human beings does not constitute or socially construct them as human but rather is a recognition of what we take to be an intrinsic property of these beings, namely, their humanness (with all the problems of moral realism or objectivity that this raises). Still, the context of recognition is a fundamentally intersubjective and social one, indeed one of reciprocal recognition, as Hegel argued, and I would propose that this deeply social conception of reciprocity is built into our idea of human rights themselves. They come into being as claims each has on the others and hence exist as rights only in such a social framework of recognition.

Even more suggestively from a distinctively feminist perspective, human rights can be said to emerge from a practical situation of care and concern, in the following sense: If people did not tend to care about the well-being and more generally the needs of others, then the claim that each can make on the others, however valid, would remain a bare one, and people would lack the motivation needed to take these claims of others seriously and structure society in such a way as to attempt to meet them. From this feminist perspective, then, although care may be most familiar to us in our personal relations with family and friends, its conceptual exclusion from the understanding of politics appears to reflect the male-dominated character of traditional political theory and, specifically, social contract theory,[12] in which individuals are understood as separated from each other, or even as antagonistically related to each other, in a state of nature, and thus lacking fundamental caring relations with others; or, to the degree that they are thought to have such relations, especially with their families, the public–private divide excludes these relations in principle from the political domain. Thus, if feminist ethical theorists are right concerning the centrality of care in human experience, we can analogously see that human rights themselves have some basis in the care and concern we feel not only for those close to us but also for all others, even those who are strangers to us. I have attempted to articulate such a universalization of care in Chapter 2 in connection with the concept of concrete universality.

Furthermore, the equality built into the human rights conception not only is based on an abstract and justice-based judgment concerning humans as fundamentally equal in their abstract humanness, where this is the product of purely rational reflection on our part, but also grows out of a shared feeling of commonality with others, on the grounds of common needs, suffering, and aspirations – in short, as beings like ourselves. Although we do not already know them, in recognizing others as beings with dignity, we also feel a certain empathy with them and conceive of the others in terms of potential encounters we could have with them as sharing fundamental concerns or as standing in possible relations with us. I would propose that the concept of human rights (as well as of rights more generally) has been deprived and reduced because of the effort to separate it from such a context of shared feeling, and to limit it to a purely rational and theoretical judgment. (This does not entail, of course, that reason itself is not also tied to the emotions in some important ways, but to discuss this would surely take us too far afield at this point. It also does not imply, of course, that there are not feelings of enmity and hostility that we feel toward others as well.)

If we look to this arena of care and concern, derived in part from women's experience in childraising and nurturance of others in the home and beyond it, we find also the corollary concept of responsibility. This concept, too, is a useful corrective to the more abstract notion of duty,

---

[12] See Carole Pateman, *The Sexual Contract* (Stanford, CA: Stanford University Press, 1988).

normally thought to be correlated with a right. Responsibilities are responsibilities for or to someone, and suggest immediately our ties to the
others for whom we feel responsible. Women (and men as well) responsible for the well-being of children, and perhaps also elderly relatives, are
tied to these others in ways beyond simply recognizing the rights they
have and their abstract duties to fulfill these rights. Likewise, it can be
argued at the more global level that an emphasis on shared responsibilities among states – for example, for ecological management – in place
of or perhaps in addition to the rights and duties of states might lead to
a greater concern for achieving just outcomes in international affairs.[13]
Here, the idea of responsibility for others not only suggests that one is
required to do some particular act toward another, after which one may
be said to have done one's duty, but also it calls for a more continuing
concern with taking care of the well-being of others, including a concern
with helping to bring about good and just outcomes for them.

Another implication of care for human rights doctrine is the support
this concept gives to the rights to means of subsistence, to health care,
and to education, inasmuch as these are fundamental to the life and
development of persons. Human rights instruments (and even more so
the U.S. Constitution) still tend to denigrate these economic and social
rights in favor of the civil and political rights, to the degree that they
include them at all. An emphasis on the social and political importance
of care and nurturance lends weight, then, to a requirement for meeting
people's basic needs, if it can be shown that these are aspects of what
people owe each other in societies (as discussed earlier) and not only
characterize the particularistic obligations or responsibilities that they
have to those close to them. Although as individuals we certainly cannot
fully care for all equally (and here care differs from the idea of respect,
which is susceptible of this equality), nonetheless I have proposed that
there is an extensibility of what we might call basic care that can apply
universally. We cannot take care of all others, in the sense of directly being
responsible for meeting their needs personally (in the way that we can,
for example, for our children, or at least try to do so). Nonetheless, we
can be jointly responsible for meeting the basic needs of all the others,
and this imposes some fundamental human rights obligations on each
of us. In this sense, it makes sense to speak of a human right to care, or

---

[13] See Robert E. Goodin, "International Ethics and the Environmental Crisis," in *Ethics and
International Affairs*, second edition, ed. Joel H. Rosenthal (Washington, DC: Georgetown
University Press, 1999), 443–446.

to be cared for. Yet this does not necessarily mean that we have to add yet another right to the long list of recognized human rights (although there may be arguments for doing this). But it does entail that the caring rights – such as those to means of subsistence or to health care – have a deep basis not only in the respect we have for others but also in the basic care that we collectively must have for them.

The Public–Private Distinction

Turning now to the vexing second issue as it impacts the conception of women's human rights, we can take note of the helpful work done by Hilary Charlesworth, Celina Romany, Rhonda Copelon, and others[14] to criticize the way traditional human rights doctrine has used the public–private distinction to marginalize harms to women by regarding them as pertaining to the private realm and hence outside the purview of human rights, which, it is held, properly pertain to the actions of states. Of course, many wrongs to women are perpetrated by states. Some of these harms are general, whereas others pertain primarily to women – for example, where rape is perpetrated by the police themselves against women held in custody, or various harms to women as refugees or in time of war.[15] Yet the feminist theorists have shown how both the list and the interpretation of human rights, having been drawn up primarily by men, are concerned primarily with public wrongs, at the expense of harms committed against women in domestic or more private domains of family life and interpersonal relations. These feminist authors have made considerable progress in rectifying the imbalance in human rights theory – for example, by tying rape to torture[16] or by showing how male bias has led to relative inattention in rights doctrines of considerations of bodily integrity so important to women (in reproductive rights, in protection from sexual assaults, and so forth).[17]

In more practical contexts, too, the CEDAW Convention (along with the subsequent Vienna Declaration on the Elimination of Violence

---

[14] See notes 1 and 2.

[15] In this connection, we can note the Security Council resolution 1325 (2000) concerning the impact of armed conflict on women (and girls) and their role in peacekeeping and peace-building.

[16] Copelon, "Intimate Terror: Understanding Domestic Violence as Torture."

[17] Helen Bequaert Holmes, "A Feminist Analysis of the United Nations Declaration of Human Rights," in Carol C. Gould, ed., *Beyond Domination: New Perspectives on Women and Philosophy* (Totowa, NJ: Rowman & Littlefield, 1984), 256–257. See also Charlesworth, "What are 'Women's International Human Rights'?" 73.

against Women) to a degree helps to diminish the public–private distinction (at least in principle) by insisting that discrimination against, and harms to, women cannot be tolerated even where they are carried out by private individuals, and that it falls to states to attempt to eliminate such discrimination and to deal with such harms, whether in the public or the private sphere. Thus, Article Two requires states "to take all appropriate measures to eliminate discrimination against women *by any person, organization or enterprise*" (2e). Accordingly, such wrongs as wife murder, sati, rape, female genital mutilation, forced prostitution, marital rape, woman battering, domestic abuse, and sexual harassment can all in principle be addressed, even though they may not be directly perpetrated by states but rather by private individuals or by economic, cultural, or social institutions. According to CEDAW, it is incumbent on states to put laws in place to eliminate these and other forms of discrimination. This helpful development (although one that is still mostly theoretical at this point inasmuch as it has not been implemented much in practice) has largely proceeded on the grounds offered over the past several decades by feminist theory – namely, that the personal is political, in that power relations of a customary or institutional sort permeate the private sphere, and legitimate oppressive and unequal treatment of women by men, and that these harms should not be beyond the scope of law and jurisprudence.

Yet many difficult issues remain unresolved in this critique of the distinction between public and private, and some of these bear on our understanding of women's human rights themselves. For one thing, privacy on a certain interpretation is appealed to, at least in the United States, as the main ground for preserving women's reproductive rights regarding abortion. Even apart from this, although the "private" sphere of the family clearly should not be an area where gender-specific violence, or indeed any violence, is tolerated (supposedly, but objectionably, on grounds of "family privacy"), still some sense of privacy is surely worth preserving. After all, we quite rightly would object to the state meddling in our choice of partners, our sexual relations, and, in a very different context, in our communications with others through the mails or the Internet, or again, in regard to medical records and the like. Different strategies are possible here for carving out a domain of privacy that merits protection by right. For one thing, much of what is included in the idea of privacy – including the support it provides for abortion rights – can in fact be captured by an idea of autonomy or freedom, from which the requirements of privacy follow. Thus, we can protect individual choice in the cases just specified by seeing it as a matter of (equal) freedom more fundamentally and of privacy by derivation from that. In this case, we would insist it is a matter of freedom to be able to choose sexual partners, have a child, or again, to control information about oneself and so on.

Beyond this, as far as women's privacy is concerned, we would probably benefit from conceiving privacy in more relational ways than on traditional views that emphasize the separateness of persons. Accordingly, what merits protection is not only my private space but also the shared space of those close to me. An important proviso here, though, would be that violence or other serious harms not be tolerated within this space, and that relations within it proceed on the basis of equality[18] or at least the absence of oppression or discrimination. In this way, a conception of privacy can be preserved at the same time that we recognize the need for a certain degree of public scrutiny of "private discrimination."

However, rethinking privacy in these ways is not sufficient. There is a correlative need to reconceptualize the public sphere, as well as to argue that human rights apply to all these contexts and to nonstate actors within them. In this view, "the public" is extended to the institutional domain of economic and social life, in short, to the domain of organizations such as firms and voluntary associations beyond the interpersonal. The distinction then becomes one between the public or institutional, on the one hand, and the private or individual or interpersonal on the other. (One interesting question that remains, though, which I cannot address here, is the status of the family in this division.) It is interesting to observe too that the concept of nonstate actors, widely used in human rights discussion, in fact applies to two rather different sets: private individuals, on the one hand, and economic, social, and cultural entities on the other. Human rights and responsibilities for their implementation properly fall on all of these, as argued in Chapter 1 and as developed somewhat further at later points in this work.

Women's Social and Economic Rights

The public–private distinction and the case of gender-specific harms – such as domestic violence – directed toward women have been treated primarily in connection with civil and political rights. Yet it seems to me that the sharp separation between these and the social and economic rights

---

[18] On this issue, see the essays in Susan Okin et al., *Is Multiculturalism Bad for Women?* (Princeton, NJ: Princeton University Press, 1999).

within human rights theory and practice is unfortunate, not only in a general sense but also in its specific impact on understanding women's human rights. The status of women's social and economic rights is the third issue enumerated earlier, and here I would like to argue that the relative neglect of such crucial economic and social rights of women as those to means of subsistence, health, and education directly contributes to women's oppression as women and even contributes to several of the gender-specific harms cited earlier. First, as discussed in Chapter 2, Amartya Sen and others have shown how the lack of regard for women's right to life or subsistence – whether through selective abortion or infanticide of girl fetuses or babies, or severe malnutrition due to selective inadequate provision for their subsistence needs, together with their lack of access to adequate health care – has led to millions of missing women worldwide.[19] Women's literacy rates and their lack of rights to work in many countries also differentially harm their life chances.

But we can additionally observe that the deprivation of these economic and social rights negatively impacts women's abilities to protect themselves from the harms to their persons customarily treated in the civil or political domain, and also makes it difficult for them to exercise their rights to political participation. Indeed, several of the abuses considered under the heading of gender-specific violence have strong economic components. Examples here include forced prostitution, where girls or women are sold for material motives; dowry killings or beatings, such as in India, which often proceed on crudely economic grounds;[20] and woman battering and domestic abuse, which at the very least reflect a lack of recognition of women's economic equality. (In the United States, these may be perpetrated by men who resent women's work, as well as by those in deficient financial circumstances, although of course not only by them.) Again, in the case of female genital cutting, African feminist activists have proposed that in addition to cultural factors, this practice is tied to economic advantage through the requirement of protecting or enhancing women's marriageability status, and the material as well as psychological gain that belonging brings.[21] Perhaps even more clearly, many of these abuses can be meliorated only if attention is also given to equalizing women's standing in economic and social matters, including

---

[19] Amartya Sen, "Gender Inequality and Theories of Justice," in *Women, Culture, and Development*, eds. Jonathan Glover and Martha Nussbaum (Oxford: Oxford University Press, 1995), 259.

[20] See Nussbaum, "Religion and Women's Human Rights," 89–90.

[21] Nahid Toubia, "Female Genital Mutilation," in *Women's Rights, Human Rights*.

by access to work and the independent income it can provide and by equal access to education and welfare as well as health care and contraception. (Along these lines, Sen has also shown how, in the case of the Kerala province in India, women's social and economic standing, particularly in terms of education, is a central factor in ensuring generally higher levels of well-being for the population.[22])

It seems apparent, then, that remedying women's oppression requires considerably more attention to their economic and social rights, beyond the often-cited issue of overcoming the public–private distinction. Yet, as Charlesworth has suggested, the prevalence of this distinction itself impacts these economic rights by reinforcing their interpretation as applying to the public, in the sense of institutional, sphere of economic life – as, for example, the well-known requirement of equal pay for equal work – while applying less or not at all to women's economic independence within the family.[23] Clearly, reinterpretations are required if these economic and social rights are to become more fully applicable to women's experience.

On the importance of social and economic rights, women's human rights activists from Africa, Asia, and Latin America have been in considerable agreement. And this striking consonance in views raises the final question of how to deal with the areas of diversity in cultural approaches to rights and to women's oppression. Before turning to that question, discussed at some length in Chapter 2, I would like to briefly address the fourth issue outlined earlier.

The Status of Differentiated Rights for Women

If we regard some of the human rights as "special" to women or as sex-differentiated, does this violate the universality of human rights or the requirement of equal treatment under the law? The CEDAW Convention in fact skirts this issue by framing its concerns in terms of eliminating discrimination against women, and it therefore specifies certain particular rights by way of assuring women equal treatment. However, the question remains as to whether we should include any sex-specific rights not only as interpretations of human rights but also as rights themselves

---

[22] For a recent statement, see Amartya Sen, *Development as Freedom* (New York: Knopf, 2000), Chapter 8.

[23] Hilary Charlesworth, "Human Rights as Men's Rights," in *Women's Rights, Human Rights*, 108.

and, more generally, what the status of such gender-specific rights might be.

If we understand human rights to be based on a mutual recognition of all humans as equally free in a fundamental way, we can observe, as argued in Chapter 1, that this freedom (as positive freedom) entails their rights to the conditions needed for any human activity whatever and also to those necessary for their fuller self-development. The first set of human rights – to the conditions of human agency in general – include the basic rights, especially those of life and liberty, where "life" signifies not only a right not to be killed but also access to means of subsistence as well as rights to health care, basic education, and certain others. The second set of what we might call nonbasic human rights include those to the conditions for the higher development of human agency in differentiated forms.[24] Unfortunately, as I see it, there is no comparable distinction in human rights documents, which instead treat all of the human rights as equally fundamental, from liberty to the right to a paid vacation. In principle, though, I believe that there is a certain distinction to be made; the basic ones are necessarily very general, inasmuch as they are prerequisites for any human activity whatever, whereas the nonbasic ones are open to more differentiation according to the diversity of human needs and interests, compatible with the equality entailed in the fundamental idea of equal freedom.

Thus, if we are to treat people equally, we must often treat them in differentiated ways, as argued earlier in this part, in view of their different needs and to a degree their different interests. The case of disabled people with special requirements of access and support services is perhaps the most obvious case, as cited previously. But this principle extends far beyond this one instance. Concrete differences between men and women are also among the differences that may need to be recognized. Of course, one can argue that differences between men and women affect not only the nonbasic rights but also the basic rights, in view of the human biological or social requirements of pregnancy and childbirth. I believe that the account I have given can accommodate this, although I do not see that it affects the enunciation of the basic rights themselves, which necessarily remain general. Beyond this, we can observe that all the rights require interpretations, a sort of inevitable casuistry, in which they are interpreted for the concrete social and historical world as it presents itself, and here too differences between people, including sexual difference, sometimes

---

[24] Ibid., especially 202–204.

rightly enter. In short, then, I am arguing that the equality entailed by human rights is fully compatible with, and indeed sometimes requires, differential but equivalent treatment, if this equality is to be realized.

Traditional Cultures Versus Women's Equality in a Human Rights Framework

Let us turn finally to the question about the multiplicity of cultures in connection with conceptualizing women's human rights. We can note that, as suggested in Chapter 2, the question is how to deal with the Western dominance in human rights discourse – with its commitment in principle to women's equality and the need for nondiscrimination, its strong public–private divide, its priority to the individual, and its preference for first-generation civil and political rights over second- and third-generation economic, social, cultural, and development rights – in relation to the diversity of cultures worldwide, many of which explicitly advocate sex-stratified societies in which men are dominant. The number and scope of the reservations that various states have registered to the CEDAW Convention are testimony to this contested situation. And given that feminists have been among the most sensitive toward recognizing differences among women as relevant to their theories, we may ask again whether this entails the requirement of accepting cultural norms that we may regard as oppressing women, especially when these norms may be endorsed or implemented by women themselves.

Continuing the argument in the earlier chapter, we can observe in this context that we need to avoid not only essentializing women's experience or gender norms more generally but also essentializing cultures, regarding them as uniform and as static or unchanging over time. In fact, there is a diversity of perspectives within cultures, and an important issue for women is that of "Who speaks for the culture?"[25] As we know, women have been relatively silenced in many cultures, at least in the public domain. Thus, in most cases, those who articulate and interpret cultural norms have been men. This inegalitarian and undemocratic situation is beginning to be rectified in many countries, where increasingly we find women's social movements gaining new influence, and we can hope to see more women in the role of interpreting cultural doctrines as well. Thus it is unacceptable for states or the men within them to assert the

---

[25] See Arati Rao, "The Politics of Gender and Culture in International Human Rights Discourse," in *Women's Rights, Human Rights*, 167–175.

priority of their traditional cultures if they retain for themselves the sole power to interpret them and to speak for these cultures.

If we recognize that not only gender norms but also cultures are constructed and transformed over time by the people within them as well as through interaction more globally, then, as suggested in the preceding chapters, we can find in this capacity of people to change themselves and their cultures that very agency that is recognized so centrally as the ground for human rights themselves and that bears some relation to the idea of human dignity, also embodied in these rights. Furthermore, the centrality of the social interaction within and across cultures supports the idea that human rights have a basis in these concrete social relations and not only enunciate an abstract human equality and universality; and I proposed earlier that this gives rise to a norm of concrete universality. It is therefore appropriate to see human rights as emerging from these practical contexts and also as properly subject to interpretation according to changing social and historical mores and practices.

Moreover, if we look at the full range of human rights doctrine, as discussed previously there has been a process of intercultural determination of these rights, and this process needs also to be intensified. This is premised not simply on the idea of a global dialogical community (with Habermassian influences), to which some feminists have appealed,[26] but also on the more concrete social interactions that emerge within and across cultures when people are engaged in common projects and joint social movements, and when they come to feel care for those at some distance from themselves. In these more positive manifestations of globalization – to the degree that they can actually come to the fore in the face of nondemocratic forms of global dominance – we can see the basis for a more open and genuinely intercultural constitution of human rights, as well as more diversity in their interpretation. Still, hard questions remain here, and these brief remarks are not intended to put this difficult issue to rest.

It is also worth observing that, when construed in this open way, it is the human rights themselves that can set appropriate limits to the tolerance of diverse cultural practices, including those oppressive to women. Thus when women's rights to freedom from domination and bodily harm are violated within a given culture as part of its tradition, the approach proposed here gives priority to women's equality and bodily integrity,

---

[26] See Seyla Benhabib, "Cultural Complexity, Moral Interdependence, and the Global Dialogical Community," in *Women, Culture, and Development*, 235–255.

as among the basic human rights, over regard for such cultural differences. While a general right to the preservation and development of cultural differences may be counted among the human rights (as argued in Chapter 5), it cannot legitimate actions that violate the basic human rights of others. In short, there is a normative limit to cultural difference: Pernicious differences – those that violate basic human rights – cannot be claimed as a matter of cultural right.[27]

One final proviso is in order and emerges rather directly from the preceding: Obviously, women's human rights are insufficient by themselves to effect full change in the situation of women. Not only rights but also actual social change in oppressive social relations are needed, with the grassroots movements and activism that this entails. And we require not only more theory but also social critique, as well as efforts to connect the human rights principles discussed here to concrete social relations, which necessarily remain both their ground and their reference point.

---

[27] For further discussion, see Carol C. Gould, "Cultural Justice and the Limits of Difference: Feminist Contributions to Value Inquiry," *Utopia* (Athens), Vol. 21 (July–Aug. 1996): 131–143; and in revised form in *Norms and Values: Essays in Honor of Virginia Held*, eds. J. G. Haber and M. S. Halfon (Lanham, MD: Rowman & Littlefield, 1998), 73–85.

PART III

GLOBALIZING DEMOCRACY IN A HUMAN
RIGHTS FRAMEWORK

7

Evaluating the Claims for Global Democracy

We are now in a position to consider the issue of globalizing democracy, which is adumbrated at the practical level in the emergence of regional political bodies, such as the European Union and smaller-scale crossborder democratic communities of various sorts, and envisioned at the theoretical level in the very general normative requirement for democratic decision making presented in this work and in that of other democratic theorists. However, when we take democracy so generally it is clear that new issues come to the fore, especially questions of the proper scope and extent of a viable democratic community. We can thus be led to ask, is this globalization of democracy really a helpful direction for democratic theory? What does it entail specifically about who participates in which decisions? What in fact do political philosophers mean when they speak of global or cosmopolitan democracy, as they are increasingly doing?

In this chapter, I begin with a brief sketch of some of the key features of contemporary globalization in their import for democracy and then assess the main models that have been advanced for global or cosmopolitan democracy, notably those put forth by David Held, Daniele Archibugi, Richard Falk, and Thomas Pogge. Given the somewhat schematic nature of these theories, however, I move back to a more elemental approach and take up the question of how to formulate the proper scope of democratic decision making – that is, who has a right to decide about a given issue? Is it "all those affected" by a particular decision, and what would this really mean? The discussion of this and other possible criteria can then provide some guidance for how we can think about the issue of democracy beyond borders, and of democratizing supranational organizations. In the latter part of the chapter, I take off from the arguments given earlier in this book but extend them in new, more cosmopolitical directions.[1] The characterization of "those affected" is revisited in Chapter 9 in connection with the issue of democratizing globalization and the realization of economic and social human rights.

Globalization and Democracy

It should be clear that this chapter employs the terms "global democracy" and "cosmopolitan democracy" in rather normative ways. Yet the empirical aspect of this issue – the understanding of globalization in its impact on democracy – is also of considerable interest and has received much attention recently.[2] "Globalization" (together with cognate uses of "global") is a term of art that has come into increasingly popular use both in the academy and in public discourse. A generation ago, the idea was vividly introduced in Marshall McLuhan's term "global village," connoting the shrinking of geographical distance and the effective disappearance of national borders brought about by the ubiquity of instantaneously transmitted words and images in the new technologies of worldwide communication. More recently, the term "globalization" has been used to characterize the rapidly developing interconnectedness and interdependence of national economies within the world economy, with respect to production, trade, finance, and labor markets, as well as the related universalization of technologies not only of production but also of communication. Yet inasmuch as this economic interdependence has entailed dominance by global corporations and lack of input into multilateral organizations by those impacted by their decisions, such economic globalization has increasingly been the subject of critique and protest. To a degree accompanying these economic and technological aspects, we have also taken note of a substantial globalization in the cultural, primarily in the proliferation of Western (and, particularly, American) cultural modes – for example, in music, film, and dress – but also in greater access to diverse cultures worldwide, including non-Western ones.

To an extent, we can also speak of political globalization, in the sense of the emergence of supranational regional bodies, most notably, the

---

[1] I used this term in the final chapter of *Rethinking Democracy: Freedom and Social Cooperation in Politics, Economy, and Society* (Cambridge: Cambridge University Press, 1988), 307–328, and I believe that in many ways it is more suitable than the simpler term "cosmopolitan."

[2] See, for example, Joseph E. Stiglitz, *Globalization and Its Discontents* (New York: W. W. Norton, 2002).

European Union – and in the growing role of international bodies, especially the United Nations, both in terms of its peacekeeping and its monetary and financial functions. There has also been the emergence of a certain globalization of democratic forms of governance, in the sense of their extension to increasing numbers of nation-states, especially in the movements that took place for political democracy and self-government (notably, among the republics of the former Soviet Union and the countries of Eastern Europe, although this democratization has sometimes been accompanied by exclusivist and chauvinist nationalist and ethnic struggles). In addition, we have observed the emergence of the conditions for a degree of transnational democratic decision making, as seen, for example, in the European Parliament, as well as at the United Nations and in certain other delimited international contexts. It is also often remarked that the new telecommunications technologies have increased communication among people remotely situated and thus have opened new possibilities for democratic dialogue – not yet, however, put to much use despite the increasing number of websites devoted to participatory democratic decision making in various formats. I return to these "democratic networks" in Chapter 11.

The new theories of global or cosmopolitan democracy – while they could be advanced as purely normative proposals, such as along eighteenth-century lines – most often take off from the claim that key features of contemporary globalization have rendered the nation-state somewhat less central and less appropriate as the locus for all democratic decision making than it previously was. Although sometimes eschewing a direct attack on the idea of state sovereignty, the theorists have pointed to several features of globalization that have worked to break down the effectiveness and appropriateness of political borders for delimiting the scope of democratic decision making. As noted, these features concern the interconnectedness of individuals and communities worldwide and the emergence of complex and overlapping networks of states and of nonstate actors situated at a distance from each other. At the social level, we can also observe the increasing regionalization or internationalization of associations in a process that can be called *intersociation*.

In this new situation, the main factors thought to require new forms of democratic organization may be summarized as follows: (1) the development within economic globalization of increasingly prominent activities of the financial markets, the growing power of transnational or global corporations and of international banking and trade, and the emergence of such international institutions as the IMF, the World Bank, and the WTO;

(2) the new communications and media interconnections, facilitated by computers, across national boundaries (and especially the Internet); (3) regional and global environmental problems, clearly visible as being beyond the scope of any given nation-state; (4) the development of international law and especially doctrines of human rights and their increasing institutionalization; and (5) the emergence of large numbers of transnational civil society organizations, NGOs (nongovernmental organizations), and regional or even global social movements. In this complex and diversified context, it is argued that we need to work out forms of democracy that can cope with these powerful transnational influences, which, in any case, it is suggested, are thrusting this requirement on us, whether we like it or not.

These developments pose additional problems for democratic theory, which can be further noted here:

1. What form of democratic accountability, if any, do such supranational entities as the International Monetary Fund and the World Bank or similar international agencies have to the constituent peoples in the countries affected by them? Or are these global institutions bureaucratic or technocratic entities that function autonomously, independent of the political processes of democracy?

2. What legitimates the authority of decision making by supranational bodies (of these or more political sorts) when such decisions impinge on the sovereignty of existing nation-states? Do the agreements to set up regional or global agencies by member-states for the purposes of economic, political, military, or cultural cooperation signify a surrender of national sovereignty by the constituent nation-states or a ceding of democratic control to a supervenient body? This issue is posed not only with respect to institutions or international agreements concerned with cooperation or regulation, such as the UN or the WTO, but even more sharply with respect to regional federations or political unions, such as that constituted by the European Union.

3. What effect does globalization have on the emerging democracies or developing nations that are highly dependent economically and unstable politically? Are these capital-deficient and economically transitional states vulnerable to external control and manipulation by supranational bodies or in a different way by multinational corporations? Does this in effect undermine internal democratic practices and the authority of democratic decision making? For

example, if the International Monetary Fund establishes requirements for the adoption of stringent austerity programs, does this amount to political coercion that compromises the internal democratic decision making in the client states? In sum, do such supranational bodies now take the role that was formerly played by powerful nations in economically and politically coercing their weaker neighbors?

In this context, a normative issue for democratic theory is how to effect democratic control of supranational bodies. The premise here is that there ought to be such control, and the general argument advanced for this is that people have the right to participate in decisions about matters that importantly affect them. Earlier, I presented a somewhat different normative argument for determining where democratic participation is called for. This argument bases the requirement for democracy on the equal right of individuals to participate in decisions concerning frameworks of common activity defined by shared goals. Both this argument and the one that refers to those affected raise the question of how such participation could be even remotely feasible with respect to global bodies for which there are no correlate political constituencies, practically speaking.

One could argue that since such supranational agencies as the UN (or its member institutions such as the International Atomic Energy Agency), such regional alliances as NATO, or such economic organizations as the WTO are constituted by voluntary member-states that therefore the citizens or people of these states are indirectly represented by their appointed delegates or functionaries; and furthermore, that such bodies are at their appropriate level "democratic," insofar as the member-states share in the decision making on a free and equal basis or in some fair manner of proportional representation. This would be at best a kind of second-order representative democracy, which, although very tenuous, would provide some accountability of the supranational bodies to the populations affected by their decisions, at least to the citizens in their member-states. But this model of democracy would be viable only on three conditions: first, that the member-states were themselves internally democratic polities and that their decisions about membership in the international body and about the policies to be pursued by the nation's representatives on such bodies were subject to the scrutiny and decision-making authority of the citizenry; second, that the citizenry were both privy to, and educated enough to understand, in broad terms, the matters that such supranational agencies act on;[3] and third, only if the supranational agencies were constituted so as to give each member-state – or where they are not fully international, all affected states – due representation.

In fact, none of these conditions is met, and therefore in practice there is no real democratic accountability of global bodies to the constituent citizenries of member-states. It may be that a democratic state by virtue of the influence that its citizens have on the government is more representative of their will in an international body than would be the case if it were an authoritarian undemocratic state. But even in this case, the degree of democratic input into the actual functioning of a global bureaucracy or technocracy or even a deliberative body such as the General Assembly of the UN is minimal at present. Nonetheless, it is on the basis of some minimal degree of democratic participation and representation that there could be any progress toward the realization of the conditions listed earlier.

Furthermore, it is conceivable that a supranational body could itself be an instrumentality for increasing the democratic accountability of its member-states to their own citizens. It would have to be the case that the international body required, as a condition for membership in that body, that the prospective or actual member-states meet a criterion of internal democracy. Of course, the situation in which a supranational body would become the instrumentality for the democratization of national states seems farfetched at present. But if such international agreements as the UN Declaration on Human Rights were implemented in a strong sense, these norms could become criteria for the legitimation of governments seeking to participate in global or supranational bodies. Of course, there have been rogue nations that were denied membership in international bodies or participation in international treaties on the grounds that their governments had behaved in ways that excluded them from the community of nations or were not legitimate governments. However, the

---

[3] At the level of supranational bodies, this presents a somewhat parallel problem to that posed by the issue of democratic control of technology within a state, in that, in the latter case, policy and funding decisions would be subject to democratic control only if there is a functioning system of representative democracy and a reasonable level of technological literacy among the citizenry. This is part of a more general normative question concerning the accountability of bureaucratic or technocratic institutions to the citizens of the relevant polity. If one conceives of democratic control as requiring accountability to all those affected by these decisions, this would pose the difficult questions of how such a constituency could be defined and, even more problematically, how it can be democratically represented.

absence of internal democracy has not been a criterion for such exclusion heretofore.

Alternatively, one could conceive of a more direct mode of democratic accountability of global institutions that would be based on something like world citizenship, on an extranational basis. This would entail a means of democratic participation on a global scale, including opportunities for deliberation, voting, and referenda in some viable international forum, as well as representation in elective bodies empowered to legislate, regulate, and make policy. Thus with respect to the issues within the decision-making domain of such global bodies, this would be a limited form of world government. This sort of model, advanced by some theorists, is implausible, certainly in the near term, and it is questionable whether it would be desirable if it entailed an abandonment of the diversity of political communities, as discussed later.

It is more realistic and perhaps also more reasonable to conceive of regional supranational unities or federations that would decide on issues of joint concern and in which there would be participation by the citizens of the various nation-states taken collectively. Such a development is the European Union with its Parliament, at least in principle, in which the representatives are elected by the citizens of the member countries. This is the most advanced case of globalization, albeit on a regional scale, where democratic participation by citizens of the member-states is designed to be transnational, and where the issue of European citizenship has been broached. Realistically, the European Parliament still has relatively little political clout, and the locus of effective political democracy still rests primarily within the structures of the various European nation-states. In fact, the future development of the European Union may proceed either as a federal union in the strong sense of a United States of Europe on the model of the United States of America, or, as currently seems more likely, as a confederation in which the sovereignty and national identity of member-states is retained.

Aside from the emergence of supranational bodies, political or economic, the question of globalizing democracy is also prompted by the appearance of new transborder communities that sometimes operate democratically. These include regional crossborder communities addressing matters of shared concern, especially environmental, where issues such as acid rain or other forms of pollution cross national borders, as well as ethnic or cultural communities in which these national or ethnic groups extend across existing political borders. Likewise, there are a host of smaller voluntary associations, civil or professional, as well as global activist groups, that increasingly use the Internet to communicate to far-flung members. These transborder associations raise the possibility of achieving agreements democratically from remote locations and again break the traditional image of nation-states (and smaller political communities within them) as the sole arena for democracy. Finally, of course, there are the increasingly shared interests in a viable global ecology and economy, and these shared interests pose the issue of more global sorts of accountability of decision makers and the question of implementing more democratic modes of deciding about such matters that affect everyone. It is in this complex new context that the possibilities of new modes of globalizing democracy arise.

Models of Global or Cosmopolitan Democracy

Before we consider some of the proposed models of global democracy, it is important to distinguish between *moral cosmopolitanism*, pertaining to universalistic approaches to people worldwide in their status as moral beings or persons, together with their various duties and rights, and *political cosmopolitanism*, which is the concern in the theories of democracy that I consider here. The political view takes democracy to concern global governance and, sometimes more abstractly still, global order. It tends to appeal to a system of cosmopolitan law, where this is not identical with international law as we know it, but rather goes beyond it in proposing the full institutionalization of a system of human rights across borders and in specifying a universal requirement for democratic decision. By contrast to such cosmopolitan democracy, what has been designated as transnational democracy or democracy across borders concerns the more delimited issue of applying democratic decision making to new communities that cross political boundaries, without any necessary implication of a comprehensive global scheme.

A helpful typology of approaches to transnational democracy is offered by Anthony McGrew, who distinguishes between three models: liberal internationalism, communitarianism, and cosmopolitan democracy.[4] Whereas the first sees the possibilities of democracy as emerging in the relations among nation-states within the current international regime as we know it and stresses especially reforms in the United Nations, the second approach, communitarianism, emphasizes the development of alternative sites for democratic decision, particularly in new functionally

[4] A. McGrew, "Democracy beyond Borders?" in *The Global Transformations Reader*, eds. D. Held and A. McGrew (Cambridge: Polity Press, 2000), 405–419.

defined and nonterritorial authorities (e.g., concerned with trade, the environment, or health). This second approach sees democracy as emerging from the efforts of certain nonstate actors in civil society, especially social movements and NGOs. McGrew then views David Held's cosmopolitan democracy as a sort of synthesis of these two models. This third approach shares with the first a constitutional and legal emphasis in the weight it gives to a new democratic public law – where international appeals to human, and especially democratic, rights become possible – and shares with the second an emphasis on embodying democracy in new communities that will be able to deal somehow with the powerful market influence of transnational corporations. Held's model sees these communities as regional and global sites for democratic decision making, territorially defined, where people are regarded as citizens of a variety of nested associations or communities at the local, regional, and global levels.

Whereas McGrew's typology does help to bring some order to this otherwise somewhat confusing literature, we can question whether in fact Held's views are the true synthesis of the other two. A more cosmopolitical, in place of a purely cosmopolitan, approach, one that more fully acknowledges the diversity of political communities, might better capture the realism that is characteristic of the first – liberal international – perspective. I return to that later. In addition, the communitarian approaches that McGrew discusses most often seek to establish new communities along functional rather than territorial lines, as is especially evident in the "demarchy" proposed by Burnheim, in which people are to be chosen by lot to represent others in matters in which they have a material interest.[5] By contrast, Held largely remains a committed territorialist in his approach. Furthermore, although Held insists that his model seeks to preserve diversity in people's community memberships – inasmuch as they can be members of numerous nested communities and are supposed to regard themselves as citizens of various communities at all levels – still his willingness to conceive of his scheme as one of global order, however democratic, might raise for some observers the old specter of global tyranny.

As for McGrew's characterization of the communitarians, too, we might well want to leave room for more territorially inclined communitarians. These theorists see new opportunities and new needs for democratic decision making among smaller crossborder communities, which may

---

[5] John Burnheim, *Is Democracy Possible?* (Cambridge: Cambridge University Press, 1985) and "Power Trading and the Environment," *Environmental Politics*, Vol. 4, no. 4 (1995): 49–65.

be ecologically or economically linked, rather than simply arguing for functionally defined communities. Thus, for example, ecofeminists such as Mies and Shiva and a communitarian like Dahbour propose that such small, ecologically defined communities, either within nation-states or in transborder situations, should replace larger ones and should be sites of democratic decision making.[6] Or again, more traditional communitarians like Sandel argue that we need, as he puts it, a common civic identity to provide a basis for democracy, and this leads him to return to the nation-state as a proper locus for decision making.[7] Kymlicka, too, displays a concern along these lines, arguing against too much globalizing of democracy on the ground that people need to share a language, in his view, if they are to actively participate in political parties, which he sees as a key element of democracy (noting in this connection the absence of political parties that span the European Union).[8]

Let us look a little more closely at the cosmopolitan democratic model, as it is enunciated by various theorists, and especially by David Held, in his book *Democracy and the Global Order*[9] and a series of articles. Held puts great weight on what he calls democratic public law, and on its "entrenchment" or "enshrinement" in constitutions at national and international levels and in the functioning of international courts.[10] This law essentially involves a set of rights (and corresponding obligations) that enable people to be free and equal within a process of self-determination. They include seven basic rights categories: health, social, cultural, civic, economic, pacific, and political.[11] While this seems close to the list of human rights, Held does not define the cosmopolitan legal structure in these terms, although it is not clear why he does not do so. Thomas Beetham, in his book *Democracy and Human Rights* does interpret the basic rights in these explicit terms.[12] We can observe that the institutionalization of

---

[6] See Maria Mies and Vandana Shiva, *Ecofeminism* (Halifax, Canada: Fernwood, 1993) and Omar Dahbour, "The Ethics of Self-Determination: Democratic, National, Regional," in *Cultural Identity and the Nation-State*, eds. Carol C. Gould and Pasquale Pasquino (Lanham, MD: Rowman & Littlefield, 2002), 1–17.

[7] Michael Sandel, *Democracy's Discontent* (Cambridge, MA: Harvard University Press, 1996), 342.

[8] Will Kymlicka, "Citizenship in an Era of Globalization: Commentary on Held," in *Democracy's Edges*, eds. Ian Shapiro and Casiano Hacker-Cordón (Cambridge: Cambridge University Press, 1999), 120–125.

[9] Held, *Democracy and the Global Order* (Stanford, CA: Stanford University Press, 1995).

[10] Ibid., 272.

[11] Ibid., 190–194.

[12] Thomas Beetham, *Democracy and Human Rights* (Cambridge: Polity Press, 1999), 136–148.

these rights across borders, where they would presumably provide both the conditions for and the framework of decision making, points to an important relation between the heretofore separate concepts of human rights and democracy, as discussed further in Chapters 8 and 9. We can note too that the views of both of these theorists give equal priority to economic and social rights along with civil and political ones, and this indicates how such approaches to democracy can be seen as supporting the need for a so-called third way in the reorganization of political economy in the present global context. Thus they seem to call for a certain degree of economic equality and hence at least for regulated forms of market capitalism, as well as, in Held's case, for greater democratic participation in corporate decisions, in a sense not yet specified. (I return to the issue of democratic management in firms in Chapter 10.)

Whereas democratic public law is the core of Held's idea, it does not exhaust it. The cosmopolitanism of his conception involves democracy as "a common structure of political action." He writes, "The whole planet's population could, in principle, be embraced by this framework. . . ." and further that "the cosmopolitan model creates the possibility of an expanding institutional framework for the democratic regulation of states and societies."[13] On his view, states "would no longer be regarded as sole centres of legitimate power within their own borders."[14] The concept of sovereignty is no longer seen as applying to fixed borders and territories but instead to networks of states and to "diverse self-regulating associations, from states to cities to corporations."[15] Held writes, "Cosmopolitan law demands the subordination of regional, national, and local 'sovereignties' to an overarching legal framework, but within this framework associations may be self-governing at diverse levels."[16] He maintains that this may well lead to increased participatory democracy at local levels, in addition to the public assemblies that he seeks to introduce at a wider global level (including, specifically, a people's assembly at the United Nations). Thus he explicitly calls for "an effective transnational legislative and executive, at regional and global levels, bound by and operating within the terms of the basic democratic law."[17]

Since there would be a division of powers and competencies at different levels of political interconnectedness, where these levels "correspond

[13] Held, *Democracy and the Global Order*, 232.
[14] Ibid., 233.
[15] Ibid., 234.
[16] Ibid.
[17] Ibid., 272.

to the degrees to which public issues stretch across and affect populations,"[18] Held sees his view as situated between confederalism and federalism; it would not entail a unified state structure. He often refers to the networks of democratic associations in terms of the idea of "overlapping communities of fate," a term that I find unfortunately reminiscent of Heidegger's "Geshick," although here it is at least extended to a variety of communities and not only a national one. The concept of fate is presumably intended to highlight the fact that contemporary globalization throws people together in such a way that they come to share a future. However, this concept remains rather unanalyzed in Held's account. It is also interesting to observe that despite this fatefulness, Held wants to maintain that the regional and global associations would initially be voluntary. Thereafter, however, they would not remain so, and the legal regulations would have to be backed by coercive power, in a way that he does not clearly specify.

Despite the emphasis that Held places on the diversity of associations, we may wonder whether his model in fact leaves enough room for pluralism in the range of institutional arrangements and in the organization of the various associations at all levels. While this need not extend to a tolerance for nondemocratic regimes, which Walzer seems to call for,[19] Held's conception seems to bind all associations to a unitary framework, at least of law if not also of democracy. Yet, beyond human rights, which we can agree ought to be given a universal implementation, it is difficult to know what Held's proposed universalistic structure for democracy would entail and what it would look like in practice. Especially with the coercive backing that it requires, we can worry that it would be open to one-sided domination by powerful interpreters (such as the United States in the present situation). In addition, the entire scheme certainly appears to lack the bottom-up quality that most participatory democrats seek.

Of considerable interest, too, is Held's effort to define the scope of these communities of governance in terms of the idea of "those affected." He appeals to this traditional idea in proposing the test of extensiveness and intensity in being affected by a collective problem or policy question in order to determine how to organize these units and the degree to which they should be subject to national, regional, or global legislation or intervention. In the second part of this chapter I return to this important "all affected" criterion and scrutinize it more closely. But here

---

[18] Ibid., 236.
[19] Michael Walzer, "Governing the Globe," *Dissent* (Fall 2000): 44–52.

we can note that it would be a large and often conflictual task to allocate decisions to these different levels, and Held does not indicate how this would be done. It is not clear whether this is something to be taken care of constitutionally, or by the courts, or indeed by some preexisting democratic decision, but by whom we do not yet know from his writings. We can also suggest that this "all affected" criterion might sometimes be in conflict with Held's proposed structure of governance, which, although it adds layers above and beneath the nation-state, and across it for certain functional purposes, does not seem to make room for crossborder communities. Thus, an important case for transnational democracy is presented by the emergence and self-consciousness of such communities, where people across borders may be similarly affected by a given factor – whether it be ecological, such as acid rain, or ethnic nationalism – and Held's view seems to have no way to approach such cases beyond the possibilities of occasional crossborder referenda or else negotiation between the states themselves.

It is helpful at this point to take note of some of the other cosmopolitan democratic theorists and consider how they may contribute to our understanding of this model. Daniele Archibugi, an Italian peace theorist, has argued for a conception of cosmopolitan democracy as entailing not only democracy within states but also democracy between them, as well as globally.[20] In his view, global democracy entails such institutions as a World Parliament, through which individuals' voices would be heard in global affairs.[21] Archibugi explicitly identifies the aim of cosmopolitan democracy as that of attempting "to achieve a world order based on the rule of law and democracy."[22] Following Held, he too sees this enterprise as falling between confederalism and federalism, although again the references to world order pose the worrisome concern with the possibility of global tyranny or, at least, a potential stifling of difference. The degree to which this is the case would depend, however, on whether it would be possible to institutionalize opportunities for effecting genuine change in these arrangements from the bottom up, or whether there would be too much opportunity for the tyranny of majorities, even with such institutionalized modes of transforming the institutions.

---

[20] Daniele Archibugi, "Principles of Cosmopolitan Democracy," in *Reimagining Political Community*, eds. Daniele Archibugi et al. (Stanford, CA: Stanford University Press, 1998), 198–228, and "Cosmopolitical Democracy," *New Left Review*, Vol. 4 (July–August 2000): 137–150.

[21] Archibugi, "Cosmopolitical Democracy."

[22] Archibugi, "Principles of Cosmopolitan Democracy," 198.

Archibugi's approach to global governance seems largely territorial, as certainly is that of Thomas Pogge, who in a 1994 article, "Cosmopolitanism and Sovereignty" lays out a proposal for institutional cosmopolitanism based on human rights, where political authority would be dispersed over vertically nested territorial units.[23] He says that "persons should be citizens of, and govern themselves through, a number of political units of various sizes, without any one political unity being dominant and thus occupying the role of the state."[24] On Pogge's view, "commonalities of language, religion, ethnicity, or history are strictly irrelevant" to the constitution of these units. In that case, however, it becomes unclear why he gives such weight to the contiguity of territory in the formation or reformation of these political units, which he wants to see as the product of voluntary association. In regard to our issue of the criterion for participating in a particular decision, Pogge makes the following claim, which he sees as tantamount to the idea of democracy itself: "[P]ersons have a right to an institutional order under which those significantly and legitimately affected by a political decision have a roughly equal opportunity to influence the making of this decision – directly or through elected delegates or representatives."[25] A footnote explains that the term "legitimately" affected is introduced in order to rule out such claims as that people should have a vote on the permissibility of homosexuality worldwide because they find it distressing to hear that homosexual acts are performed elsewhere.[26] I shortly return to this account of affectedness to see whether it will suffice for delimiting who should be able to participate.

We can finally note the work of the global order theorist Richard Falk, who has emphasized the role of global civil society, including social movements and the large range of international NGOs, in providing a basis for global democracy. While he recognizes the dangers of romanticizing these movements and organizations, he nonetheless regards them as the seeds for a grassroots or bottom-up approach to extending democracy. He also advocates a range of concrete reform proposals for change in the United Nations in order to make democracy among nation-states more effective.[27] Although both of these approaches are certainly

[23] Thomas Pogge, "Cosmopolitanism and Sovereignty," in *Political Restructuring in Europe*, ed. Chris Brown (London: Routledge, 1994), 89–122.
[24] Ibid., 99.
[25] Ibid., 105.
[26] Ibid., 120n28.
[27] Richard Falk, "The United Nations and Cosmopolitan Democracy: Bad Dream, Utopian Fantasy, Political Project," in *Reimagining Political Community*, 309–331.

unobjectionable, it is hard to see how the voluntary associations of civil society can produce global forms of democracy sufficiently powerful to tame the nondemocratic forces of global capitalism, or how the changes at the United Nations – such as the abolition of the veto in the Security Council or a "second assembly" in addition to the General Assembly that would be accountable to electorates rather than governments – will amount to a genuine transformation from state sovereignty to cosmopolitan democracy.

This review of various approaches to transnational, cosmopolitan, or global democracy suggests an alternative typology to that of McGrew, which, although inferior in being relatively insensitive to the intellectual antecedents of the various models, is perhaps simpler and more comprehensive. This typology would distinguish *international* models, which focus on democracy among states, from *transnational* or crossborder models, which conceive of the democratic associations as beyond existing states but not fully global, and finally the *global* models, which posit some unified framework. In the last two models – the transnational and the global – the associations or communities can be seen as either territorially based or not. There is also the possibility of mixed models, either within transnational or global approaches or among any of the three main models themselves. We might add that all the approaches, or at least the latter two, call for increased democratic decision making at local levels. The global ones put more weight on a comprehensive scheme and on increasing democracy from the outside, as it were, through legal and constitutional structures that protect and institutionalize democratic rights in a variety of associations. The transnational ones emphasize more localized or regional democratic communities, or else the emergence of new democratic associations or the democratization of existing ones – whether in civil society or more fully political in some sense – short of a fully global or cosmopolitan scheme. They may also propose various mechanisms of a rather temporary and near-term sort to deal with crossborder issues. Mention might be made here of Michael Saward's interesting set of proposals presented in his critique of Held, which include deliberative forums, reciprocal representation (a term introduced by Philippe Schmitter), functional representation (e.g., of crossborder cultural groups), complex accountability, and crossborder referenda and initiatives.[28]

---

[28] Michael Saward, "A Critique of Held," in *Global Democracy: Key Debates*, ed. Barry Holden (London: Routledge, 2000), 39–43.

Criteria for Determining the Scope of a Democratic Community

I now turn to a closer analysis of a key theoretical issue for global democracy, not much addressed in the literature, as a partial basis for advancing this discussion and suggesting which model of those presented might be most helpful for further research in this area. Of course, beyond the issue of theoretical clarity, another basis for choice of models is the analysis of empirical possibilities, and I return to that question at the conclusion of this chapter.

The theoretical issue to be considered here concerns the normative grounds for determining the proper scope of democratic decision making. Specifically, who has the right to decide about which issues? It is worth recalling the even more fundamental question of the meaning of democracy itself in its import for cosmopolitan democracy. Clearly, as discussed earlier in this work, it would be inadequate to characterize it, as several theorists do, simply in terms of elections and voting, or representation, or more generally, in exclusively procedural or formal terms, however important these may be. The protection of individual rights is another aspect of its meaning often appealed to, but this function also does not exhaust the meaning of the term. Views that link democracy to popular control or some interpretation of self-determination or self-rule are more relevant. Yet it is clear that any such understanding of democracy entails a conception of who has a right to decide or to participate. And at least where we are contemplating the need for more transnational democratic communities, giving the traditional liberal answer of "the citizens of a state" would be question-begging in regard to determining the proper scope for democratic decision. Thus, democracy normatively understood entails a conception of the *demos,* or the collectivity that has the right to participate in decision making, and this is a difficult issue for global democratic theory.

Indeed, it gives rise to one of many paradoxes of democracy, inasmuch as the issue of who gets to make democratic decisions – the scope of the *demos* – cannot itself be settled democratically without an infinite regress. It seems, then, that the *demos* must be specified by other means. Of course, there could be a consensual process of deciding on a constitutional framework specifying the nature and scope of democratic procedures, where this framework is regarded as literally constitutive of the political community. And this is in fact the view implicit in several liberal democratic arrangements. Nonetheless, the makeup of any ultimate body authorizing the subsequent democratic procedures cannot itself be democratically arrived at, strictly speaking, and this is why these theories have turned instead to concepts of consent or consensus, among other justifications. It would thus seem that issues of membership in a *demos* (or citizenship), as well as the more general question of who has rights to participate in collective decision making, require an appeal to concepts beyond those of self-determination or self-rule per se.

I want to consider two main possibilities here, which I refer to as the "all-affected" principle and the idea of *common activity* – the latter being central in the account I offered earlier in this book and in *Rethinking Democracy*[29] – and examine the problems of each view as well as the guidance they can give for this new area of global democracy. But first, it might be helpful to return briefly to the traditional answer of citizenship in a nation-state as grounding equal rights to participate in political decisions concerning the commonweal. Recall that Sandel (among others) appeals to this conception in speaking of the need for a common civic culture, with shared values and identities, as a ground for democratic participation. Yet another citizenship-based approach could stress instead that it is simply a matter of being situated together with others within boundaries, where these may be historically given or even arbitrary, that gives rise to rights to participate. Indeed, the historical view at least has the advantage of being realistic, and I return to it later. Yet if the ground for democratic rights is to be citizenship in either of these senses, then we would still have to address the question of whether such citizenship does or does not apply transnationally, and what it would mean in that new application. And we would also have to specify more fully what it is about citizenship that gives rise to rights of democratic participation.

The view that I developed earlier, which will need some supplementation for transnational associations, is that (at the most general level of analysis) rights of democratic participation arise from rights to self-determination in the context of common or joint activities. At its root, it can be argued that people should be equally free to control the conditions of their own activity and that, where their activity is social or common, this gives rise to rights to codetermine it if they are not to be under the control of others. Common activity can be defined as activity in which a number of individuals join together to effect a given end. To the degree that they choose for themselves the end of this activity and the good it serves, it essentially involves the cooperation and coordination of many individuals in the realization of their joint projects or purposes. Yet such

---

[29] Gould, *Rethinking Democracy*, especially 78–85.

common activity can be seen to be among the conditions that people need for their own freedom as self-development, in that it provides a social context for reciprocity and makes possible the achievement of ends that cannot be achieved by an individual alone.

At the most general level, then, as I argued in Chapter 1, the requirement of democracy can be seen to follow from this conception, together with the idea of equal agency or equal (positive) freedom. Furthermore, inasmuch as this is joint activity defined by common purposes, it requires a form of participation in the common decisions that bind all the members of the group. Its appropriate form is then codetermination or shared decision making among equals. This proposes the extension of democracy beyond the sphere of political life alone to decision making in economic and social institutions as well, for so much of common activity takes place in these domains. It is probably helpful to give this an institutional or broadly public interpretation, and to see this democratic right of participation as pertaining in the first instance to those who are engaged with others as members of these political, economic, or social institutions.

The motivation for this emphasis on spheres of common activity is in part to place weight, in somewhat Aristotelian fashion, on the active rather than passive side of social life, and also to provide a very general and preexisting criterion not deriving from democratic decision itself to indicate the context in which this participation is justified. A second motivation is to avoid the evident difficulties with the "all affected" criterion. Paramount among the difficulties with that view is the impossibility of specifying all who would be affected, since decisions obviously have unintended consequences and their reach is potentially unending. A second crucial difficulty, sketched in more detail later, is that various people are differentially affected by given decisions, which would therefore entitle them to participate differentially rather than equally, where such equality is presupposed as part of the core of democratic citizenship.

Yet there are also some problems with the common activity view itself, and these problems indicate a need to supplement it with additional considerations. There are two main ones: First, it is apparent that not only those belonging to or taking part in an institutional framework of common activity have a stake in the realization of the goals of the activity; so, to a degree, do those importantly affected by its functioning (despite the other criticisms one can make of this latter idea). Second, perhaps especially in view of globalization, we seem to be much less frequently agents at all, either as individuals or jointly with others with whom we share goals, but instead often feel ourselves to be rather passive subjects of forces beyond our (or perhaps anyone's) control. Of course, this is not a new development in human history, but the global scope of the forces affecting us (e.g., the greenhouse effect, nuclear disasters, and other environmental impacts; or again the workings of global financial markets and large-scale capital) gives pause to anyone who would wish to stress an exclusively agential approach in the present, even one that emphasizes social activity. Granted that numerous global factors are in fact due to the actions of other people and thus may be in principle subject to political regulation, we are nonetheless faced with the reality that no political community or set of them currently seems in a position to bring these forces under substantial control.[30]

Turning to the "all affected" criterion, we may wonder whether there is an interpretation of it that will make it more adequate than the first approach as a way of demarcating the constituents for a given deliberative process or for establishing rights of democratic participation. Consider two versions of it that we have come across. We can cite again Pogge's version, namely, that "persons have a right to an institutional order under which those significantly and legitimately affected by a political decision have a roughly equal opportunity to influence the making of this decision – directly or through elected delegates of representatives."[31] But to say that those significantly affected by a political decision are those who should have an equal opportunity to influence it seems question-begging if it is to lay out what is to constitute a political decision. Also, Pogge's use of the idea of "legitimately affected" raises the issue of who will decide about this legitimacy.

In the second case, David Held is rightly concerned with developing modes of participation for people affected by such transnational issues as AIDS, BSE (bovine spongiform encephalopathy), the management of nuclear waste, the use of nonrenewable resources, the instability of global financial markets, and so forth.[32] As I noted, Held formulates tests of extensiveness and intensity that attempt to assess "the range of peoples within and across delimited territories who are significantly affected by a collective problem and policy question" and "the degree to which the latter impinges on a group of people."[33] However, as Saward importantly points out, the use of this principle might actually restrict constituencies

---

[30] Cf. Zygmunt Bauman's discussion of this in his *Globalization: The Human Consequences* (Cambridge: Polity Press, 1999), 55–76.

[31] Pogge, "Cosmopolitanism and Sovereignty," 105.

[32] David Held, "The Changing Contours of Political Community," in *Global Democracy*, 28.

[33] Held, *Democracy and the Global Order*, 236.

within political communities to those who could be said to be "affected" with respect to a particular issue.[34] Saward continues, "Further, it falls down in seeming to require a different constituency – in effect, a new political unit – each time a collective decision needs to be made."[35] Yet Saward endorses the use of this affectedness principle for relatively transitory decision making, using the mechanisms I cited earlier. In addition to all these problems with the concept, we are reminded of the ones noted earlier concerning the ultimate difficulty of knowing all who are or could possibly be affected by a decision, problem, or policy.

Nonetheless, the "all affected" criterion, like the common activity discussed earlier, captures certain important features of an account of who has rights to participate. Perhaps we could specify "all affected" as "those importantly affected" or perhaps "relevantly affected." Yet another direction would be to add to the idea of joint activity a conception of common interests and shared needs. We could then argue that not only those who belong to an institutional framework have rights of democratic participation, but so do those who have common interests in the particular course of action or the policy under consideration, even if they are not participants in the activity itself. This suggestion might help to avoid some of the difficulties we have noted but would still require considerable specification, in terms not only of explicating the idea of common interest but also of demarcating the social and political common interests that support democratic rights from the more interpersonal ones that do not. Likewise, a conception of shared needs that can be realized only through cooperation could ground rights to participate in decisions about them, including even at global levels inasmuch as these are incorporated in some human rights. I return to this connection between affectedness and human rights in Chapter 9, where, on a certain specification, it will be seen to have considerable import for the issue of democratizing globalization. The proposal that I develop there is that people at a distance are to be regarded as affected by a decision if their human rights are affected, where these include economic and social, as well as civil and political, rights.

We may finally want to propose the relevance of both of the criteria discussed here but see them as applying in two, sometimes overlapping, domains. Thus, the idea of equal membership in a community characterized by persistently interconnected activities over time, where this activity

---

[34] Michael Saward, "A Critique of Held," in *Global Democracy*, 37.
[35] Ibid., 37–38.

is defined by shared goals, could support the requirement of democratic decision making both in large-scale, territorially based societies and in the smaller associations of various institutional sorts – economic, social, and cultural. We might turn to the idea of being significantly affected by decisions to demarcate an additional layer of democratic networks where people have a right to provide input into making it. This latter criterion would apply especially to transborder economic and ecological matters produced as an effect of globalization, where being affected in such cases might support a variety of methods for contributing to decisions about these matters. Aside from the standard ones of being represented by one's nation-state in international decision making about these regional or global concerns, there may be innovative ways to facilitate input that are both more informal and more personal. Some of this input might be gathered through computer networks, as discussed in Chapter 11.

Both criteria for the scope of democratic decision making are relevant to the difficult issue characterized earlier in this chapter of achieving democratic control over supranational economic organizations such as the IMF, the World Bank, and the WTO. As already suggested, democratic accountability of these institutions is required, inasmuch as their financial and commercial policymaking directly bears on well-being levels in the countries to which their policies apply and also bears on environmental conditions that have a local or more global impact. Since these are economic and environmental conditions for the common (and individual) activities of people in the relevant countries, they have a right to participate in decisions about these conditions. Similarly, insofar as they are importantly affected, they ought to be able to participate in making these decisions or in selecting representatives to do so. Both of these criteria thus support the idea that beyond the idea of accountability itself, membership in these supranational bodies should be fully representative of those whose activities are impacted by the policies and decisions of these bodies. It also implies that it is wrong to leave these decisions to representatives only of the financial or commercial interests in the various countries; workers and the public more generally need to be represented as well. Moreover, given the increasingly globalized impact of some of this policymaking, particularly concerning the environment, newer methods of incorporating input from dispersed groups and individuals have to be devised. New models of networked democratic decision making may be required if we are to take account of the disparate relevance of decisions to different groups as well as their proximity to the issues at hand. Needless to say, the often-cited requirement of transparency of the deliberations of these supranational bodies is clearly necessary in all these contexts of decision, since opening up the policies to a broader public requires that such participants can become familiar with the relevant issues and not be deceived about the social or economic impacts of any of them.[36]

Some Implications for Cosmopolitical Democracy

Let us now return to the various models of global democracy discussed in the first section to briefly consider in which direction this analysis of the scope of democratic association points. It is helpful here to keep in mind the criticisms that I advanced earlier of the various models, as well as the obvious need to avoid purely utopian projections of a nineteenth-century sort. Thus proposals for reform and transformation need to be grounded on an understanding of empirical possibilities.

Recalling McGrew's three models – liberal internationalism, communitarianism, and cosmopolitan democracy – the analysis I have given lends support in various ways to the second and third of these. But before casting aside the first approach of liberal internationalism, which has in fact advanced some helpful proposals for the near term democratic reform of international institutions, we should keep in mind the caution raised by Richard Bellamy and R. J. Barry Jones in their article "Globalization and Democracy – an Afterword." They write, "In the absence of global institutions, any weakening of established state-level public government could create a serious regulatory hole that might all too readily be filled, in the short and medium term at least, by undemocratic structures of private governance."[37] They continue, "The financial sector provides merely the most marked example of the shortcomings of private governance in general, and on matters of public concern in particular."[38]

The analysis of common activity and of shared interests and needs as a framework for democratic decision making, as well as the idea of those importantly affected, underwrites a communitarian approach to transnational democracy by seeing such decision making as relevant to emerging associations and communities that share aims and interests. Because of the rather general scope of the idea of institutionalized forms of activity,

---

[36] For other suggestions concerning reforms in procedures of these organizations, see Stiglitz, *Globalization and Its Discontents*, 214–252. I also discuss this issue in Chapter 9.

[37] Richard Bellamy and R. J. Barry Jones, "Globalization and Democracy – an Afterword," in *Global Democracy*, 212.

[38] Ibid., 213.

we can see that these communities can be both local and intrastate (from voluntary associations through economic or social units of various sorts to more traditional political communities), as well as regional or crossborder, and they can be of varying sizes depending on the aims and interests they serve; similarly, they include functional and territorial associations, whether established or new. I have introduced the term "intersociative democracy" to refer to the range of such associations, especially calling attention to new crossborder ones as well as to the attitudes of openness and transnational solidarity required within them, as suggested in the earlier discussion of concrete universality in Chapter 2.

It is evident, then, that of the alternative set of models I proposed – the international, transnational, and global – the emphasis here falls primarily on the transnational one, at least for the present. And the interpretation of this remains communitarian to the degree that it leaves room for a variety of forms of democracy in diverse contexts. It regards the processes of social decision making involved in self-determination as an important value that should not be underestimated, as it sometimes is by the cosmopolitan theorists. Indeed, the approach here is willing to see any decision procedure that all members of a group agree on, and that is compatible with human rights, as democratic in being chosen freely by participants (provided, of course, that they do not yield up their ultimate powers of decision without any term). It therefore does not envision the conception of democratic processes of self-determination as limited exclusively to those that are most familiar in Western political democracies.

Yet considerations of common interests and needs, where these can be given a universalistic interpretation, lead us also to give considerable weight to the third model of cosmopolitan democracy and its parallel in my alternative set of models, the global level of democracy. This is so especially with regard to the centrality of human rights to meeting basic needs and interests, where these rights have to be not only enunciated but also given effect at the global level, through new international law and effective international courts, and through democratic governments at all levels. Indeed, the conception I have presented here is fully cosmopolitan in giving a certain priority to these human rights over the self-determination of groups, inasmuch as the collective's right to self-determination can be shown to presuppose several of these human rights and to depend on their recognition. In addition, I have emphasized the role of care, empathy, and solidarity, applying also to nonmembers and to those at a distance, as important aspects of the idea of intersociative democracy.

Despite these cosmopolitan features, the view developed here remains wary of world-order theories, both because of their potential exclusion of a plurality of modes of self-determination and, even more, if they call for a global executive with coercive powers. I do not yet see how this sort of organization can securely avoid the possibility of the centralization of power and authority on a global scale.

In earlier work, I characterized a view of the sort I have presented here as *cosmopolitical democracy*. This term seems to me to aptly capture the combination of regard for cosmopolitan doctrines, implementation of human rights, and cooperation on transnational and global levels, together with respect for social self-determination by diverse people and groups in local, national, and transborder contexts. With its incorporation of the concept of the political, a cosmopolitical conception of democracy also recognizes the need for continued political struggle to implement democracy, from the bottom up and on the ground, as it were. But the term is perhaps somewhat misleading for the present situation, where we also need to focus more narrowly on the opportunities for developing more delimited forms of transnational decision making, which, as I have suggested, current directions in globalization are making increasingly more urgent.

8

Are Democracy and Human Rights Compatible in the Context of Globalization?

In this chapter, I want to put the earlier discussion of globalized democracy into relation with human rights, an issue that I also pursue in a different context in Chapter 9. Yet framing their relation as a question of compatibility, as expressed in the title of this chapter, is likely to evoke a certain puzzlement. On the face of it, the question of the compatibility of democracy and human rights in the present would normally be answered with a resounding, "Of course they are." Such an answer could appeal to two related considerations. The first is that democratic participation is in fact one of the human rights, whether in the less explicit form that it takes in Article 21 of the Declaration of Human Rights or in its fuller formulation in Article 25 of the International Covenant on Civil and Political Rights, although regrettably (and probably for political reasons at the times of their drafting), neither article uses the term "democracy" itself. Article 21 of the Declaration approaches a conception of democratic political participation by stating that

(1) Everyone has the right to take part in the government of his country, directly or through freely chosen representatives....

(3) The will of the people shall be the basis of the authority of government; this will shall be expressed in periodic and genuine elections which shall be by universal and equal suffrage and shall be held by secret vote or by equivalent free voting procedures.

The somewhat more explicit version in Article 25 of the Covenant states that

Every citizen shall have the right and the opportunity, without ... unreasonable restrictions:

(a) To take part in the conduct of public affairs, directly or through freely chosen representatives;
(b) To vote and to be elected at genuine periodic elections which shall be by universal and equal suffrage and shall be held by secret ballot, guaranteeing the free expression of the will of the electors. . . .

There is much of interest to discuss about the approach to democracy taken in these documents, but that is not the focus of this chapter. Rather, I here want to use them simply to point to one obvious compatibility between democracy and human rights at the level of the human rights instruments themselves, namely, that democracy is one of the human rights.

A more complex but related answer to our question is provided by the linkage that is drawn between democracy and human rights in the idea of "liberal democratic states," which are distinguished in the literature from illiberal states. Thus as Thomas Risse and Kathryn Sikkink observe in the introductory chapter of the collection *The Power of Human Rights*, referring to the work of Thomas Franck and Ann-Marie Slaughter,[1] "Some legal scholars now discuss a community of 'liberal states' seen as a sphere of peace, democracy, and human rights, and distinguish between relations among liberal states, and those between liberal and nonliberal states."[2] Risse and Sikkink add that "[h]uman rights norms have special status because they both prescribe rules for appropriate behavior, and help define identities in liberal states. Human rights norms have constitutive effects because good human rights performance is one crucial signal to others to identify a member of the community of liberal states."[3] They then contrast this category with that of "authoritarian" or "norm-violating states," which are held to have quite different interests. They further point out the coherence between requirements for democracy and human rights in the case of the European Union, where "only democratic states with good human rights records can join the club," as they put it,[4] and in the case of the OAS's Managua Declaration of 1993, which

---

[1] Thomas M. Franck, *The Power of Legitimacy among Nations* (New York: Oxford University Press, 1990); Ann-Marie Slaughter, "International Law in a World of Liberal States," *European Journal of International Law*, Vol. 6 (1995): 139–170.

[2] Thomas Risse and Kathryn Sikkink, "The Socialization of International Human Rights Norms into Domestic Practices: Introduction," in *The Power of Human Rights: International Norms and Domestic Change*, eds. Thomas Risse, Stephen C. Ropp, and Kathryn Sikkink (Cambridge: Cambridge University Press, 1999), 8.

[3] Ibid.

[4] Ibid., 9.

specifies "the need to consolidate, as part of the cultural identity of each nation in the Hemisphere, democratic structures and systems which encourage freedom and social justice, safeguard human rights, and favor progress."[5]

This second response to my initial question about the compatibility of democracy and human rights can thus take a conceptual direction, which asserts the necessary linkage of these ideas, or a more empirical one, which we see adumbrated in the last set of suggestions of Risse and Sikkink regarding the shared interests of liberal democratic states and their contrast with authoritarian ones. A related empirical linkage between our two terms can also be found in the democratization literature, where a correlation is observed between such democratization and the implementation of protections of human rights within nation-states. This may consist in the observation that democratic governments are more capable of and more likely to protect the human rights of their citizens or, perhaps more generally, of the people living in them.[6] Thus Rhonda Howard and Jack Donnelly observe, "In the inevitable conflicts between the individual and the state, the liberal (democratic state) gives prima facie priority in the areas protected by human rights, to the individual."[7] By contrast, they hold that "in communist societies, the possession and enjoyment of all rights are contingent on the discharge of social duties."[8] These comments reflect one standard liberal approach to asserting the compatibility of democracy and human rights.

In a contrasting mode, a very different answer can also be given to our initial question by those critical of practices in liberal democratic societies that disregard or violate certain human rights. One thinks here of critics of capital punishment in the United States, who hold that it is a human rights violation. Their response to the question of the compatibility of democracy to human rights would be a resounding no. In this response, human rights are taken somewhat more broadly than the narrowest construal of civil and political rights (although even these may be violated in contemporary democracies), while it would seem that the term

---

5 Ibid., 9, citing Viron P. Vaky and Heraldo Muñoz, *The Future of the Organization of American States* (New York: Twentieth Century Fund Press, 1993).

6 See, for example, Zehra Arat, *Democracy and Human Rights in Developing Countries* (London: Lynne Rienner Publishers, 1991).

7 Rhonda E. Howard and Jack Donnelly, "Human Dignity, Human Rights and Political Regimes," *American Political Science Review*, Vol. 80, no. 3 (1986): 803, 816.

8 Ibid., 810.

"democracy" continues to refer to the standard conception applicable in self-identified liberal democratic states.[9]

In this chapter, however, I want to go beyond these various answers – each of which to a degree operates with current and rather limited conceptions of both democracy and human rights – and address the opening question in a perspective that takes seriously certain developments and trends associated with globalization, especially in its political and legal dimensions. Let me introduce this formulation of the problem by taking note of two examples from human rights jurisprudence. I then go on to clarify in what sense my initial question is in fact a serious one and then, in the rest of the chapter, make some proposals concerning how the potential incompatibility between democracy and human rights can be addressed.

The Development of Human Rights Law and the Framework of Globalization

The cases I wish to start with are drawn from the European and Latin American contexts. Interestingly, both have a bearing on the extension of human rights to violence against women because of their treatment of the so-called private sphere of the family (discussed in Chapter 6), but this feature is not essential to the use I want to make of them here. The first case is *X and Y v. the Netherlands*,[10] which involved a sixteen-year-old woman with learning disabilities who lived in a private institution, where she came to be sexually assaulted by the son-in-law of the directress. No prosecution was brought in this case. The European Court of Human Rights, however, found that Article 8 of the European Convention on Human Rights requires that the state take positive measures to ensure that the right to respect for private and family life is not violated by private parties, in addition to protecting individuals against arbitrary interference by public authorities. The court held that the choice of the ways to secure compliance with this Article was to be decided by each state (and fell within the so-called margin of appreciation left to each

---

9 This approach can also proceed to a deeper critique of the self-congratulatory tendency of some Western liberals, who valorize their own form of democracy and human rights as the ultimate development of these ideals.

10 *X and Y v. the Netherlands* (1986), 8 EHRR 235, para 23. See the discussion of this case in Susan Millns, "'Bringing Rights Home': Feminism and the Human Rights Act 1998," in *Feminist Perspectives on Public Law*, eds. Susan Millns and Noel Whitty (London: Cavendish, 1999), 197–198.

European state). Yet it also held that the Dutch government's argument that a criminal sanction in this case was too intrusive and a civil remedy more appropriate was not correct, and that the protection afforded by civil law is not enough where fundamental values and aspects of private life are at stake. The court held that there was in fact a violation of the European Convention in this case. Other well-known cases decided by the European Court have included the rights of homosexuals, issues of blasphemy, and also electoral democracy, as in *United Communist Party of Turkey v. Turkey*, which found that, contrary to the decision of Turkey's Constitutional Court, the government's dissolution of the Communist party infringed the freedoms of assembly and association of the Convention's Article 11.[11]

In the Inter-American context, as Henry Steiner and Philip Alston observe in their overview of the regional protection of human rights, "the Court plays a more restricted and modest role than does its equivalent in the European system. Its governing provisions bear a close relationship to those for the European Court of Human Rights."[12] The best-known case here is that of the Inter-American Court's decision in *Velasquez Rodriguez v. Honduras*,[13] which importantly "can be read to establish a principle of complicity in (and therefore state responsibility for) state failure to implement its human rights obligations."[14] This case concerned the disappearance of Angel Manfredo Velasquez Rodriguez. He was seized by seven armed men dressed in civilian clothes, who were members of the National Office of Investigations, and later abducted in an unlicensed car. He was detained and subject to "harsh interrogation and cruel torture."[15] The court held that under Article 1 of the American Convention, which requires the state to "ensure...the free and full exercise of...rights and freedoms," the Honduran government was responsible for politically motivated disappearances even if they were not overtly carried out by government officials,[16] because the state apparatus failed to prevent the disappearances or punish those responsible and thus failed to implement its human rights obligations.

---

[11] See the discussion in Henry Steiner and Philip Alston, *International Human Rights in Context*, second edition (Oxford: Oxford University Press, 2000), 840–853.

[12] Ibid., 881.

[13] Inter-American Court of Human Rights, 28 I.L.M. 294 (1989).

[14] Celina Romany, "State Responsibility Goes Private: A Feminist Critique of the Public/Private Distinction in International Human Rights Law," in *Human Rights of Women*, ed. Rebecca J. Cook (Philadelphia: University of Pennsylvania Press, 1994), 101.

[15] Steiner and Alston, *International Human Rights in Context*, 881–882.

[16] Romany, "State Responsibility Goes Private," 101.

These cases have many interesting theoretical implications, but here our main concern is with the regional interpretation of human rights documents as holding against the states within them. The European jurisprudence is of course more extensive in this context; although the court has been careful to avoid trespassing on what it takes to be the function of national authorities, nevertheless in considering international responsibilities of the state, it has scrutinized certain aspects of domestic law, and its decisions are binding on the contracting states. The new development here raises the possibility of individuals (if they have the requisite standing) appealing to regional and perhaps eventually international courts of human rights against actions by their own government or even more generally in regard to the actions of private individuals within their nation-state.

This is usually taken as an issue of the possible infringement of the sovereignty of nation-states. But I would suggest that this emerging jurisprudence brings before us the more general issue of the proper relation of regional or international human rights documents to nation-states' own human rights documents and jurisprudence, as well as to the internal order and proceedings of these nation-states, and in fact to the democratic self-determination that is possible within them. The interesting questions for us arise, then, with the growing role of cosmopolitan human rights law, or what has been called the emergence of a human rights regime. The body of human rights instruments has of course grown substantially since its birth in 1948 with the UN Declaration.[17] Although only the European Convention, among current rights instruments, specifies, according to its preamble, that it is taking "the first steps for the collective enforcement of certain of the rights stated in the Universal Declaration," it is not far-fetched to project a similar movement in other contexts of international human rights law.

Before squarely addressing our compatibility issue, we can pause to observe that the legal globalization just described is also accompanied by a certain political globalization, as discussed in Chapter 7. This involves the spread of democratic forms of governance, usually defined in terms of periodic elections, universal suffrage by citizens, and majority rule decision procedures. Although this political globalization has for the most part remained confined to an increase in democratic forms and procedures within existing states, we have observed the emergence of transnational or crossborder communities with limited democratic

---

[17] Of course, human rights were recognized in various ways before that date.

decision making, where these communities are not fully global, but rather regional, in three senses – in certain regions within nation-states, in some self-consciously crossborder communities, or in a multinational regional sense – in the European Union, but perhaps incipiently elsewhere.

Whether such political and legal globalization is a byproduct of economic and technological globalization or in fact antithetical to it remains an open question. Yet it is clear that certain aspects of the spread of technology have been put in the service of democracy, in particular the increased communication and openness made possible by the Internet (from Tiananmen to Seattle).[18] Again, despite the many negative consequences produced by the increased scope and power of global corporations (considered in part in Chapter 9), it is plausible to argue that economic globalization as a continuation of modernization has played a certain role in extending the reach of democratic forms of governance and has sometimes helped to disrupt local tyrannies and authoritarian modes of government.[19] In some ways, globalization has also contributed to increased levels of economic well-being in developed countries if not in developing ones, and this in turn has sustained democratic modes of decision making, at least where inequities in distribution of wealth and income have not been too great.

We are faced then, in the first place, with a new cosmopolitanism of human rights, in which everyone worldwide is equally regarded as a global citizen and a bearer of a wide range of human rights. Furthermore, and this is important to the argument, as will be evident, these rights are increasingly regarded as including a range of economic, social, and cultural rights, if not also group rights and development rights, beyond the initially recognized set of civil and political rights. In the second place, we see a somewhat increased role for democratic participation and decision making in various nation-states (although not necessarily any increase in the established democracies). While the spread of democratic forms is also a manifestation of cosmopolitanism to the degree that it responds to the recognition of each person's human right to democratic participation, nonetheless the more bounded sense of democracy's scope as pertaining to the political community within a given nation-state constitutes a communitarian rather than a cosmopolitan moment. Yet this

---

[18] For further discussion, see Chapter 9, which discusses democratic networks.

[19] This was recognized even by Karl Marx himself, most notably in his *Grundrisse*. See the discussion in Carol C. Gould, *Marx's Social Ontology: Individuality and Community in Marx's Theory of Social Reality* (Cambridge, MA: The MIT Press, 1978), 1–2, 22–26.

communitarianism is qualified by a somewhat diminished role of nation-states in the context of newly emergent regionalism, most especially, of course, in the European Union but also to a degree in some other regions.

Elaboration of the Problem

The compatibility issue that I pointed to at the outset, which at present remains mostly a theoretical concern, can be posed in simple terms as follows: If human rights become institutionalized in regional and global frameworks of law, then they can restrict the democratic decisions of communities. This would, after all, be one of their functions: to be sure that these decisions as well as the actions of the government and its members do not violate human rights. But the value of democracy itself may then be delimited by the superior power of these rights in a way that mirrors the issue of the relation between constitutional rights protections at the national level and the legislative (or, more generally, democratic) decision making that takes place within that framework. The internationalization of these rights protections in fact exacerbates the latter issue, which has been discussed at length in recent years, especially by legal constitutional scholars (e.g., Dworkin and Ely[20]). Yet these scholars have not focused on the new issue of the further constraint on democratic decision making that may eventually be posed by the elevation of the international rights instruments.

The question of sovereignty and not only democracy is implicated here as well, as has been noted especially by right-wing critics of the new internationalism (reaching a fever pitch in regard to the International Criminal Court). To the degree that sovereignty can be seen as an expression of the autonomy of a self-determining community, it has a connection via this idea of self-determination to the concept of democracy itself. Thus, a new preeminence to human rights would seem to threaten the scope of democratic decision making, especially as it is instantiated in sovereign democratic communities. In short, the emergence of cosmopolitan law seems to intensify the problem discussed in this country of the relationship of individual rights (often protected through

[20] Ronald Dworkin, *Taking Rights Seriously* (Cambridge, MA: Harvard University Press, 1978) and *Freedom's Law: The Moral Reading of the American Constitution* (Cambridge, MA: Harvard University Press, 1996); and John Hart Ely, *Democracy and Distrust* (Cambridge, MA: Harvard University Press, 1980). See also Mark Tushnet, *Taking the Constitution Away from the Courts* (Princeton, NJ: Princeton University Press, 2000).

a constitutional bill of rights and judicial review) and democratic self-determination. Where new systems of international law can further constrain not only national courts but also national legislatures, it would seem that human rights and democracy can pull in different directions. This is even more fully the case if the list of human rights is extended to the full range of economic, social, cultural, and developmental rights, where these are interpreted as standards to be met by each community. The arena for democratic decision making would seem on this reading to become quite narrow.

A further complication of this problematic concerns the derivation of human rights themselves. I have so far spoken of them as though they are self-evident and universally agreed to. Of course, this is far from the case, and there are conflicts over their scope and interpretation (although less so over their existence). To the degree that these rights are arrived at and agreed to by quasi-democratic consensual procedures, we are faced with a possible vicious circularity if we seek to use the rights to constrain democratic procedures. This is the problem that I have previously called the constitutional circle.[21] But leaving this largely philosophical problem aside here, we still have the issue of differing cultural and ideological interpretations of the human rights themselves, and this disrupts a too easy cosmopolitanism. Furthermore, it can exacerbate our issue of relating democracy and human rights by suggesting that Western conceptions of rights can limit forms of quasi-democratic self-determination elsewhere.

Yet another complication is that human rights are dominant at present largely in name only. The United States, for example, regards them in the form they take in international documents as rights applicable only to other nation-states and not to it, except to the degree that some of them are embodied in the U.S. Constitution, and especially in its Bill of Rights and certain other amendments. And there is of course a more general absence of human rights enforcement worldwide, although human rights concerns have recently been instrumental in supporting armed humanitarian interventions in various regions of the world. There is also the further question of the degree to which international human rights can be satisfactorily implemented via national (hopefully democratic) interpretations, the current approach in the main body of international law, or whether they in fact need to be further codified at an international level and given full priority over national constitutional interpretations. While human rights law has developed primarily along the first line, in

[21] Chapter 1 in this book.

which these rights are held to be open to national constitutional inter-pretations, they seem gradually to be gaining an autonomy and scope of their own and, I would argue, legitimately so. It is this development of their international scope and potential power that most sharply presents the challenge I have described to national democratic decision mak-ing. Especially if such decision making is rightly constrained by the very rich list of human rights – civil, political, social, economic, cultural, and developmental – then it might seem to become so severely delimited in range that the will of the people (to the degree that it is expressed via representative government) is ultimately very seriously attenuated.

Two Approaches to This Issue: Beetham and Dworkin

In the remainder of this chapter, I consider some directions for approach-ing, if not entirely resolving, the putative incompatibility just described, which, I have suggested, is exacerbated in the relatively new framework of economic and political globalization. I begin by considering a recent ex-plicit attempt to address the relationship of democracy and human rights offered by Thomas Beetham, and I briefly take note of Ronald Dworkin's approach to the issue of individual rights and democracy within a nation-state context before moving to some proposals of my own in the final section.

As I have remarked, the two discourses of democracy and human rights have largely been separate until recently, and Thomas Beetham usefully adds to this observation that they have in fact been confined to two dif-ferent disciplines: law in the case of human rights and political science in the case of democracy.[22] His approach to our compatibility issue is to first distinguish the human rights into three groups: the civil and political rights, the economic and social rights, and the cultural rights, focusing especially in this last case on group rights. He then argues that the first group, the civil liberties and political rights (freedoms of expression, press, association, assembly, etc.), are intrinsically related to the concept of democracy as popular control inasmuch as they make democracy pos-sible, as much as do the political institutions with which it is customarily associated. As Beetham puts it, "The guarantee of these basic freedoms is a necessary condition for people's voice to be effective in public affairs and for popular control over government to be secured."[23] This importantly

---

[22] Thomas Beetham, *Democracy and Human Rights* (Cambridge: Polity Press, 1999), 90.
[23] Ibid., 93.

reminds us that the close connection between democracy and human rights that was asserted at the outset in the claim that democracy is one of the human rights can be supplemented by the additional observation that the other civil and political rights are themselves requirements for democratic participation.

In Beetham's view, when there is a conflict between a majority decision and individual rights, it is not then a tension between democracy and human rights. Rather, he helpfully suggests, as others have also,[24] that

[i]t would be more accurate to describe such a conflict as one between a particular expression of popular opinion, on the one hand, and the conditions necessary to guarantee the continuing expression of that opinion, on the other; between a particular "voice" and the conditions for exercising that voice on an ongoing basis. It follows that democracies have necessarily to be self-limiting or self-limited if they are not to be self-contradictory, by undermining the rights through which popular control over government is secured; although any such limitation in turn requires popular consent to the basic constitutional arrangements through which it is secured.[25]

However, this approach remains quite limited in that it justifies the civil and political rights in reference to democracy but not in any sense intrinsically. As I argued earlier in this work, where these rights are not justified in themselves but only instrumentally for their contribution to democracy, great weight is ultimately placed either on majorities for maintaining and interpreting them or on stronger requirements of democratic consensus about constitutions and the rights they embody. But this in turn raises philosophical issues of an infinite regress: Would there have to be a prior determination of the rights that delimit the initial democratic process of constitution making in order to introduce constitutional guarantees of rights? Or it entails a circularity – that of constitutional guarantees of rights being established by a consensual or democratic procedure, which in turn presupposes some of the rights to be institutionalized. The consensus process among free and equal participants seems to presuppose the very rights that it is designed to authorize.

Beetham does offer another ground for the intrinsic relation of civil and political rights to democracy, and this is close to the view I presented in my earlier work, although Beetham somewhat unhelpfully phrases the matter in terms of human nature. He suggests that both democracy and

---

24 See, for example, Robert Dahl, *Democracy and Its Critics* (New Haven, CT: Yale University Press, 1989).

25 Beetham, *Democracy and Human Rights*, 93.

human rights entail related "assumptions about human nature"[26] or, better, "a common assumption about human capacities; and the same anti-paternalist argument, to the effect that there are no superiors competent to decide for us what is for our good, whether individual or collective, except in so far as we specifically, and within clearly defined limits, authorize them to do so."[27]

As to economic and social rights, Beetham sees not an intrinsic connection to democracy, but rather a relation of mutual requirement or presupposition. That is, following the arguments of Henry Shue and others, Beetham holds that a certain degree of well-being for individuals is required if democratic participation is to be possible for them and also makes the commonplace (although important) observation that undue wealth can distort political processes.[28] Conversely, he argues that opportunities for democratic participation are the best guarantee of economic and social well-being, at least to the degree that these latter are protected not simply instrumentally but as rights. (In these terms, he rejects arguments as to the superiority of authoritarian regimes for producing such well-being, also disputing the empirical support for such claims.[29]) Finally, in regard to cultural rights, particularly as group rights, Beetham proposes that their relation to democracy is to necessitate a rethinking of democracy along multicultural lines, to qualify majoritarianism and winner-take-all policies where there are established cultural minorities, and in these cases to introduce some form of power sharing "to guarantee to members of minorities their due place in the polity."[30]

These are sound suggestions about second- and third-generation human rights, but we can ask whether the relation between economic and social rights, on the one hand, and democracy, with the civil and political rights that it entails, on the other, is in fact so extrinsic as Beetham portrays it. His account tacitly endorses the problematic liberal preference for the civil and political rights, an endorsement that seems to give the human rights an ineluctable Western cast. Although he grants that we need to be alive in order to exercise our civil and political rights and also the right to democratic participation, his formulation renders the crucial right to means of subsistence subordinate to these others. I believe it is

---

[26] Ibid.

[27] Ibid., 94.

[28] Ibid., 97.

[29] Ibid., 103–107.

[30] Ibid., 112.

more helpful to regard the rights to life and liberty as equally basic and to read life as entailing both a right not to be killed and a right to means of subsistence. But such a position does not characterize these rights only as instrumental to democracy, as Beetham seems to. Furthermore, although Beetham importantly recognizes that we "need institutions at the international level which could modify the systematic global inequalities that lie at the root of much human rights abuse,"[31] this formulation implies that these inequalities fall outside the range of human rights – presumably, primarily the civil and political ones – whereas in fact they are themselves violations of crucial social and economic rights.

Ronald Dworkin explicitly wrestles with the relation between rights as laid out in a constitution and democratic processes in a way relevant to our account, among other places in the introduction to his 1996 book, *Freedom's Law*.[32] He argues against what he calls the "majoritarian premise" and in favor of a "constitutional conception of democracy," which takes the defining goal of democracy not to be arriving at collective decisions with majority support but rather "that collective decisions be made by political institutions whose structure, composition, and practices treat all members of the community, as individuals, with equal concern and respect."[33] He explains that this approach, although requiring much of the same structure of government as majoritarian views do, including especially periodic election of officials, requires this out of a concern for the equal status of citizens and hence permits also nonmajoritarian procedures when they enhance this status. His conception of democracy is one that signifies "government subject to conditions – democratic conditions – of equal status for all citizens."[34] This conception justifies basic requirements and rights to preserve this equality and establishes a basis for declaring laws unconstitutional if they violate these conditions. He also insists that "political decisions that affect the distribution of wealth, benefits, and burdens, must be consistent with equal concern for all."[35]

Yet Dworkin's account remains largely tied to the historical record of the United States[36] and focuses on the case of a nation-state with a constitution. It is not clear how he would extend his account to human rights and whether he would hold them to have import only to the degree

---

[31] Ibid., 145.
[32] Dworkin, *Freedom's Law*, 1–38.
[33] Ibid., 17.
[34] Ibid.
[35] Ibid., 25.
[36] Ibid., 11.

that they were incorporated within each nation-state's own constitution. In addition, his account leaves little or no room for divergent conceptions of democracy or of individual, let alone human, rights. Still, it is suggestive for our present problem by tying democracy to a broader principle of what he calls equal concern and respect.

Some Proposals

I would like now to approach the incompatibility issue by recalling the framework developed in Chapter 1, which relies on a conception of equal positive freedom as a basis for theorizing both the requirement for democracy and that of human rights. Without repeating the arguments in detail here, we can say that democracy has value inasmuch as it serves freedom, where this is understood not simply in the liberal sense of freedom of choice, but rather as self-development, or perhaps in even less culture-bound fashion, the self-transformative power of people (as discussed in Chapter 2 on universality). Since freedom in this general sense is characteristic of all humans, they can be said to have equal rights to it. But this freedom requires access to conditions for its realization – both material and social – and this in turn gives rise to a set of human rights, both basic and nonbasic, that specify these conditions for people's transformative activity. As presented earlier, the conception of equal rights to the conditions of freedom as self-development or self-transformation also gives rise to a requirement of democratic decision making in contexts of common activity, where this serves as one of the main conditions for people's free activity. If people are to be self-determining in regard to such common activity, then they have rights to participate in decision making concerning both the ends and the means of this activity (although they can choose to delegate some of their powers here to others). On this account, both the value of democracy and the role of human rights derive from the mutual recognition of the character of humans as freely acting beings.

Inasmuch as human rights are expressions of and serve to protect and give meaning to human freedom, they should not be violated by democratic procedures and therefore can legitimately constrain democracy, as rights against majorities. Yet democracy, in the rich and pervasive sense employed here, is itself one of the human rights and is directly required by this value of freedom in all contexts of joint activity, where the latter, as one of the main forms of social interrelation, is a central aspect of human activity itself. So we are still faced with our difficulty, in that if human rights are taken in their full scope, it would seem that democratic decision procedures properly executed might be limited to a ratification (or, at best, an explication or implementation) of these norms, given in advance. As I suggested in the earlier chapter, we need to avoid the implication that the democratic process is an exercise of freedom of choice only when it is "correct," or that it can be trivialized by being easily overturned.

Although it is important to avoid the path of assuming too easy a congruence between democracy and human rights, still some progress can be made by considering their relation from the standpoint of both formal (or procedural) and substantive democracy, as discussed in connection with the hard question of the relation between justice and democracy. We can see that human rights constraints do not in fact overly constrict, or worse, marginalize, formal democracy, where democracy is taken as a set of procedures, inasmuch as these remain untouched if a particular outcome of the decision procedure were to be overridden by a court on human rights grounds. Yet the act of participation would become rather pointless if such overriding were taken to an extreme. Thus, an appeal to a more substantive conception of democracy is required here; the argument is that the exercise of democracy deserves to remain ineffective when its outcome is such that it violates the very rights and liberties for the sake of which democracy itself has been instituted. For if democracy is required by equal rights to self-development, the decisions made should not be allowed to undercut democracy's own ground. Here the conception of democracy is substantive in referring to an activity of self-development or self-transformation on the part of participants in which people reciprocally recognize each other's freedom and equality in the process of making collective decisions. If the function and justification of democracy are that it serves freedom in this way, a democratic decision that violates these very conditions of recognition is inconsistent with democracy itself in this sense and undercuts it in practice. Yet, as I suggested in the earlier discussion, good judgment is required in order to avoid excessive judicial constraints that would marginalize democracy, as well as the violation of rights in abuses of the freedom of decision making.

As political globalization proceeds, we see the emergence of regional and more generally transnational communities, which may seek to decide matters democratically. As these new intersociative contexts develop, claims for the centrality of national self-determination lose some force. But the concept of self-determination as democratic self-determination, that is, rights of participation in decision making within democratic communities, remains relevant. It is evident, too, that these new domains for decision increasingly require regional or international frameworks of human rights law to protect and enhance the rights of those within them. We can see then that the ideas of democracy and self-determination remain central, although they may be delinked from nation-states or, perhaps better, added as layers above and beneath these latter. Inasmuch as democratic communities continue to be central in this way but are regarded as subject to human rights constraints, the view presented here strives to combine a communitarian emphasis with a cosmopolitan one. Whereas I previously called this a conception of cosmopolitical democracy,[37] it could also be referred to, as Bellamy and Castiglione do, as a cosmopolitan communitarianism.[38]

Still, human rights cannot remain so static as the account in this chapter has presented them. As considered in earlier chapters, in the framework of globalization, with its new international networks of relations, it is ever clearer that the account of human rights has to be open to revision and change. Here, the intercultural (or interactive multicultural) conception of human rights that I introduced previously plays a role. To the degree that both democracy and human rights as conceptions emerge from our embedded social relations and are constructed out of our social practices, they need to be understood as legitimately drawing on the variety of cultural traditions that have contributed to them and as open to critique from these and other sources. The increasing universalization that globalization supposedly heralds must therefore be taken not simply in the abstractly universalist terms of the old human nature arguments but as a concrete universality created through specific and more widespread interaction and association, which I have called intersociation. As noted, the conception of human rights has benefited from this universalization, which has moved it beyond liberal rights toward including also economic, social, cultural, and developmental ones. As an open concept of this sort, however, it does not lose its critical thrust, both because it can draw on a variety of divergent perspectives and also because it retains at its core the recognition of humans as fundamentally self-transformative in both individual and shared ways, and hence as free.

---

[37] Ibid., Chapter 12; see also the discussion in Chapter 7 of this work.

[38] Richard Bellamy and Dario Castiglione, "Building the Union: The Nature of Sovereignty in the Political Architecture of Europe," *Law and Philosophy*, Vol. 16, no. 4 (July 1997): 423, and "The Normative Challenge of a European Polity: Cosmopolitan and Communitarian Models Compared, Criticised, and Combined," in *Democracy and the European Union*, eds. Andreas Follesdal and Peter Koslowski (Berlin: Springer Verlag, 1997), 265.

Furthermore, when we take this somewhat more open and contextual approach to the understanding of human rights, we leave room for seeing them not only as a rationally derived list of requirements but also as responsive to the care and concern that people may come to have in practice for those at some distance from them. The growing linkages in globalizing practice, including in common projects, can support an increasing recognition of people's shared needs and mutual concerns, and this can in turn provide the basis for the more universalistic dialogue and deliberation that many democratic and human rights theorists appeal to.

Finally, it is worth reiterating that the concept of democracy itself can usefully be put into such an interactive cultural context so that it becomes more open than heretofore to a certain diversity of implementations, compatible with the root ideas of equal rights of participation, and popular control or self-determination. So long as there is no overarching hierarchy or authoritarian structure and people do not give up the power of decision without term, a range of democratic forms of organization can be compatible with the fundamental conception. However, this range can probably not be specified in advance but remains to be developed with further and more universalized interactions in social, economic, and political life.

Nonetheless, there is an apparent disanalogy between human rights and democracy in regard to this issue of the diversity of their forms. Although my argument is that both democracy and human rights have to remain open to a variety of interpretations and forms of implementation, there is probably a greater need for provisional agreement on human rights than on the forms of democracy, which can range more widely. The distinction between the two norms here arises from the required development of regional, if not fully international, frameworks of human rights that would permit appeal for enforcement of these rights across borders and against nation-states or nonstate actors that violated them. At the present time, effective regional frameworks, rather than fully international ones, could suffice for these purposes, with the advantage of allowing for a continuing local diversity in rights interpretations. It should be clear too that, were such regional human rights instruments to be introduced widely (beyond the borders of the European Union), these instruments would not replace constitutional protections of human rights at the national level but rather would reflect new agreements across a given range of nation-states.

A regionalization of this sort – emerging as it does from the growing interconnections between peoples and states – can indeed also be expected to have some effect on the forms of democracy. Still, there is no need to limit the range of these democratic forms or to come to the wide agreement about them that seems to be necessary in the case of human rights. Yet even with regard to the institutionalization of human rights across borders, I have suggested that we can look for the emergence of more intercultural understandings of their scope and interpretation than exist at present. Such diversity in people's understanding and interpretation of the human rights would accompany the more substantial diversity in the actual conditions that are required for people in every culture to achieve fuller freedom and dignity.

9

The Global Democratic Deficit and Economic Human Rights

We have observed that economic globalization, especially in the form of global capitalism, raises important normative issues; two of its implications in particular have elicited considerable concern on the part of political philosophers. One impact can be characterized as the *global justice deficit*, that is, the wide discrepancy in wealth, income, and, more generally, development, between diversely situated people or countries. Related to this is the failure to realize the economic human rights – and specifically, the right to means of subsistence – of the large numbers of people worldwide who remain in impoverished conditions.[1] The second normative impact is what has been called the *global democratic deficit*, in which there is a lack of input and participation, and a correlate lack of accountability, concerning decisions by intergovernmental and other transnational organizations that increasingly affect people's lives, both in developed and in less developed countries. This latter critique has been launched most strikingly against the World Trade Organization and the International Monetary Fund but applies to global corporations and to governments as well.

These two deficits – one of justice and the other of democracy – are clearly related to each other, although each has tended to be discussed separately. One of the aims of this chapter is to highlight some of the conceptual relations between these discourses. But even more important here is to consider some of the remedies that have recently been

---

[1] According to Thomas Pogge, "About one-quarter of all human beings alive today, 1.5 billion, subsist below the international poverty line." See his "Priorities of Global Justice," in *Global Justice*, ed. T. Pogge (Oxford: Blackwell, 2001), 7.

proposed, especially on the democracy side, for extending accountability on the part of intergovernmental and transnational organizations and, more generally, of increasing the opportunities for crossborder decision making, a topic introduced in Chapter 7. In this connection, I offer a new and more globalized interpretation of what is there called the "all affected" principle. Furthermore, the consideration here of what can be called the globalization of democracy (and of its reciprocal, namely, democratizing globalization) suggests a way of addressing the justice deficit and the related deficiency in the realization of economic human rights. The chapter concludes with an articulation of some of the complex interrelations between democracy and human rights in the context of economic, political, and legal globalization.

Current Proposals for Democratizing Globalization Processes

Proposals for the extension or intensification of democratic participation in decision making concerning transnational or global issues have ranged from short-term minimalist (although important) proposals by economists for providing input from NGOs into the decision processes of the WTO and the IMF (e.g., by Joseph Stiglitz[2] and Peter Willetts[3]) to the maximalist proposals, discussed earlier, for cosmopolitan democracy or global citizenship (e.g., by Held[4] and Archibugi[5]), arguing for institutionalizing a nested series of territorially based spheres of decision from local communities through nation-states up to the global level. Whereas the more minimal approaches look for so-called accountability by intergovernmental institutions to civil society by means of input from transnational NGOs, the maximal approaches argue for a broader and

---

[2] Joseph Stiglitz, *Globalization and Its Discontents* (New York: W. W. Norton, 2002), chapter 9.

[3] Peter Willetts, "Transnational Actors and International Organizations in Global Politics," in *The Globalisation of World Politics*, second edition, eds. J. B. Baylis and S. Smith (Oxford: Oxford University Press, 2001), 356–383; and "Civil Society Networks in Global Governance: Remedying the World Trade Organization's Deviance from Global Norms," paper presented at the Colloquium on International Governance, Geneva, Sept. 20, 2002 (http://www.staff.city.ac.uk/p.willetts//CS-NTWKS/CSGG0902.HTM).

[4] David Held, *Democracy and the Global Order* (Stanford, CA: Stanford University Press, 1995), and "The Changing Contours of Political Community," in *Global Democracy: Key Debates*, ed. Barry Holden (London: Routledge, 2000), 17–31.

[5] Daniele Archibugi, "Principles of Cosmopolitan Democracy," in *Reimagining Political Community*, eds. Daniele Archibugi et al. (Stanford, CA: Stanford University Press, 1998), 198–228, and "Cosmopolitical Democracy," *New Left Review*, Vol. 4 (July–August 2000): 137–150.

richer system of worldwide participation in decisions by all those who are affected by them. I analyze this "all affected" principle in Chapter 7 and present some criticisms of it, as well as of the approaches that aim to institutionalize it. Here, we can reiterate the central difficulty that arises when the issue of global democracy is put in these terms: If democracy requires that all affected by a given decision have a right to participate in making it, then how can this be implemented in a transnational situation, where the number of those affected is very great and ranges far afield, and where people may be affected by a given policy or proposal to very different degrees? In nation-states with a stable citizenry, this issue is usually settled by giving citizens an equal vote in governmental affairs, but it is difficult to articulate a reasonable framework for comparable implementation at the global level. Indeed, as noted in Chapter 8, most theorists, even Held, are understandably reluctant to talk about world government, and therefore the significance of the idea that all affected have a right to participation or at least input into relevant transnational decisions remains in question.

In the face of this difficult issue, some theorists have recently argued for a less demanding approach, yet one that presumably goes beyond the minimalist calls for consultation with NGOs and accountability to them. These theorists in different ways have suggested that we take a "pragmatic" or "problem-solving" approach to democracy and recognize that democratic networks spontaneously emerge when people come together to deal with the contemporary vexing problems to which globalization gives rise. I have in mind here two quite different proposals along these lines, one by Frank Cunningham[6] and the other by Joshua Cohen and Charles Sabel.[7] Without analyzing these in the depth they deserve, we can take note first of Cunningham's idea that democracy is a matter of degree and thus can, and ought to, be implemented in a variety of contexts, without the expectation that full democratic participation will result in each case. This provides a helpful caution against the idea that because democracy cannot be fully realized globally we therefore should not even try to introduce it.

---

[6] Frank Cunningham, *Theories of Democracy: A Critical Introduction* (London: Routledge, 2002), Chapter 11, and "Democracy and Globalization," in *Civilizing Globalization*, eds. Richard Sandbrook (Albany: State University of New York Press, 2003), 139–156.

[7] Joshua Cohen and Charles F. Sabel, "Sovereignty and Solidarity: EU and US," in *Governing Work and Welfare in a New Economy*, eds. Jonathan Zeitlin and David M. Trubek (Oxford: Oxford University Press, 2003), 345–375; and Cohen and Sabel, "Directly-deliberative Polyarchy," *European Law Journal*, Vol. 3/4 (1997): 313–340.

Cohen and Sabel's conception, which they sum up under the designation of "democratic deliberative polyarchy," is somewhat different. Developed mainly as a characterization of decision making within the European Union (EU), and particularly of regulation produced through the decentralized and comparative determination of standards involved in the Open Method of Coordination (OMC) employed there, Cohen and Sabel's approach gives central place to the requirement of problem solving by way of a deliberative give-and-take and a process of mutual adjustment among different participants.[8] They describe with approval the emergence of what I have called democratic networks, where input into decisions is dispersed and at times even episodic, and where these networks arise around specific problem issues. The input from diverse participants motivated to come to agreement about such matters of common concern can form a public, in a way reminiscent of John Dewey's view. This is not a public unified within a governmental framework, and furthermore, it is one that can reconstitute itself as the tasks and problems are redefined. The more encompassing public of the polity at large is no longer understood as an undivided sovereignty but rather as made up of such smaller-scale and shifting publics and as empowering them.[9] This approach contrasts with a view such as Held's, which emphasizes the development of new, permanent governmental institutions for global decision making. With a somewhat similar pragmatic orientation, Cunningham approvingly cites Michael Saward's emphasis on the variety of parameters that may be available for enhancing transnational decisions, ranging from the permanent ones of Held to the more temporary governmental ones cited earlier, such as crossborder referenda and reciprocal representation in parliament, to temporary and nongovernmental ones such as consultations with issue-oriented NGOs.[10]

The allure of pragmatism in either of its variants lies in its openness to new and possibly shifting and overlapping forms of crossborder groups, alliances, or communities that may come together for purposes of regulation or harmonization of interests and in its lack of restrictive and overly demanding criteria for democratic participation. Yet, in regard to Cohen and Sabel's proposal, to the degree that it is meant to extend beyond the context of the EU, we may wonder whether it is possible to so completely

[8] Cohen and Sabel, "Sovereignty and Solidarity," 362–373.

[9] Ibid., 362.

[10] Cunningham, *Theories of Democracy*, 216–217, citing Michael Saward, "A Critique of Held," in *Global Democracy*, 32–46. See also Cunningham, "Democracy and Globalization," 144–145.

avoid the question of the proper scope and level of democratic decision making. While these authors say that the new publics they propose are to be inclusive rather than exclusive, it remains a question, I think, of who is to have a right to participate in which decisions and who should therefore be recognized as an equal participant in the dialogue. Moreover, in their own deliberative account of democracy, the grounds for the admirable requirement of nonexclusivity is not entirely clear, beyond the suggestion that it is based in the value of democracy itself. Furthermore, the rights required to ensure that these processes are democratic are said to be determined at least in part by the course of deliberation itself, and thus such rights are left open for redefinition. Yet, as discussed in Chapter 1, it is not clear on such a view how the list of rights to structure the deliberation process can be drawn up and how these rights come to have the interpretation they do.

Although there is clearly a role for shifting problem-solving publics within the new forms of democracy required by transborder interactions in global society, I propose that the issue of scope remains, in order to determine who has a right to participate in these and other decision contexts. For certain purposes, it may indeed be sufficient to say that anyone with an interest or opinion should be able to have it considered, and, where intergovernmental organizations are concerned, that any NGO, for example, should be able to have some form of input into the deliberations. Clearly, too, the often-mentioned requirement of transparency in the functioning of these organizations is of great importance. But this does not get us very far in addressing the issue of how such consultations can be implemented and institutionalized, which would seem to require some specification of who can officially participate. Indeed, even progressive proposals for the reform of the WTO, for example, which call for systematic consultation with NGOs along the lines of existing UN consultations, propose that such consultations should be with NGOs already recognized by the UN and not simply any that might form.[11] Although there should be ways for new NGOs to gain the required recognition, it is perhaps too demanding to require such intergovernmental organizations to meet with anyone at any time. Thus, beyond the role of ad hoc and shifting problem-solving publics, it is still necessary to consider criteria of relevance in order to determine the scope of participation in decision making, that is, who gets to decide what issues. Of course, none of this is to diminish the importance of arguments for a general right of

[11] See Willetts, "Civil Society Networks in Global Governance."

consultation or input within the WTO, where such input would indeed be an important advance over the present situation.

The Global, the Local, and Eliminating the Democratic Deficit

To further consider the import of these questions of scope and mode of participation for the problem of globalizing democracy, it would perhaps be useful to briefly recall the various senses of globalization discussed in Chapter 7 and take note of the correlative new conceptions of the local that are beginning to emerge. As Held puts it, globalization can be understood generally as "the growing interconnectedness of states and societies."[12] In more extended terms, he writes,

Globalization can be understood in relation to a set of processes which shift the spatial form of human organization and activity to transcontinental or inter-regional patterns of activity, interaction and the exercise of power (see Held et al. 1999). It involves a stretching and deepening of social relations and institutions across space and time such that, on the one hand, day-to-day activities are increasingly influenced by events happening on the other side of the globe and, on the other, the practices and decisions of local groups or communities can have significant global reverberations (see Giddens 1990).[13]

In somewhat similar ways, Ulrich Beck distinguishes this sense of globalization from *globalism* (the ideology of free-market world capitalism) and writes that it "denotes the *processes* through which sovereign national states are criss-crossed and undermined by transnational actors with varying prospects of power, orientations, identities and networks."[14] He points out that the globalization process not only creates "transnational social links and spaces" but also "revalues local cultures." In this way, he suggests that the concept of the local becomes transformed into the "glocal" when personal and local ties lose their former territorial boundedness, as, for example, they do to a degree through Internet communications.

As indicated in previous chapters, the key features of globalization and its impact on nation-states, as described by Held, Beck, and others, include most centrally global economic processes – especially the free movement of capital and trade – which result in constraints on democratic governments by unelected economic powers that are not bound by

---

[12] Held, "The Changing Contours of Political Community," 17.

[13] Ibid., 19, citing Held, McGrew, et al., *Global Transformations: Politics, Economics and Culture* (Cambridge: Polity Press, 1995) and Anthony Giddens, *The Consequences of Modernity* (Cambridge: Polity Press, 1990).

[14] Ulrich Beck, *What Is Globalization?* tr. Patrick Camiller (Cambridge: Polity Press, 2000), 11.

requirements to represent citizen interests. Another aspect is the world-wide spread of information and communications technology and the global reach of the media. Held further associates this with certain cultural changes, including the domination of the English language in several fields. Global environmental challenges also are crucial – for example, global warming, in which the actions of nation-states centrally impact others and in which their fortunes can no longer be understood in territorial terms. Additionally, there is the strengthening of international law and especially the growth of a human rights regime, discussed in Chapter 8, in which individuals can begin to initiate proceedings against their own governments. There is the increased emphasis on transnational security and defense policies, as well as organizations, such as NATO, that involve collective defense and cooperative security arrangements. Finally, an additional feature, which arises from the feminist analysis, might be added to the usual list just cited. This is a certain globalization of care and affiliations more generally, in which people's concerns more frequently extend to others at a distance (in part due to new media technologies and the communication relations they facilitate with widespread others).

As we have seen, these various factors lead Held and other theorists to the conclusion that political power can no longer be assumed to be concentrated in nation-states, but instead consists in power sharing between national, regional, and international actors.[15] Furthermore, globalization in several of the senses just discussed entails that central determinants of people's life chances are beyond the reach of these nation-states, although the latter remain highly significant.[16] This raises the issue of who should be accountable to whom in this new context.[17] And if powerful geopolitical interests ought not to settle issues simply in terms of their own aims because they have the power to do so, then new modes of accountability are required. As we have seen, Held goes on to propose the creation of political institutions that would coexist with the state system but would be able to override them concerning activities having transnational impact, such as economic regulation, environment, global security, and world health. Examples proposed are the European Union and a democratically reformed United Nations.[18]

---

[15] Held, "The Changing Contours of Political Community," 26.
[16] Ibid.
[17] Ibid., 27.
[18] Held, *Democracy and the Global Order*, 273. Richard Falk also calls for greater democracy at the UN, although without Held's cosmopolitan interpretation, in his "The United

Beyond those I discussed earlier, critical responses to Held's idea of cosmopolitan democracy and the associated idea of cosmopolitan citizenship have ranged from Dahl's objections to the very possibility of democracy of this sort[19] to the objection offered by Will Kymlicka and others that Held's approach undervalues the efficacy and scope of national policymaking in dealing with transnational problems.[20] Accordingly one might propose that the global democratic deficit can to a significant degree be remedied by addressing the national democratic deficit.[21] For example, when nation-states influence the WTO to support powerful corporate interests, they most often do so under the influence of powerful domestic interest groups. If indeed the nation-states or the regional bodies such as the EU were made more accountable to their own citizenry rather than exclusively to these powerful groups within them, there would be less need for new supranational regulation. A similar argument could be made with regard to the unrepresentative groups within the United States that have blocked the move to cooperatively address climate change. Furthermore, it might be observed that an additional source of the domestic democratic deficit is the lack of political interest and participation by national populations themselves. It can then be argued that correcting this would lead nation-states to more responsible actions in the new transnational environment.

However well taken these points may be concerning the need to address the domestic democratic deficit, and granted that remedying this deficit would be very beneficial in dealing with the transborder issues raised by globalization, nonetheless they do not argue against the need for new forms of democratic decision making in crossborder contexts. As suggested earlier, the key reason for this is that wherever people are engaged in common activities defined by shared aims, there is a requirement for rights of democratic participation. And to the degree that there are in fact emergent communities across borders with such joint activities and interests, democratic rights pertain to them, and thus we need to address the question of the forms that these might take. In the example of

---

Nations and Cosmopolitan Democracy: Bad Dream, Utopian Fantasy, Political Project," in *Reimagining Political Community*, 309–331.

[19] Robert A. Dahl, "Can international organizations be democratic? A skeptic's view," in *Democracy's Edges*, eds. Ian Shapiro and Casiano Hacker-Cordón (Cambridge: Cambridge University Press, 1999), 19–36.

[20] Will Kymlicka, "Citizenship in an Era of Globalization: Commentary on Held," in *Democracy's Edges*, 112–126.

[21] This formulation is given by Alon Laniado in an unpublished paper.

acid rain, noted earlier, there are increasingly recognized shared interests among communities, including certain Midwestern states in the United States along with neighboring parts of southern Canada. This would represent a new crossborder locality that seemingly has no place in a model such as Held's, which simply adds layers above existing nation-states. The pragmatic proposals considered earlier seem better able to deal with this sort of emerging community of need and interest (and indeed my own view shares their presumption for democratic decisions across a wide range of associations); but some of the pragmatic views in turn seem to offer no guidelines beyond that of being open to democratic input and deliberation in such emergent communities.

The very different case of democratic input into NGOs in the WTO also escapes both approaches. Held's view does not discuss the sort of functional rather than territorial representation that would justify this necessary participation, whereas again democratic pragmatists would endorse this but do not show how it is normatively required beyond the suggestion that all organizations should be somehow inclusive. It is worth noting that such an emphasis on NGOs and social movement participation in directing globalization processes has more generally been articulated in connection with the idea of global governance. In regard especially to multilateral organizations such as the WTO, the IMF, and the World Bank, which play an increasingly important role in facilitating economic globalization and development, it has been argued that these organizations need to be considerably more open to input from civil society as represented by these NGOs and social movements, and need to be held accountable to them and more generally to the people and societies affected by their policymaking. Specific proposals have been made to ensure greater accountability and representation, ranging from requirements of transparency in deliberation to institutional reforms such as broadening the functions of the WTO secretariat, to much more extensive consultation with NGOs, and to bringing the WTO within the framework of the UN.[22] Likewise, proposals have been made for "re-regulation" of globalization, for mandating increased social responsibility by transnational corporations, and for the introduction of Tobin taxes on transnational currency transactions,[23] which could be used to ameliorate the defects of unregulated financial markets

[22] See Willetts, "Civil Society Networks in Global Governance."
[23] See, for example, the Tobin Tax Initiative, Center for Environmental Economic Development, http://www.ceedweb.org/iirp/factsheet.htm.

and also to aid in social and economic development where urgently needed.

These diverse proposals contribute to the "globalization from below" that Richard Falk and others have called for[24] and would, if implemented, make the processes more accountable, if not fully democratic. More radically still, other theorists have sought ways to permit certain local regions, whether within nation-states or crossborder, to "opt out" of globalization processes that are directed in part by these multilateral organizations.[25] To the degree that decisions by supervenient trade organizations, for example, proceed in a wholly undemocratic manner, on these proposals localities could choose not to be bound by decisions that applied to them but to which they had no input. (This priority to the local would certainly constitute a radicalization of the principle of subsidiarity or decision at the lowest level possible, now widely recognized in regional transnational arrangements and taken by Held and others as a model for cosmopolitan democracy.)

Criteria for Democratic Participation in Global Institutions

Without addressing the political economy of globalization further here, we can focus on the democratization issue, from the standpoint introduced earlier of the conceptual analysis of the scope of democratic decisions and the alternative criteria for demarcating this scope. As suggested in Chapters 1 and 7, the criterion that all those who take part in a common activity, defined by shared aims, should be able to participate in decisions about it can presumably be applied to social and economic institutions at any level and also to the larger systems of social cooperation involved in the idea of a politically organized society, whether on a local or a national scale. In the latter case, it has traditionally taken the form of equal citizenship rights.

As noted previously, in placing emphasis on taking an active role in common projects, this view contrasts with the more usual account of such democratic rights. These accounts appeal to the idea that, as Andreas Follesdal puts it, "Those equally affected by practices and institutions should also have an equal say in how the institutions should be shaped."[26]

---

[24] See Richard Falk, "Global Civil Society and the Democratic Prospect," in *Global Democracy*, 162–178.

[25] On this and some of the other suggestions, see James Mittelman, "Alternative Globalization," in *Civilizing Globalization*, 242–245.

[26] Andreas Follesdal, "Citizenship: European and Global," in *Global Citizenship*, eds. Nigel Dower and John Williams (New York: Routledge, 2002), 80.

Follesdal applies this to European citizenship, on the ground that "Europeans are now so interdependent due to their common institutions that they must also have an equal say in how they are governed. The institutions of the Union, including Union citizenship, must be shaped to ensure such democratic accountability."[27] He then goes on to extend this to the idea of global citizenship, writing that

This line of argument can serve as a model with regards to claims to institutionalize global citizenship. Globalisation reduced the significance of state borders, due largely to the digital and transnational economy. Our decisions increasingly affect others across borders, increasing the interdependency of foreigners. In so far as global regimes have global implications, normative cosmopolitanism requires that they must also be under political control where all have an equal say.[28]

Follesdal is certainly right to call attention to global interdependence, especially in terms of economy and technology, and to argue for the importance of cosmopolitan democratic input into decisions. I also agree, as discussed previously, that the "all affected" principle has a role to play here, providing a rationale for permitting significant input into decision making at a distance. The question, as we have seen, is whether this principle is sufficiently determinate, taken simply as stated, to provide guidelines in devising more democratic transnational institutions. To the degree that decisions are at a great level of generality, people may indeed be equally affected; but most transnational decisions are not of that level of generality, and people are most often differentially affected. In addition, the principle is difficult to apply concretely because it cannot always be known in advance who is going to be affected.

As discussed earlier, these difficulties do not require that we completely abandon this "all affected" principle in global contexts. I think it importantly supplements the first idea – that those active in an institution or in a system of cooperation have democratic rights within it – by expanding the range of those who should have some input beyond the members, citizens, or those most closely involved. However, we need to further specify this criterion – to be able to say, for example, that those affected by the actions of a transnational corporation or by the WTO or other governmental or intergovernmental bodies have a right of input into the decisions. One possible specification, given earlier, is to introduce a conception of being importantly affected or materially affected by a decision, but this idea still needs to be fleshed out.

---

[27] Follesdal, "Citizenship," 80–81.
[28] Ibid., 81.

Here I would like to propose that we take one meaning of being affected as given by human rights, where these rights include not only the
mostly negative civil and political rights but also the more full-bodied
social and economic rights. More specifically, a person is to be regarded
as importantly affected if the decision in question impacts the basic freedom, needs, or central interests that are protected by human rights, or
if the decision has significant effects on that person's ability to realize
these human rights. Again, this does not apply only if the decision deprives people of civil rights or threatens their person but also applies if
it would deprive them of the opportunity to gain means of subsistence.
The strong interpretation of the human rights entailed here is of course
fairly innovative on the world stage, where such rights tend to be taken in
a more anemic reading, as constraints against the actions of states in the
public sphere, in regard to torture, political voting rights, and so forth.
Nonetheless, inasmuch as human rights specify the conditions necessary
for people's freedom – not only in the sense of their free choice but
also as their ability to develop or transform themselves individually or
with others – I would say that impact on the basic freedom, interests,
and needs that are protected and realized by human rights provides a
criterion for determining when someone at a distance is affected by a
decision. Oversimplifying a bit, on this view we can say that people are
importantly affected when their human rights are affected.

Relating Democracy and Human Rights

This suggestion provides an interesting and unnoticed connection between human rights and democracy. In Chapter 8, I propose that a cosmopolitan framework of human rights can provide a legitimate constraint
on democratic decisions, whether national or transnational, as a generalization of the idea that constitutionally established rights are needed to
protect minorities from majority decisions. I argue that inasmuch as both
democracy and these human rights are required by people's equal freedom, then if democratic decisions violate these basic conditions, which
protect and make real the freedom for the sake of which democratic participation is also instituted, such decisions can properly be overturned. I
also have indicated that rights protection of this sort requires the further
elaboration of a human rights regime at regional, and more fully global
levels.

Yet another deep connection between democracy and human rights
is reflected in the proposal introduced here to take human rights as

indicating one meaning of "affected" in global contexts, an interpretation that would give rise to democratic rights by those so affected to have a say in the decisions in question. Of course, this proposal does not yet settle the issue of where full equality of participation is required and where some degree of input would suffice. Addressing this question would require further consideration of the scope of the matters under discussion – in particular, how global they are – as well as giving some assessment of how centrally human rights are affected and whether these impacted rights fall within the basic or nonbasic rights, as I have discussed these previously.

A further connection between democracy and human rights is the obvious one that democracy is itself one of the human rights. Recognizing this, however, might be thought to pose a problem of circularity for the suggestions made above, namely, that impact on human rights gives rise to rights of democratic participation, or again, that human rights, including presumably the right of democracy itself, can legitimately constrain democratic decisions. Yet, this sort of circularity is avoided in the proposal above, by characterizing affectedness in terms of impact on the basic freedom, needs, and interests of people, which are in turn protected by human rights. Likewise, there is no circularity entailed in the proposal that particular democratic decisions must not undermine people's basic right of democratic decision or their other fundamental rights. At a deeper level, as argued in Chapter 8, circularity is avoided by recognizing that both human rights and democratic participation itself have their basis in the prior idea of freedom. Human rights specify the social and material conditions necessary for protecting this freedom and making it effective, while rights of democratic participation arise as an expression of this freedom in contexts of common, rather than simply individual, activity, where such participation is itself one of the social conditions that human rights are concerned with. I have also maintained here that to the degree that this or other central features of people's freedom and well-being (protected and recognized by human rights) are importantly impacted by decisions at a distance, people thereby gain rights to participate in some ways in decisions about these matters, again on the grounds of their equal freedom.

Turning to the practical circumstances of the global impacts of decisions, a simpler interpretation of being affected may often suffice, where it means something like importantly and relevantly affected. For example, if a particular trade policy under consideration concerns steel, then the steelworkers in the countries or regions under discussion would be materially impacted, in the sense that the policy would likely affect their livelihood. This interpretation would also give rise to democratic rights of input into the policy under consideration, in a way that raises for us the question of functional representation. Those who advocate a separate system of democratic representation regarding economic issues, including a more representative global body that would encompass functions now allocated to the WTO and the IMF, appeal to a criterion that those materially impacted by these policies should in this way have a right to participate in making them. Whether this representation is to take place by industry or is understood as applying to civil society as a whole remains an open question in their thinking. Still, this approach, like the democratic pragmatism considered at the outset (which emphasizes ad hoc problem solving through democratic deliberation), represents an important direction for potentially making the political economic system more democratic.

At this early stage in the discussion of institutionalizing cosmopolitan democracy, I do not think it necessary to choose only one path, whether territorial or functional. The functional approach has the virtue of allowing a wide range of crossborder groups to play a role if they share interests, such as economic ones, whereas the territorial cosmopolitanism of Held is perhaps more orderly and consonant with present nation-states and the emerging transnational regionalism. It is plausible and consistent, I think, to advocate moving ahead in all of these ways at present and to endorse a multiplicity of paths to seeking greater democratic participation and representativeness in globalization processes.

Finally, I would like to consider a little more fully the human rights framework needed for globalizing democracy in the ways discussed and point to the dialectical relation between democracy and human rights in this new context. I have already suggested two of these relations, beyond the idea that democracy is itself one of the human rights: first, the notion that human rights can legitimately constrain democratic decisions (and a fortiori, constrain unilaterally taken decisions, e.g., by transnational corporations that may sometimes act in a way to deprive people of such rights or fail to take actions to protect them[29]); and second, the idea that impact on people's human rights serves as one interpretation of when they can be said to be importantly affected by a decision and therefore have a democratic right to participate in making the decision. Yet a further

---

[29] See the discussion in Thomas Donaldson, "Moral Minimums for Corporations," in *Ethics and International Affairs*, ed. Joel Rosenthal (Washington, DC: Georgetown University Press, 1999), 455–480.

connection between these concepts is that we can speak of the realization of human rights as a goal for democratic decisions within states, as well as at the level of intergovernmental agencies. The concept of democracy "for the people" and not only "by the people" articulates this idea.[30]

However, this analysis still leaves out of account two crucial dimensions of interrelation between these normative concepts. To see these connections, we can reflect on the inadequacy of democratic deliberation when systems of exploitation and dependence are in place. Indeed, a weakness of the deliberative account of democracy taken alone is that it does not directly address the requirement that deliberation to be effective needs to be among equal participants with relatively equal economic rights (who are not distracted by poverty or other salient needs). There are, in short, economic and social conditions for democratic decision making, and these go beyond the idea that people need some resources in order to be able to vote. Rather, it can be observed that discrepancies in power and control over resources go hand in hand with discrepancies in influence over decisions. It follows then that injustice and the lack of economic and social human rights needs to be rectified in order to make real progress in facilitating the globalization of democratic decision making. Conversely, however, it is apparent, as I have noted, that the creation of new democratic networks and the implementation of greater democratic participation by those affected is one of the main ways to ensure the realization of economic and social rights. Redistributive considerations alone are insufficient without input and participation by those who would be impacted by decisions.

Before we throw up our hands in the face of the seeming dilemma this poses for us, namely that democracy and the human rights appear to presuppose each other in order to be realized, we can turn this into the more positive requirement to move ahead on both fronts, with the understanding that such a double-sided approach is in fact required. Human rights are thus needed not only as a constitutional framework for appeal within nation-states, within regions, and in a more cosmopolitan sense as well, but also should be taken as a goal in the construction of social and economic systems to realize them in national and crossborder contexts. However, I have also proposed that one main way of limiting the control by some over the resources needed by many others and thereby achieving equality in economic and social human rights is indeed by extending

[30] See Ross Zucker, *Democratic Distributive Justice* (Cambridge: Cambridge University Press, 2001), 277.

democratic participation more globally, such that economic and social institutions as well as political ones operate more democratically and such that those importantly affected by decisions have a say in making them.

We can observe finally that human rights as used here retain their generality as valid claims that each person can make on all others or on society at large, as discussed in Chapter 1. In the view here, they cannot be restricted to constraints on governments or on actors in the public sphere, as they have been traditionally; accordingly, the new moves to apply them to nonstate actors are salutary. Furthermore, given the central role of social cooperation and of economic, social, and political institutions in the meeting of needs and in the provision of the conditions specified in these human rights, it is not sufficient to talk about individuals and governments refraining from infringing on them. The primary requirement is the construction of institutions and social forms that function in a way to provide for these rights. And whereas such institutions previously existed mainly at the level of nation-states, the growing interconnectedness of economies gives rise to the need for international institutions that can work to ensure a more universalized protection of and availability of human rights, including the economic and social ones. Accordingly, the functioning of the international economy and of politics must not deprive entire sets of people of their rights,[31] and, more positively, should contribute toward the realization of these rights, by cooperation to make access to material and social conditions more equally and more universally available. Yet it is worth reiterating the suggestion in this chapter, that the most important institutional innovation that can effect such a realization of rights is in fact the extension of democratic decision making in global contexts.

---

[31] See Thomas Pogge, "Human Rights and Human Responsibilities," in *Global Justice & Transnational Politics*, eds. Pablo De Greiff and Ciaran Cronin (Cambridge, MA: The MIT Press, 2002), 151–195. Although Pogge helpfully emphasizes the global order and its functioning in the realization of human rights, especially economic ones, his account remains closely tied to the traditional conception of rights as holding against governments, where they are a matter of "official conduct." Furthermore, his emphasis on the negative requirement of avoiding the imposition of a coercive order that deprives people of their rights loses the positive sense in which we can each make a claim on others for the construction of social, economic, and political institutions that function to provide the basic conditions specified in these rights.

PART IV

CURRENT APPLICATIONS

10

Democratic Management and the
Stakeholder Idea

In this final part of the book, I take up certain outstanding contemporary social and political issues to which the previous analysis of democracy and human rights can usefully be applied. These practical contexts are normally addressed within business ethics, computer ethics, and international ethics, respectively. They concern, first, the question of democratic management in firms; second, the use of computer networks for democratic decisions; and third, ways of understanding and responding to terrorism. I believe that the framework advanced in the earlier parts of this work, in which democracy and human rights are seen to pertain to the personal, the plural, and the global, has helpful implications for applied ethics, as these three cases show. The consideration of these applications also reciprocally helps to refine and concretize aspects of the theory presented previously.

One of the key arguments in earlier chapters is that rights to democratic participation should extend broadly across society and pertain not only to entire political societies but also to smaller-scale institutions in political, economic, and social life (in addition to their crossborder applicability, discussed in Part III). One of the most controversial aspects of this claim consists in the proposed extension to economic firms. This older issue, which used to be denominated as that of "worker self-management," remains of current interest, although it has come to be overwhelmed in importance among those critical of economic life under capitalism by the critique of economic globalization and its effects. In this chapter, I revisit this question of democratic participation in firms and consider it especially from the standpoint of the dominant theoretical approach within business ethics, namely, stakeholder theory. I ask, does stakeholder theory itself in fact require democratic management in corporations? And, if so, what forms might such democratic management take?

We can usefully begin with a statement by R. Edward Freeman, whose work is often associated with the historical introduction of the stakeholder idea. In his "Stakeholder Theory of the Modern Corporation," Freeman strikingly asserts, "The task of management in today's corporation is akin to that of King Solomon."[1] In making this somewhat offhand remark, Freeman is referring to the balancing and adjudication of diverse stakeholders' interests that a wise and capable manager is called upon to accomplish. Although he is not seriously intending to analogize the manager to a king, Freeman's suggestion of rule raises the following question: If the manager is not to be an autocrat of any sort, as business ethics has generally insisted, should the authority of managers be construed as like that of a governmental official – a bureaucrat? an elected representative? a town selectman? Or are these metaphors unhelpful in understanding managerial authority in organizations and in particular in corporations?

In his 1994 work *Authority and Democracy*, Chris McMahon argues for the accountability of managers to their workers in decision making, understood as requiring democratic input into managerial authority on the part of the employees.[2] As noted, this proposal has a long history in the idea of employee participation or, more strongly, workplace or corporate democracy.[3] Notwithstanding much important analytical work on this theme, as well as actual instances of implementation of participation in companies and empirical studies of these cases, this democratic direction for management has receded in the current theory and practice of corporate ethics. Yet, despite the numerous criticisms lodged against schemes of employee participation, several business ethicists and political theorists have continued to argue for the normative relevance of some sort of

---

[1] R. Edward Freeman, "Stakeholder Theory of the Modern Corporation," in *Ethical Issues in Business*, seventh edition, eds. Thomas Donaldson et al. (Saddle River, NJ: Prentice-Hall, 2002), 44.

[2] Christopher McMahon, *Authority and Democracy: A General Theory of Government and Management* (Princeton, NJ: Princeton University Press, 1994). See also Christopher McMahon, "The Political Theory of Organizations and Business Ethics," *Philosophy and Public Affairs*, Vol. 24, issue 4 (Autumn 1995): 292–313.

[3] See, for example, Carole Pateman, *Participation and Democratic Theory* (Cambridge: Cambridge University Press, 1970), Chapter IV; Robert Dahl, *A Preface to Economic Democracy* (Berkeley: University of California Press, 1985), especially Chapter 4; and Sidney P. Rubinstein, *Participative Systems at Work* (New York: Human Sciences Press, 1987).

employee participation in management decisions.[4] However, in all these participatory approaches, the scope of this input and the specification of the form it optimally should take remain to be clarified: How much input is required, and what modalities can make it practicable?

In contrast to the lack of support for participative management schemes, *stakeholder theory* has emerged over the past few decades as a leading approach to business ethics, with its suggestions that managers need to take seriously into account the interests of the variety of groups affected by their decisions – not only the stockholders but also employees, suppliers, customers, banks and other lenders, the local community, and even the government and the public at large. Managers are said to have a multi-fiduciary relation to these other stakeholders, in addition to that which they have toward stockholders. Some theorists have also argued that non-social stakeholders – for example, the environment – merit consideration as well. Despite the popularity of this stakeholder approach, however, ethicists have increasingly pointed to a certain vagueness in stakeholder theory's directives. For example, Donaldson and Dunfee write that prevailing normative approaches, including stakeholder theory, philosophical deontology, or utilitarianism, "provide general guidance but fail to reflect the context-specific complexity of business situations. . . . [With respect to a variety of problems often confronted by a multinational manager] [s]takeholder approaches are merely able to advise this manager to consider both the interests of stockholders and other 'stakeholders,' (i.e., employees, community residents, customers, etc.)."[5]

We thus have a situation in which workplace democracy has come to seem too stringent a requirement for management, while stakeholder theory is too vague. It is interesting to observe, however, that stakeholder theory itself likely originated within the theory of industrial democracy. Thus in his account of the history of the stakeholder concept in the *Encyclopedic Dictionary of Business Ethics*, Freeman notes, citing the work of Nasi,[6] that "[t]he Swedish management theorist Eric Rhenman, who is perhaps the originator of the term, was instrumental in the development

---

4 See, for example, Robert Grady, "Workplace Democracy and Possessive Individualism," *The Journal of Politics*, Vol. 52, issue 1 (Feb. 1990): 146–166; and Denis Collins, "The Ethical Superiority and Inevitability of Participatory Management as an Organizational System," *Organization Science*, Vol. 8, issue 5 (Sep.–Oct. 1997): 489–507.

5 Thomas Donaldson and Thomas W. Dunfee, "Toward a Unified Conception of Business Ethics: Integrative Social Contracts Theory," *The Academy of Management Review*, Vol. 19, issue 2 (Apr. 1994): 254–255.

6 J. Nasi, *Understanding Stakeholder Thinking* (Helsinki: LSR-Julkaisut Oy, 1995).

of stakeholder thinking in Scandinavia, where the concept became one of the cornerstones of industrial democracy."[7] And even in the work of Freeman himself, we find echoes of this view. Thus he lays out his view as follows:

Stakeholders are those groups who have a stake in or claim on the firm. Specifically, I include suppliers, customers, employees, stockholders, and the local community, as well as management in its role as agent for these groups.... [E]ach of these stakeholder groups has a right not to be treated as a means to some end, and therefore *must participate in determining the future direction of the firm in which they have a stake.*[8]

Or again, with regard to employees who must follow management instructions most of the time, Freeman writes, "Where they are used as means to an end, they must participate in decisions affecting such use."[9] And finally, in speaking about fair contracts as a ground for stakeholder theory, he enunciates the *principle of governance*. This important principle "translates into each stakeholder never giving up the right to participate in the governance of the corporation, or perhaps into the existence of stakeholder governing boards."[10] Indeed, as we shall see, a connection with participation or governance is suggested by the very terms of the stakeholder formulation itself, at least as Freeman presents it, namely, that those groups are stakeholders who are affected by and affect the corporation's functioning or the managers' decision making. It is a very short step indeed from this to the further claim that those affected by the decisions in question, or subject to the firm's authority, have a right to participate in its decision-making processes.

Although Freeman's approach may in fact have these democratic implications, he does not go on to develop its import in explicitly democratic terms, and this is certainly not the way that stakeholder theory has functioned in the business ethics literature. Thus, Donaldson and Preston's important review article, "The Stakeholder Theory of the Corporation: Concepts, Evidence, and Implications" makes no mention of these governance aspects of stakeholder theory. Instead, they begin by observing that "[s]takeholder analysts argue that *all* groups with legitimate interests participating in an enterprise do so to obtain benefits and that there

---

[7] R. Edward Freeman, "Stakeholder Theory," in *Encyclopedic Dictionary of Business Ethics*, eds. Patricia H. Werhane and R. Edward Freeman (Malden, MA: Blackwell, 1997), 602.

[8] Freeman, "Stakeholder Theory of the Modern Corporation," 247, italics mine.

[9] Ibid., 251.

[10] Ibid., 255.

is no prima facie priority of one set of interests and benefits over an-other."[11] Then, after considering the descriptive and functional uses of the stakeholder idea, they focus on its normative aspect and propose a ground in a pluralistic and extended conception of property rights. They then state that "[a]ll that is necessary is to show that such characteris-tics, which are the same as those giving rise to fundamental concepts of property rights, give various groups a moral interest, commonly referred to as a 'stake,' in the affairs of the corporation."[12] Finally, it follows that "[i]t is the responsibility of managers, and the management function, to select activities and direct resources to obtain benefits for legitimate stakeholders."[13] The import of stakeholder theory here is thus limited to a requirement on managers to consider and take account of the interests of the other stakeholder groups in the managers' own decision processes. But it does not extend to a requirement of participation by central stake-holders, and especially employees, in management decisions and indeed explicitly rejects any prima facie priority that we might be inclined to give to the interests of employee stakeholders over others.

A similar limitation of the stakeholder idea emerges clearly in Donaldson and Dunfee's book *Ties That Bind*. There, they lay out the re-quirements of stakeholder theories – at least as ordinarily understood – in a similar way:

An important task for business ethicists is to define when firms should consider the interests of stakeholders in their decisions. The extant conventional wisdom requires managers to act as follows: 1) identify the full range of stakeholders for a given firm and decision, 2) identify the stakes at issue in the decision, 3) assess the legitimacy of the stakes, 4) allocate priority among conflicting stakeholder claims, 5) identify strategic options for responding to the legitimate stakes having priority, 6) assess the viability of the options within the framework of corporate governance, including any special consideration to be given to the interests of stockholders, and 7) make a final decision.[14]

Thus the full weight of the theory falls on the managers themselves in this account. It is also relevant to observe how, after laying out this approach, Donaldson and his collaborators point out the vast scope sometimes given

---

[11] Thomas Donaldson and Lee E. Preston, "The Stakeholder Theory of the Corporation: Concepts, Evidence, and Implications," *The Academy of Management Review*, Vol. 20, issue 1 (Jan. 1995): 68.

[12] Ibid., 85.

[13] Ibid.

[14] Thomas Donaldson and Thomas W. Dunfee, *Ties That Bind: A Social Contracts Approach to Business Ethics* (Boston: Harvard Business School Press, 1999), 236.

to the stakeholder notion, along with the attendant vagueness of its application beyond the immediate constituencies within the corporation and closely allied to it.

We can now ask, has stakeholder theory perhaps lost some of its bite by becoming largely divorced from the democratic conceptions of participation that in part gave rise to it? Yet if we want to return stakeholder theory to its normative linkage with some conception of participative or democratic management, then we might again seem to weaken its range by coming up against overly demanding desiderata of workplace democracy. Certainly, an interpretation that would require all possible stakeholders to participate in management decisions within a firm would be hopelessly cumbersome, if we could make sense of such a requirement. We seem then to confront the following dilemmatic situation, with regard to the import of stakeholder theory for decision making: Either we need to accept stakeholder theory as it is, with its limited and unfortunately vague recommendations for accountability, or we need to return to a demanding requirement not only of employee participation in decision making but, even more stringently, some participation by all relevant stakeholders.

In the rest of this chapter, I try to make some progress on this issue by examining the basic claims of stakeholder theory to see whether they indeed require participative, or what I call democratic, management and, if so, consider who may be said to have a right to participate and to what degree. This entails an analysis of the normative justification for such a democratic approach to management, which draws on the account given earlier in this book. I also analyze the proposal that the manager is properly considered as standing in a fiduciary or trustee relation to employees or other stakeholders and consider whether a more participative understanding of the manager's role is more appropriate. By putting stakeholder theory into the context of this earlier discussion of the requirement for participative management, I hope to lend greater specificity to some of the desiderata of this stakeholder theory. At the same time, I want to suggest how stakeholder theory, with its analysis of the diverse relations that managers have to various stakeholders, can in fact help to make theories of workplace or corporate democracy more practicable and realistic by showing how they can be appropriately qualified and interpreted for modern corporations. Clearly, these are all large tasks, and my goal is more narrowly to initiate this discussion in this chapter.

Normative Justifications for Democratic Management and Stakeholder Theory

We can start from Freeman's broad definition of stakeholder, widely echoed in the literature: "any group or individual which can affect or is affected by an organization."[15] Elsewhere, Freeman clarifies that "[t]he concept of stakeholders is a generalization of the notion of stockholders who themselves have some special claim on the firm. Just as stockholders have a right to demand certain actions by management, so do other stakeholders have a right to make claims."[16] The formulation that those who are affected by the decisions of an organization have rights to make claims on it may in turn suggest to us (as it did to Freeman himself) a version of the democratic principle, as we have discussed this previously. And indeed, this conception is reflected in Freeman's principle of governance, referred to earlier, which states that each stakeholder does not give up the right of participation and may even entail what he calls "stakeholder governing boards."

Bracketing here the concern with the efficiency of such stakeholder participation in management decisions,[17] it seems that, in this account, "being affected by decisions" requires a right (although not necessarily a duty) of participation in decision making in the firm. Where direct participation is not possible, representation comes into play, and stakeholders would presumably at least have the right to select representatives to make decisions about matters that affect them. Perhaps they should be accorded the right to select the managers themselves.

As I argued in Chapters 7 and 9, however, defining the scope of a strong requirement for rights of democratic participation in terms of the idea of "all those affected by" a decision is too broad. The main difficulty, as we saw, is that of determining all those who may be affected. Decisions usually

---

[15] Freeman, "Stakeholder Theory," *Encyclopedic Dictionary of Business Ethics*, 602.

[16] Freeman, "Stakeholder Theory of the Modern Corporation, 250.

[17] There is a wide literature on the relative efficiency of participatory management, as well as of stakeholder-oriented firms, in comparison with more traditional examples of corporate governance. In general, much of this literature is supportive of gains in efficiency, but this issue is too broad to consider within the normative analysis given here. See, for example, Samuel Bowles and Herbert Gintis, "A Political and Economic Case for the Democratic Enterprise," in *The Idea of Democracy*, eds. David Copp, Jean Hampton, and John E. Roemer (Cambridge: Cambridge University Press, 1993), 375–399; and Edward E. Lawler, S. A. Mohrman, and G. E. Ledford, *Employee Involvement and Total Quality Management* (San Francisco: Jossey-Bass Publishers, 1992).

have unintended consequences that in some cases reverberate across various contexts outside the organization or even through generations yet unborn. In such cases, it is impossible in principle for all those affected by the decision (or their representatives) to participate in making it. Indeed, this problem may affect stakeholder theory as well, inasmuch as it urges managers to consider the impact on all affected. This "all" can be a rather indeterminate class in many cases. If we want to insist that consideration be given to all affected, then it might seem to follow that stakeholder theory ought to eschew a democratic interpretation. For it might be possible for managers to imagine the impact on all (or most) affected, but it would be impossible for all of these to participate in making the management decision itself.

Nonetheless, we cannot jettison the idea of democratic management so quickly, in the first place because there are other justifications for participation in decisions that may apply to corporate management as to nation-states. Perhaps we can also find ways to narrow the participation requirement so as to make it more manageable (a point that I return to in the final part of this chapter). One alternative justification, elaborated earlier, focuses on the idea of being a member of an organization with common goals and aims, giving rise to rights to codetermine its decisions. On such an approach, we can say that while members of an organization have a right to participation, outsiders ought to have their interests heard and considered to the degree that they are affected by the decisions of the organization, although they may not yet have a right of democratic participation in governance.

A related avenue for justifying democratic input into corporate decisions asserts that those who are subject to managerial authority, whether in states or corporations, have a right to participate in this management, at least by way of selecting the managers. This is the argument given by Christopher McMahon, as noted earlier. This approach shares with the one I have advanced the reservations about founding democratic rights primarily on "being affected." In the context of rejecting general stakeholder participation in corporate governance while validating employee participation, McMahon writes,

There is a deeper philosophical issue that counts against "stakeholder" participation in corporate governance. The suggestion that representatives of such groups should participate is associated with a widely held, but I believe fundamentally mistaken, conception of democracy. This is the view that democracy requires that, or is more fully realized to the extent that, people have a say in what affects them. A little reflection shows that this is not a principle that we accept in the political sphere. Virtually everyone in the world is affected by the foreign policy decisions of the U.S. government, but we do not suppose that they therefore have a right to participate in making these decisions or in choosing those who make them.[18]

Both his view and mine instead propose that a crucial ingredient in the requirement of democracy consists in membership in an organization in which one's actions will be guided by the decisions in question.[19] And, in my version, it is freedom or self-determination, where this takes the form of group self-determination, that gives rise to the requirement of democratic participation. Yet, in this context as in economic globalization more generally, it is evident that being affected by decisions does have an important role to play, to which I return later.

Although most recent normative justifications of stakeholder theory ignore Freeman's suggestion of the need for participative management, Donaldson and Preston, in the review article cited earlier, justify it in a way that permits such a democratic interpretation (although this is not the direction of their own view). There, these ethicists seek to ground the requirement for considering stakeholder claims on a newer, more plural conception of property rights, as including the requirement to do no harm. In their view, a conception of shareholders as able to do what they will with the corporation as their property disregards several of these dimensions of property right itself. For Donaldson and Preston, such property rights are grounded in a theory of distributive justice, whether one that emphasizes the meeting of needs, a return for ability or effort, or the implied understandings among individuals or groups regarding appropriate distributions or uses of property.[20] Rejecting a single theory of distributive justice, they prefer a plural approach. They explain that "for example, the 'stake' of long-term employees who have worked to build and maintain a successful business operation is essentially based on effort. The stake of people living in the surrounding community may be based on their need, say, for clean air or the maintenance of their civic infrastructure. Customer stakes are based on the satisfactions and protections implicitly promised in the market offer, and so on."[21] On their view, these groups have a corresponding moral interest, or "stake," in the affairs of the corporation.

---

[18] McMahon, *Authority and Democracy*, 11.
[19] Ibid., 12.
[20] Donaldson and Preston, "The Stakeholder Theory of the Corporation," 84.
[21] Ibid., 84–85.

However, although Donaldson and Preston do not themselves draw a more radical conclusion, it can be argued that these conceptions of justice and the correlative ideas of property justify the more participative approach to managing stakeholder interests discussed here.[22] Certainly, their prohibition on harmful use serves to narrow property right considerably. Robert Dahl develops some further implications of this sort of restriction. For him, "[None] of the reasoned arguments for private property justify a right to the unlimited acquisition of private property. If anything, they would justify a right to a minimum collection of resources, particularly the resources necessary to life, liberty, the pursuit of happiness, the democratic process, and primary rights."[23] And Dahl, as well as McMahon after him, goes on to argue that fairness and equality, both aspects of a conception of justice, require equal rights of participation in decision making concerning binding collective decisions by those subject to them.[24] On the view I presented earlier, as well, these democratic rights are in fact derived from a principle of equal (positive) freedom, itself a principle of distributive justice.

The Interpretation of Stakeholder Theory and the Requirement for Participative Management

What are the implications of this normative analysis for understanding stakeholder theory, and how should we construe a reasonable requirement for democratic or participative management? It seems clear in the first place that the approach here gives priority to those stakeholders who are inside the corporation or members of it – in particular, employees and managers themselves, as well as the board of directors, and, in a different way, stockholders (who, while outside the corporation, are clearly decisively important to it). Other stakeholder groups can be seen

---

[22] More recently, however, Donaldson and Dunfee suggest that stakeholder theory is grounded in their integrative social contract theory, with its important concept of hypernorms. For them "hypernorms" refer to "deep moral values," widely accepted, and seem to include the human rights that Donaldson has emphasized elsewhere. The question would be whether more participatory or democratic forms of decision making are required as a hypernorm not only in politics, as they would presumably grant, but also in all contexts of common activity, including of an economic sort. Whereas they describe certain crucial aspects of stakeholder theory as supported by hypernorms and other less essential ones as supported by community norms, at this point they would presumably not accept a requirement for democratic management as discussed here. See Thomas Donaldson and Thomas W. Dunfee, *Ties That Bind*, especially Chapter 9.

[23] Dahl, *A Preface to Economic Democracy*, 82–83.

[24] Ibid., 57–58, and McMahon, *Authority and Democracy*, 129–130.

to have certain significant rights but are not entitled to participate directly in governance. This approach thus leads us to introduce a trifold division among stakeholders, in place of the more common binary division between the groups closely related to the corporation (traditionally including customers and suppliers, even though they are not insiders) and the more tangential outside groups and interests, where the latter includes both social and nonsocial (e.g., environmental) components. On the view favored here, there are (1) the members of the corporation, along with the stockholders, (2) outside stakeholders having close and regular contacts with it – especially suppliers, customers, financiers, and the local community, with its local environment, and (3) a more distant group, including the public at large, the government, and even global social and political entities, with their broader economic and environmental interests. Furthermore, this division suggests that management may well have a fiduciary or trustee relation to the latter two groups but a more fully representative relation to the first set.

We can also observe that within the corporation, employees have a special place among stakeholders. One reason is that the other groups who may be regarded as part of the economic organization of the corporation usually have a considerably greater ability than employees do to exit from the organization. Possessing "exit," they need "voice" less than do the employees. Although it is tempting to regard employees as free agents who may choose to work for anyone, this applies mainly to those possessing highly valuable skills. For the others, there is clearly the potential for a coercive element in obedience to management guidelines – namely, they must do so on pain of losing their employment. Indeed, they may be hard pressed to find another. Along these lines, Robert Dahl analogizes workers to the citizens of a state in respect to the difficulty of exiting. He writes,

[I]s not "exit" (or exile) often so costly, in every sense, that membership is for all practical purposes compulsory – whether it requires one to leave a country, a municipality, or a firm? If so, then the government of a firm looks rather more like the government of a state than we are habitually inclined to believe: because exit is so costly, membership in a firm is not significantly more voluntary or less compulsory than citizenship in a municipality or perhaps even in a country.[25]

Even leaving aside this consideration of the special status of employees, who generally cannot easily leave, we can assert the more general principle that as long as people are part of an organization defined by

---

[25] Dahl, *A Preface to Economic Democracy*, 114–115.

joint and cooperative activity in pursuit of shared aims, whose own activity will be guided by decisions about these aims and the means to achieve them, then all those who are active in the organization have a prima facie right to participate in controlling their own joint activity. This need not entail what Carole Pateman characterizes as "full participation; that is, . . . 'a process where each individual member of a decision-making body has equal power to determine the outcome of decisions.'"[26] In practice, a requirement for employees to have a full say in all decisions in the firm would be cumbersome if not unworkable, and it seems beyond what the current argument requires. It is more plausible to interpret this requirement as one for significant input into major decisions concerning the firm, as well as all those applying to conditions of work. Beyond this, the members of a corporation include more than the employees, at least as conventionally defined – namely, managers and the board of directors. (In practice, of course, there may be considerable overlap among these groups; for example, some employees may also be managers.) Furthermore, as things currently stand, self-management rights have to be put into relation to the property stake that stockholders have in the corporation, which currently is interpreted to support a sort of governance right, namely, their right to elect directors and to set long-term company policy. (In practice, of course, boards can sometimes be self-perpetuating, dominated by high-ranking executives; and many stockholders have no interest in setting company policy but instead just endorse the directions proposed by the board or top management.)

In this diversified and more practical context, then, there are various possible forms for democratic management within the corporation. In a 1997 article, "The Ethical Superiority and Inevitability of Participatory Management," Denis Collins summarizes the range of alternative proposals in very broad terms as follows:

> . . . employee representatives on boards of directors, labor-management committees, joint task forces, Scanlon-type gainsharing plans, quality circles, sociotechnical work teams, suggestion systems, employee attitude surveys, goal setting, job enrichment, codes of ethics, ethical analysis, an employee bill of rights, and employee stock ownership plans . . . These participatory management features differ according to size, scope, and form of employee involvement. They increase employee involvement in the company's decision-making process while enabling managers to intervene when employee decisions fail to achieve organizational goals.[27]

---

[26] Pateman, *Participation and Democratic Theory*, 71.
[27] Collins, "The Ethical Superiority and Inevitability of Participatory Management as an Organizational System," 501.

In his book on managerial authority, McMahon more forcefully proposes that the form of employee participation should be primarily the election of managers, who should be accountable to the employees.[28]

In my view, a helpful approach to enhancing participation for the near term is advanced by Charlotte Villiers in her discussion of necessary changes in European company law. She argues for "shared control of company decisions," with participation taking place at three levels: The first would be employees sharing control with managers over work allocation and methods. The second would be that of management, shared by having worker representatives discuss with managers the terms and conditions of work, including environment and facilities. And the third would be at the level of corporate policy, where her proposal is to have a dialogue between shareholders and employees, with each holding equal votes and equal access to the board of directors.[29]

Clearly, these proposals involve rather dramatic change in the prevailing situation, where, according to a 1992 report, only 11 percent of *Fortune* 1,000 corporations even used quality circles, 13 percent had suggestion systems, and 8 percent had labor/management committees.[30] Further complicating the introduction of such changes, as Villiers herself points out, are practical obstacles to their implementation, especially in regard to the proposed dialogue between shareholders and employees: For example, larger companies have dispersed shareholders, making this communication difficult; individual investors often are not interested in the policy decisions, preferring to leave these to managers; institutional investors often prefer to deal directly and discreetly with managers; and in multinational or widely dispersed companies, there would be very substantial practical difficulties in arranging meetings of the sort called for.[31] Despite these practical difficulties, she argues that some such reorganization is required in principle.

As a precondition for such changes in participation, there is also the need for fuller provision of information, especially to employees but indeed to all stakeholder groups, if management is to be responsive to these constituencies. As Michael Saward has argued, this information flow must be coupled with a constant process of public notification of decisions,

---

[28] McMahon, *Authority and Democracy*, 13.
[29] Charlotte Villiers, *European Company Law – Towards Democracy?* (Aldershot, England: Ashgate, 1998), 221.
[30] Collins, "The Ethical Superiority and Inevitability of Participatory Management as an Organizational System," 500.
[31] Villiers, *European Company Law – Towards Democracy?* 221–222.

options, and outcomes.[32] It seems evident that access to shared information is a prerequisite for effective participation. On these grounds, disclo-
sure of information can be seen to be important not only for stockholders
but also for employees, who are obviously interested in the economic situation of their employers.[33] The threefold distinction among stakeholders
that I introduced earlier may also be of use in this context in determining
the degree of transparency required with regard to company matters. It
suggests that corporate "members" and stockholders have a prima facie
stronger claim on access to information than do those outsiders having
close and regular contacts with the corporation, whereas the latter have
a stronger claim than do those stakeholder groups who stand at further
remove. Furthermore, whereas the first group has a claim to very full
access, the latter two groups need to receive information that pertains to
their assessment of their own functioning in relation to the corporation.
(Needless to say, these relatively clear requirements in theory most likely
would give rise to numerous difficulties in practical application, in regard
to determining what sort of information and what degree of transparency
are required for each stakeholder group.)

An additional methodological requirement is the need to establish
clear and recognized procedures for democratic management, whether
these take the form of those mentioned here or new ones that are suitable for a given corporation's own primary concerns and management
style. We can say that if stakeholder theory is to be given more bite by
being put into this context of participatory management – in a way
that will also avoid its use to justify self-serving managerial behavior –
then clear and established procedures for representing and taking
into account stakeholder interests would need to be agreed upon and
instituted.

It is also in place to observe here that participatory management as
implemented in the near term may in fact imply somewhat different requirements with respect to diverse management functions, in a way that
bears on the interpretation of stakeholder theory. Thus, given current
management divisions, the personnel director of a corporation, for example, would more closely have to attend to the needs and expressed
interests of employees, whereas a finance director would be more concerned with creditors and stockholders, and the head of publicity with

---

[32] See Michael Saward, "Democratic Theory and Indices of Democratisation," in *Defining
and Measuring Democracy*, ed. David Beetham, 16–17, cited in Villiers, ibid., 208.
[33] See also Villiers, ibid., 208–209.

the views of customers.[34] Relevant sorts of accountability remain to be more clearly articulated in this context, with benchmarks developed for assessing responsiveness.

We can return finally to the original stakeholder idea, that those affected by the decisions and actions of a corporation have a claim on it to have their interests taken into account. My argument has so far supported a requirement of democratic management as far as the employees, managers, and directors are concerned, although significant questions remain about how this can be implemented. But can we say anything further about other stakeholders? In contrast to McMahon's view, I would propose that here the idea of being affected comes into play and gives rise in these cases to what we might call quasi-democratic requirements on managers entrusted with decision making. Thus, as in the global case considered previously, the criterion of being affected, beyond that of membership in the organization, has implications here for a participatory interpretation of management vis-à-vis the broader range of stakeholders beyond the limits of the corporation, its managers, and employees. For if it is the case that decision makers must take into account the interests of all the major groups affected by their decisions, and if people are the best judges of their own interests, then there is the requirement of soliciting input from and listening to these external stakeholder groups and of gathering their own views of their interests before making these decisions. As noted, it would also require that these groups receive accurate information about corporate activities and their projected impact, and they would need a sound understanding of their own relation to the corporation, as conditions for making reasonable estimates of how they might be affected. The meaning of managerial trusteeship, if indeed it is an appropriate term for management in this context, would thus entail a two-way relation between managers and these other stakeholder groups, such that their direct input is actively solicited, carefully attended to, and actually taken into account in the decisions.

Where corporations are themselves increasingly global, the import of management decisions on distant stakeholders has become more significant than ever. We therefore need to go beyond such phrases as "the public at large" in assessing the impact of managerial decisions and corporate activity and in fact begin to attend more closely to the interpretation and application of the criterion of "all those affected" in such contexts. A fuller view of participative or democratic management would then have

34 Ibid., 218.

to consider not only some new modes of representation for all corporate members in governance, and not only those primary stakeholders who directly relate to the corporation, such as customers, suppliers, lenders, and the local community. It would in addition need to hear from representatives of those at a greater distance, not only the political associations, government, public, and environment of its own nation-state, but those in the more far-flung areas affected. As suggested in Chapter 9, this is of particular importance where there is impact on the human rights of these others, including on their possibilities for realizing their economic and social rights. In this respect, newer considerations of the social responsibilities of corporations to respect the full list of human rights and to introduce assessments of wider social and environmental impacts into their management decisions gain special significance. In this way, this analysis of democratic management ties into broader considerations of the relations between democratization and economic globalization.

11

Democratic Networks

Technological and Political

In previous chapters, I frequently refer to the Internet and other computer technologies as potentially facilitating transborder democratic participation, and I would like now to focus more directly on these possibilities. Our question here will be, can technological networking in fact facilitate political networking and do so in a way that has genuine democratic effects? If so, what principles can helpfully guide this process?

Technology and Politics

To frame these issues adequately, we can begin by reflecting on a little-known but interesting detail about Thomas Edison that Anthony Wilhelm cites in his book *Democracy in the Digital Age*: that the first invention on which Edison was granted a patent was a "revolutionary vote Recorder." As Wilhelm tells it, Edison sent his device in 1869 to Washington, D.C., to demonstrate it to a congressional committee in hopes that the members would appreciate the new efficiency that this innovative voting technology produced. The congressmen would only have to flip a switch at their desks, and their votes would be instantly recorded and counted by the vote recorder machine situated on the clerk's desk. Needless to say, as it turned out, the congressional leaders strenuously objected to this new device on the grounds that it made it impossible for minorities to gain advantage by changing votes or filibustering legislation. This efficient device, in short, threatened to get in the way of the longer time frame that minority groups required to persuade (or coerce) others to come over to their viewpoint.[1]

---

[1] Anthony G. Wilhelm, *Democracy in the Digital Age* (New York: Routledge, 2000), 1–2.

We might say that the possibilities of the technology were not suitable for the social and political relations of Congress at that time, and hence Edison's hopes for his invention were inevitably disappointed. Alternatively, perhaps, we might conclude that the overall impact of the technology promised to be negative as far as political deliberation was concerned.

This anecdote raises some interesting questions about the relation between a technology and the society in which it is embedded, but that general question is not my theme here. Rather, for me, as for Wilhelm in his book on digital democracy, it poses the narrower issue of the degree to which and the ways in which democratic decision making can be enhanced (or not) by various technologies, and in particular by the still rather new phenomenon of the Net, or as it is now sometimes put, the GII, or global information infrastructure. Thus in this chapter, I do not focus directly on the broader question of the relation of democracy and technology. To do so would require considering not only how technology may serve our interests in enhancing democracy both nationally and globally, but also the difficult question of how to bring about some democratic input into the design and use of technologies – what used to be called (perhaps unfortunately) the question of the democratic control of technology. Instead, I focus more narrowly on information and computer technologies as they may (or may not) facilitate democratic participation, in what is now coming to be called *cyberdemocracy* (replacing the earlier "electronic democracy" or "digital democracy").

Nonetheless, this narrower focus does bear on the broader issue of the relation of technology and democracy, not only as a case study – one that additionally raises concerns about who in fact controls its design and use – but also because technology in this contemporary period is very much entwined with politics. Thus it has been argued that we are now in what could be called the Fourth Revolution in the development of technology, in which increasingly global high technology is bound up with political power, usually still wielded hierarchically, even in democratic societies as well as in highly nationalistic or fundamentalist ones.[2] It thus can be said to be increasingly politicized, subject to political decisions by elites, and interlinked with economic and military ones (as expressed in Eisenhower's old but trenchant phrase, "the military-industrial complex").[3] Crucially, too, inasmuch as technologies increasingly have

---

[2] See the discussion in Marx W. Wartofsky, "Technology, Power, and Truth: Political and Epistemological Reflections on the Fourth Revolution," in *Democracy in a Technological Society*, ed. Langdon Winner (Dordrecht: Kluwer Academic Publishers, 1992), 15.

[3] Ibid., 16.

regional or global impacts, they seem to require the development of new transnational structures of regulation and direction. Information and communication technologies (what the British, especially, refer to as ICTs) promise to facilitate decision making about such wide-ranging technologies by virtue of their global scope and their openness to multiple and widely dispersed participants. It is hoped that they can be used for this decision making as well as for the regulation of technology itself.

Democracy and Networking Principles

Is it plausible to suppose that the use of computer technologies, and, in particular, networking, in contexts of political deliberation and decision will in fact increase democratic participation overall? The literature on this question has grown exponentially in recent years and unfortunately tends to vacillate between the extremes of overenthusiastic paeans to a new world of full and open democratic participation and deliberation online, through which citizens become empowered, and the alternative dystopian vision of a panoptican of constant monitoring, supervision, and manipulation of the citizenry, whether by a hegemonic government or by monopolistic and exclusively profit-seeking corporations in their own interest.[4] More sober and analytical assessments have also begun to appear, and I take note of some of these. But I want to delineate my own approach to these questions by beginning from the early framework for addressing political participation through the Internet proposed in my 1989 volume *The Information Web: Ethical and Social Implications of Computer Networking*,[5] placing it within the perspective developed in this work.

In an essay titled "Network Ethics: Access, Consent, and the Informed Community,"[6] I discussed certain conflicts of values – most notably, between the right of privacy and the desideratum of free and open communication – that are posed by computer network use in the context of political participation, especially to facilitate citizen–government interaction.[7] In considering such uses as government databanks, electronic polling and referenda, and the interactive applications, such as

---

4 See also the critique by David Resnick, "The Normalization of Cyberspace," in *The Politics of Cyberspace*, eds. Chris Toulouse and Timothy W. Luke (New York: Routledge, 1998), 48.

5 Carol C. Gould, ed., *The Information Web: Ethical and Social Implications of Computer Networking* (Boulder, CO: Westview Press, 1989).

6 Carol C. Gould, "Network Ethics: Access, Consent, and the Informed Community," in *The Information Web*, 11–19.

7 Another focus there was on these issues in the context of scientific research.

the QUBE system, that had recently been introduced, I noted not only the dangers of infringements to privacy and confidentiality but also the potential for manipulation and fraud that these uses posed. Another focus was on inequality of access to information, which, I argued, gives rise to a phenomenon that I called "informational poverty."[8] I proposed two ethical principles for computer networking: (1) free and informed consent to the use of information about oneself – a new application of this principle, initially discussed in medical ethics, to information use; and (2) prima facie equal access to information and to computer networks,[9] qualified by the relevance of the informational access to a given community of users.[10] The two principles can be combined in the following heuristic formulation: "[m]aximum sharing of information and maximally equal access compatible with the preservation of the value of privacy, as protected by the requirement of free and informed consent."[11]

Globalization and the New Media

In view of the changes that have taken place since that early Internet period, we can ask whether the early analysis still holds up and also what new issues need to be taken into account in developing democratic uses of these media. Probably the most salient new dimension is the increasing rate of globalization, discussed in previous chapters, both in the scope and uses of information and communication technologies and in the emergence of transborder democratic (or potentially democratic) networks. As noted, these include not only the most obvious case of the European Union but also more delimited networks that cross traditional borders – concerning shared ecological interests (e.g., regarding overfishing or toxic dumping); concerning economic production or trade (e.g., between indigenous peoples and Western consumers, or socially responsible investment); or, in a different way, concerning organization and outreach on the part of global NGOs or activist social movements (e.g., the World Social Forum).

Along with this globalization has come an even more pronounced "digital divide," the term introduced to denote the gulf between the information-rich and the information-poor. In the increasingly global

[8] Gould, "Network Ethics," 11–19.
[9] Ibid., 25–31.
[10] Ibid., 30.
[11] Ibid., 33.

context, this divide pertains not only to disparities of access to the Net between well off and less well off within the postindustrial societies themselves, but also to even more pronounced disparities between these and developing countries. Thus in her book *Digital Divide*, Pippa Norris observes the following:

> The evidence indicates that some developing nations such as Malaysia, Brazil, and Taiwan have made substantial progress in the knowledge economy. But average rates of Internet penetration have grown sluggishly, at best, in most developing nations.... [T]he global divide in Internet access is substantial and expanding: About 87 percent of people online live in postindustrial societies. The contrasts worldwide are sharp: More than half of all Americans now surf the Internet compared with 0.1 percent of Nigerians. There are currently twice as many users in Sweden than across the vast continent of Sub-Saharan Africa. In considering alternative explanations of this phenomenon, the evidence strongly suggests that economic development is the main factor driving access to digital technologies, so that the Internet reflects and reinforces traditional inequalities between rich and poor societies.[12]

Other authors further characterize the relations between the information-rich industrialized states and the information-poor Third World in terms of "cyberimperialism" or even "cybercolonialism." Here what is most often meant is a sort of economic imperialism via the Net, where corporate control over software, specialized information, and access to the Net delimits access to the elites who can afford to pay for it, including especially the "symbolic analysts" in the postindustrial North.[13] Yet another aspect of this "cybercolonialism" is of course the current domination of English as the language of the Net. As Deborah Tong puts it,

> What is taken for granted is always apparent to those who are not in its possession. Upon finally connecting to the network, the first thing a member of a developing nation would undoubtedly detect is Cyberia's lingua franca: English. English is the mother tongue of data. It encodes 80 percent of all computer messages and data content even though only slightly more than a tenth of the world's population speaks the language (including both primary and secondary language speakers).[14]

[12] Pippa Norris, *Digital Divide: Civic Engagement, Information Poverty, and the Internet Worldwide* (Cambridge: Cambridge University Press, 2001), 15.

[13] Frank Louis Rusciano, "The Three Faces of Cyberimperialism," in *Cyberimperialism? Global Relations in the New Electronic Frontier*, ed. Bosah Ebo (Westport, CT: Praeger, 2001), 19–24.

[14] Deborah Tong, "Cybercolonialism: Speeding along the Superhighway or Stalling on a Beaten Track?" in *Cyberimperialism?* 71.

It follows, as she points out, that members of developing countries who want to participate or work on the Net must be bilingual.[15] This analysis suggests that we need to add a conception of cultural imperialism to that of economic imperialism if we are to understand the restrictions on Net access in the present more global context.

It is probably worth pointing out that the problems of access are not exhausted in the raw figures regarding differential connectivity such as those given here. There are also serious discrepancies in speed of access and in the availability of advanced computers, discrepancies that further exacerbate the differences in sheer access itself. Well-off people in well-off countries obviously have advantages because of these faster modalities, which facilitate their connections and the scope of their information gathering. And, as Anthony Wilhelm and others have stressed, access is not only a matter of economic well-being, which permits computer ownership, but is also a matter of literacy and of educational levels sufficient to enable full use of these information modalities. The differences in this regard apply within given nation-states, as well as among them, or more globally.

It is clear, then, that a reflection on the new developments in the globalization of communication and information networks shows that the problem of achieving equal access to information and to networks remains a very serious one, if not entirely intractable. This necessarily qualifies any optimism we might have about the power of such networks to facilitate cyberdemocracy, since without substantially equal access to information, where this information is one of the conditions of meaningful political participation, the equality built into the concept of democracy itself cannot be realized.

Indeed, we might become even more concerned about this accessibility and inequality when we consider the growing commercialization of the Net, as described, for example, by Robert McChesney in his *Rich Media, Poor Democracy*.[16] In fact, it seems likely that this commercialization has intensified since the date of that book's original publication in 1999. Against the idea that "the Internet, or more broadly, digital communication networks, will set us free," McChesney characterizes the growing dominance of Time Warner, Disney, and other media conglomerates in

---

[15] Ibid., 72.
[16] Robert W. McChesney, *Rich Media, Poor Democracy: Communication Politics in Dubious Times* (New York: The New Press, 2000), especially Chapter 3.

this domain, along with the new threats from cable and television companies in the provision of broadband services, thereby potentially controlling Internet portals. With the growth of commercial websites, there is the additional possibility of blending commercial and editorial content, so that users may find it hard to distinguish them.

To concretize these issues, perhaps it is worth citing McChesney's description of the case of Time Warner:

> In addition to its activities as a cable company, Time Warner produces nearly two hundred websites, all of which are designed to provide what it terms an "advertiser-friendly environment," and it aggressively promotes to its audiences through its existing media. Its CNN website is now available in Swedish and other languages. Time Warner uses its websites to go after the youth market, to attract sports fans, and to provide entertainment content similar to that of its "old" media. . . . It has a joint website with Procter & Gamble.[17]

We might also take note of McChesney's own proposal for the democratic adoption of public policies to regulate the Internet and its commercial development, and especially to set aside broadband for public interest programming and network use. His argument is that there is no viable alternative to such public policy if the new networks are to serve genuinely public interests.

In the face of the sort of overwhelming commercial power just described, where corporations even more than governments have a strong interest in developing profiles of their customers together with their information and communication preferences, the old recommendation that I made of requiring free and informed consent as a basis for protecting individual privacy rights may seem hopelessly utopian. Nonetheless, the idea has resurfaced in regard to regulating individuals' control of information about themselves. Indeed, people are routinely given some choice in regard to the uses of some of this information, especially in regard to its sale or other distribution from one company to the next, and the limits on the use of "cookies." Nonetheless, there are significant costs to individuals who choose to fully opt out of providing such information in the first place, and there is certainly a lack of transparency in the uses made of this information. Thus the consent, where it exists, is not usually informed and hence is not very free. It remains to be seen whether there will be further moves to seriously implement some sort of control over personal information.

[17] Ibid., 176–177.

Does the Net Facilitate Democratic Decision Making?

Let us now turn to the central issue of assessing the possibilities that the Net or the global information infrastructure affords for facilitating democratic decision making, both on and off the Net. I have presented the two extreme views that one encounters in the literature. The more prominent, very positive outlook asserts that the decentralization of the Net and its openness to multiple and direct two-way communications among participants ideally suit it for democratic participation, which is likewise supposed to be open to all, at least to all citizens. Of course, the Net does not normally recognize nation-state boundaries, and this distinctive feature has some interesting implications, to which I will return.

The more negative view of cyberdemocracy by contrast tends to emphasize its isolating features and the relative insularity of participants. Here it is correctly observed that individuals most often choose to communicate online with like-minded others, with those who share their interests and also their biases. The crucial feature of democratic deliberation, in which one opens one's views to rational discussion with others who often disagree, is clearly missing from many of these online communities. Deborah Johnson puts it this way:

[T]here is the possibility that individuals will become even more isolated from diverse perspectives and people than they are now. Why deal with those with whom you have disagreements? Why deal with your difficult and "different" neighbors, when you can simply avoid them? Why expose yourself to news perspectives that suggest something wrong with the views you presently hold? In the past, shared geographic space has necessitated contact and joint deliberation. It has compelled diverse people to figure out how to live together. That necessity becomes weaker and weaker when the infrastructure of so many activities is global.[18]

Yet the fact that the Net can facilitate voluntary communication among like-minded people with shared interests may in fact contribute to the strengthening of what political philosophers have referred to as civil society, or in Arendt's and Habermas's terms, the public sphere. Participation in public forums, chat rooms, and email lists can establish bonds between people who share perspectives and clarify their views, and can help them to organize around issues and communicate their perspectives to others, including those holding positions of power. As Norris puts it, "[D]igital

---

[18] Deborah G. Johnson, "Is the Global Information Infrastructure a Democratic Technology?" in *Cyberethics*, eds. Robert M. Baird et al. (Amherst, NY: Prometheus, 2000), 317.

technologies have the capacity to strengthen the institutions of civic society mediating between citizens and the state."[19] In her view, this capacity especially benefits "insurgent organizations," which possess fewer traditional advantages, and, in this way, digital politics can level the playing field for "transnational advocacy networks, alternative social movements, protest organizations and minor parties, such as those concerned with environmentalism, globalization, human rights," and so on.[20] Furthermore, Norris holds that "reducing the costs of information and communication minimizes some, although not all, of the significant barriers to effective political participation at an individual level."[21]

Along these lines, we see the beginnings of substantial input into U.S. national politics by means of the Net in such organizations as MoveOn.org, which greatly simplify and thereby facilitate the process of communicating with congressional representatives via online petitions and letter-writing campaigns, and open up the possibilities for large-scale online polling and perhaps also referenda. Even more recently, we have witnessed the first U.S. political campaign – that of Howard Dean – that established itself and initially flourished through Internet organizing and fundraising. The widespread use of email lists, which facilitates large-scale discussions and the passing along of references between friends or strangers, thus presents a networking model with considerable potential power for politics. Such a network model, in which there are only interconnecting nodes with no center, has also been adopted by socially critical groups, not only for the diffusion of information, in which anyone can post messages or add new links, but also for their mobilization for protest. This organizing activity self-consciously attempts to be "horizontal," that is, nonhierarchical, consensual, and nondominating. Although important decisions are often left to face-to-face meetings among (rotating) representatives, much of the planning and organizing proceeds through the Net, in a way designed to invite the participation of those at a distance and to remain open to the diversity of their contributions to the movement.

We can grant the benefits for the public sphere that may ensue from such increasingly global connections among mostly like-minded people.

---

[19] Norris, *Digital Divide*, 19.
[20] Ibid.
[21] Ibid., 23. See also James N. Rosenau, "Information Technologies and the Skills, Networks, and Structures that Sustain World Affairs," in *Information Technologies and Global Politics*, eds. James Rosenau and J. P. Singh (Albany: State University of New York, 2002), especially 283.

But what can we say about the deliberative and participative aspects of democracy, in which it is supposed to involve reasoned discussion among people who do not share many individual interests, although they share some common ends as members of the same political community, or else share certain defined needs and interests across the borders of communities? The Net has so far not provided conclusive results in such contexts. Even the activist networks just described are still in search of ways to use the Net to delineate shared goals through discussion and to arrive at decisions across the group.[22] So far, the Net seems strong at disseminating information and facilitating communication among widespread individuals but not as strong at establishing substantial agreements, even among like-minded participants. As for connections among diverse groups of people within given political communities, cases do abound of discussions of a political nature on various websites – on message boards, chatrooms, and forums, even on sites oriented to ostensibly nonpolitical matters. Yet these have so far remained without clear ties to political decision making off the Net. We can say that at present, these discussions primarily serve to reflect and sometimes shape public opinion. Although this is hardly insignificant, it misses the key point that deliberation is more than the mere expression of opinion, but a give-and-take in which views are shared and possibly transformed, in such a way that they eventuate in, or at least influence, the actual decision-making process. Perhaps such decision making must remain mainly face-to-face, or perhaps new modalities of conversing, refining opinions, and coming to decisions will soon emerge on the Net itself.

A potentially very positive feature of networked interaction is its global character – that it offers to transcend the limits of fixed and given democratic communities of a geographical sort. Although this aspect is sometimes regarded more negatively, I see it has having the potential to help deal with emerging problems, both ecological and environmental, of a transborder or even global nature. Leaving aside the issue of agreeing on the establishment of new political units of a transnational sort, the more globalized participation that the Net makes possible can in fact facilitate the expression of views by all those affected by a given problem or policy – including those at a distance – even if they are not members of the particular geographically defined community or nation-state and thus are not immediately subject to its jurisdiction. Perhaps it will be possible in

---

[22] See Naomi Klein, "Does protest need a vision? *New Statesman*, Vol. 13, Issue 612 (July 3, 2000): 23–25.

the future to define modes of input and collective decision suitable for these more far-flung people or groups who are impacted at a distance by a nation-state's or multilateral's policies and programs.

In discussing the Net's potential for enhancing democratic participation, the argument here suggests that we need to distinguish three types of network communities:

1. There are voluntary communities or associations of like-minded individuals, which the Net already reinforces and even potentiates; in the political sphere, the communication among these individuals can contribute to activist organizing and transnational advocacy groups (not all of them positive, of course). These networks are often more international or global than heretofore and hence can be classified as a type of intersociative network, using the concept introduced earlier in this work.

2. There are the more traditional predefined political communities made up of diverse individuals who understand themselves to belong to these communities or nation-states. In this context, new modes of facilitating deliberation and collective decision making are needed, if cyberdemocracy is to be realized.

3. There are the newly emergent transborder and regional communities or networks that share some of the features of each of the first two but have certain distinctive features. The individuals within them are not yet defined as belonging to a given jurisdiction, but these groups may not be made up of individuals all of whom share some particular interest in common in the familiar sense. These networks may be organized around political issues, such as dealing with common ecological problems, or they may be economically based or social in nature. Of particular interest here are those communities or networks made up of people who are aware of being affected similarly by regional or global phenomena. As discussed in the preceding part of this work, these people have certain rights of participating in decisions about these transborder phenomena, even if they are not citizens of the relevant nation-state or members of the given community.

My intuition is that the Net is especially well suited to enhancing the participation of groups of this latter sort in political decisions. How this would work remains to be determined, and it will depend in part on the actual emergence of communities of this sort and their own articulation of their needs, aspirations, and interests. We might suggest that significant opportunities for democratic participation may be provided by new technologies that provide more full-fledged (and user-friendly) video dimensions, which could model face-to-face interactions, where desired, among participating individuals or groups. The present text-based modes of networking, by contrast, may not be the preferred mode of communication for all those who want to participate. Adding the direct visual representation of others might also help in taking them and their views more seriously and more personally. Yet the problems of setting the agenda and collecting and mediating among divergent views, as well as the difficulties due to dominant personalities and other such factors, would remain despite these new technologies.

We might add that while networking technologies may facilitate less hierarchical modes of decision and open new possibilities for democratic participation among geographically dispersed individuals, they do not, of course, necessitate such a development. Contrary to the optimistic views expressed by commentators such as James Rosenau to the effect that networks introduce horizontal modalities of interaction that contrast with older hierarchical modalities,[23] we can observe that these networks themselves are often used in hierarchical and antidemocratic ways. For example, websites may be controlled by webmasters, or discussion boards by moderators, or email lists by those who select members and post content. In addition, Internet services such as AOL or Yahoo exercise control over content, and employers often use the Net to monitor employees. In such cases, the old problem of control over decision making by technological elites rather than by users again comes to the fore. Thus we can conclude that active and self-conscious efforts are required to develop and use networks in ways that provide equal access to potential participants in discussions and that facilitate democratic interaction by the users. Otherwise, we can expect that networks will continue to be turned primarily to commercial uses or will be utilized with excessively centralized controls that in fact vitiate these increasingly global democratic possibilities.

[23] Rosenau, "Information Technologies," 281–284.

12

Terrorism, Empathy, and Democracy

In this final chapter, I want to focus on a key issue for international ethics: the normative understanding of terrorism, which has become increasingly global in its character and impact. More specifically, I consider the relation between terrorism and the concept of empathy, particularly as it emerges from feminist theory and as I have discussed it earlier in this work, and I also place this analysis in the context of the preceding discussion of democracy. I suggest that there is a close connection between the concepts of empathy and democracy, and I make some remarks about the relation of these to both terrorism and the possible responses to it.

Defining Terrorism

To concretize the discussion that follows, it is helpful to begin with a brief review of some definitions of terrorism, a widely used but rather muddy concept. The numerous definitions in the literature seem only to agree that terrorism involves violence or the threat of violence. Beyond that, there are important disagreements as to whether it is limited to the targeting of people who are noncombatants or also extends to combatants, whether it should be limited to violence perpetrated by nonstate actors or also encompass state terrorism, and whether we need to make reference to its purposes as part of the definition.

According to Michael Walzer, "Terrorism is the deliberate killing of innocent people, at random, in order to spread fear through a whole population and force the hand of its political leaders."[1] For Walzer, it

---

[1] Michael Walzer, "Five Questions about Terrorism," *Dissent* (Winter 2002): 5.

includes national liberation terrorism as well as the state terrorism of authoritarian governments spreading fear and stifling dissent among their own people and, finally, war terrorism, such as the killing of civilians (e.g., at Hiroshima) in such large numbers as to force a government to surrender. In his view, "[t]he common element is the targeting of people who are, in both the military and political senses, noncombatants."[2] Similarly, Jessica Stern takes violence against noncombatants as the core notion in her frightening account of terrorism via weapons of mass destruction. She writes, "I define terrorism as an act or threat of violence against noncombatants with the objective of exacting revenge, intimidating, or otherwise influencing an audience."[3] She continues, "This definition avoids limiting perpetrator or purpose. It allows for a range of possible actors (states or their surrogates, international groups, or a single individual), for all putative goals (political, religious, economic), and for murder for its own sake.[4]

Others, such as Bruce Hoffman in a comprehensive review of the uses of the term "terrorism" in his book *Inside Terrorism*, limit it to violent acts "perpetrated by a subnational group or non-state entity."[5] On his view,

> terrorism is ineluctably political in aims and motives; violent – or, equally important, threatens violence; designed to have far-reaching psychological repercussions beyond the immediate victim or target; conducted by an organization with an identifiable chain of command or conspiratorial cell structure (whose members wear no uniform or identifying insignia); and perpetrated by a subnational group or non-state entity.[6]

Gordon Graham, in his survey work *Ethics and International Affairs*, helpfully places an emphasis on the terrorists' purpose of controlling people. He writes, "Terror consists in the causing of widespread fear and alarm by means of violence as a way of unsettling and hence controlling other people. . . . The point of terror is to ensure that the *will* to oppose is broken, by breaking the will itself."[7]

Arguing along different lines, Andrew Valls follows Virginia Held in adopting perhaps the broadest definition. He writes, "[W]e can with great plausibility simply define *terrorism* as a form of political violence, as Held does: 'I [see] terrorism as a form of violence to achieve political

---

[2] Ibid., 5–6.
[3] Jessica Stern, *The Ultimate Terrorists* (Cambridge, MA: Harvard University Press, 2000), 11.
[4] Ibid.
[5] Bruce Hoffman, *Inside Terrorism* (New York: Columbia University Press, 1998), 43.
[6] Ibid.
[7] Gordon Graham, *Ethics and International Affairs* (New York: Blackwell, 1997), 123–124.

goals, where creating fear is usually high among the intended effects.'"[8]
"This is a promising approach," Valls continues, "though I would drop as
nonessential the stipulation that terrorism is usually intended to spread
fear."[9] Valls goes on to explicitly include damage to property among potential terrorist acts, whereas Held restricts it to harm to people. Both
are opposed to restricting terrorism to actions against noncombatants,
with Held emphasizing the case of the blowing up of the Marine bar-
racks in Lebanon in October 1983 as a terrorist attack. She might also
have referred to the Irgun terrorist attacks on British military targets before the Israeli War of Independence. Finally, in a different vein, Robin
Morgan proposes that "[t]he terrorist is the logical incarnation of patriarchal politics in a technological world."[10] While probably not intended
as a definition per se, her conception is suggestive and interesting.

Although this issue of definition may seem esoteric, it is in fact of
considerable importance, since if terrorism is understood to necessarily
target noncombatants, then it *eo ipso* seems to run afoul of the *jus in bello*
restriction against targeting "innocents," making terrorism always unjus-
tified. It is clear, then, that these definitional matters have important normative consequences, some of which I return to in the following discussion. However, my central focus in this chapter begins where definitions
leave off. My interest, in particular, lies in the applicability of the concepts
of empathy and democracy to terrorist acts and terrorists. For this purpose, I give special attention, at least in the first section concerning the
role of empathy, to the most prominent case of terrorism that affected
the United States: the World Trade Center attacks of September 11th.
Since this largely involved terrorism directed against noncombatants or
civilians, in this part of the analysis we can take this characteristic as
given.

Terrorism and Empathy

The attacks on the WTC, in which more than 2,700 people were killed,
some of whose bodies were never found, constituted a grievous set of
terrorist acts as well as a profound injustice involving gross violation of the

---

[8] Virginia Held, "Terrorism, Rights, and Political Goals," in *Violence, Terrorism, and Justice,*
eds. R. G. Frey and Christopher W. Morris (Cambridge: Cambridge University Press,
1991), 64.

[9] Andrew Valls, *Ethics in International Affairs* (Lanham, MD: Rowman & Littlefield, 2000),
67.

[10] Robin Morgan, *The Demon Lover: The Roots of Terrorism* (New York: Washington Square
Press, 2001), 33.

human rights of the victims. Yet we can observe that there was not only the violation of rights but also what we might call a wholesale lack of human fellow-feeling, an absence of caring about or empathy with the potential victims on the part of the terrorists. Pursuing this line of thinking, we can observe the apparent callousness of the perpetrators, unconcerned about the innocents affected – for the victims and their survivors. What could lead people to do such a thing? There are two questions here: one a more descriptive or explanatory one, and the other, a more ethically oriented one, concerning what must be lacking at a moral level to permit such actions. I want to focus more on the latter question, although not purely from the standpoint of the ethics of care but also in terms of a broader perspective of political morality. Yet the answer to the second question inevitably takes us by way of the first as well, that is, the question of motivations.

Let us begin with the suggestive concept introduced by Hannah Arendt, namely, the idea of the "banality of evil," which she proposed as a way of understanding Adolf Eichmann in his role during the Holocaust. Can we, in fact, understand Mohammed Atta and the other hijackers in these terms as well? In *The Demon Lover*, Morgan approvingly cites Martha Crenshaw's general analysis of terrorism, which, according to Morgan, "coolly dismisses the 'terrorists are deranged' theorists: 'What limited data we have on individual terrorists... suggests that the outstanding common characteristic of terrorists is their normality.' "[11] Certainly the pictures of the 9/11 hijackers withdrawing funds at the ATM the night before their flights suggest this sort of normality or even banality, as did their apparently routine existence in Florida and elsewhere attending flight schools, and so on. And, to the degree that these terrorists followed the orders of higher-ups, we are also reminded of the authoritarianism to which Arendt also referred.

But what about the image of Mohammed Atta and some of his associates in the nightclub shortly before the terrorist flights, in which they carried on with lap-dancing stripteasers? Is this evocative of the banality of evil as well? Perhaps, inasmuch as it is a recognizable behavior practiced by a subgroup of the male population. Yet Mohammed Atta's rather unusual strictures in his will that his genitals not be touched without gloves and that no pregnant women attend his funeral and so forth, while not unique among devout Muslims, certainly do not seem simply "banal."

[11] Ibid., 42, citing Martha Crenshaw, "The Causes of Terrorism," *Comparative Politics* (July 1981): 379–399.

By contrast, a few elements may be taken to be common to the 9/11 terrorists and to officers such as Eichmann and thus may suggest the relevant banality: in particular, the use of technology and technological rationality to nefarious ends and, more generally, the dehumanization of the subject that characterizes both contexts. Overall, however, it seems that, while several other terrorist cases can usefully be characterized in terms of a routinization and bureaucratization of violence – or as Morgan puts it, its normalization – the WTC attacks are not entirely successfully described in these terms.

Yet, another aspect of Hannah Arendt's account, which she introduced in part to help explain the phenomenon of the banality of evil, is quite helpful here. Specifically, some of her more philosophical suggestions about thinking and judging appear relevant to understanding these terrorist acts, and perhaps other cases as well. In her magnum opus, *The Life of the Mind*,[12] Arendt took off from the concept of the banality of evil to investigate *thinking* because, in her view, Eichmann and others like him lacked this, above everything. Their problem, she suggested, was that they did not *think*. By this she did not mean an absence of contemplative thought. Instead, Arendt suggests (in her separate "Lectures on Kant's Political Philosophy," published posthumously as an appendix to *The Life of the Mind*) that there may well be a defect of judging here. Arendt focuses on the judging of particulars, using imagination and common sense, as a way of understanding political community, thereby going beyond the analysis of aesthetic judgment, which was Kant's central intent in his third critique. And in place of identifying an explicitly moral defect in evildoers – which could be approached in terms of Kant's Second Critique, namely, of Practical Reason – Arendt proposes that we focus on the important ability of imaginatively bringing the others close to one and of putting oneself in the place of another.

In her interesting elaboration of Kant's approach, Arendt explains this idea as follows:

The "enlargement of the mind" plays a crucial role in the *Critique of Judgment*. It is accomplished by "comparing our judgment with the possible rather than the actual judgment of others, and by putting ourselves in the place of any other man." The faculty which makes this possible is called imagination. . . . Critical thinking is possible only where the standpoint of all others are open to inspection. . . . [By] force of imagination it makes the others present and thus moves potentially in a

---

[12] Hannah Arendt, *The Life of the Mind*, one-volume edition (New York: Harcourt Brace, 1989).

space which is public, open to all sides; in other words, it adopts the position of Kant's world citizen. To think with the enlarged mentality – that means you train your imagination to go visiting.[13]

In these terms, then, we might propose that the 9/11 terrorists evidenced a failure of imagination and of judgment. Their imaginative use of technology against itself notwithstanding, the 9/11 terrorists utterly failed to consider the standpoint of their victims and to identify with these others as striving and feeling beings like themselves.

Yet, perhaps unfortunately (from a feminist perspective), Arendt goes on to explicitly distinguish this sort of imaginative representation to oneself of the others, and the consideration of their standpoint, from the phenomenon of empathy. She writes:

> I must warn you here of a very common and easy misunderstanding. The trick of critical thinking does not consist in an enormously enlarged empathy through which I could know what actually goes on in the mind of all others. To think, according to Kant's understanding of enlightenment, means *Selbstdenken*, to think for oneself.... To accept what goes on in the minds of those whose "standpoint" (actually, the place where they stand, the conditions they are subject to, always different from one individual to the next, one class or group as compared to another) is not my own would mean no more than to accept passively their thought, that is, to exchange their prejudices for the prejudices proper to my own station. "Enlarged thought" is the result of...disregarding what we usually call self-interest.... [The] larger the realm in which the enlightened individual is able to move, from standpoint to standpoint, the more "general" will be his thinking. This generality, however, is not the generality of concept.... It is on the contrary closely connected with particulars, the particular conditions of the standpoints you have to go through in order to arrive at your own "general standpoint." This general standpoint we mentioned before as impartiality.[14]

We might propose that Arendt's critique of the relevance of empathy is misplaced here, in that, contrary to her interpretation, it should not be taken, even in extended form, to require actually knowing what goes on in the mind of all others (something that would be impossible) or accepting their viewpoint. Rather, it entails listening to others and responsibly (as well as responsively) reconstructing their views for oneself, and doing so with fellow-feeling. Yet Arendt's way of posing a requirement for a certain sort of judging in politics may actually help to address a standard objection to the empathy account, which feminists have suggested is drawn in the first instance from women's (and men's) experiences of

---

[13] Arendt, *The Life of the Mind*, 257.
[14] Ibid., 257–258.

caring for particular others. This objection has been that the sort of particularistic thinking involved in empathy is precisely what is impossible at the more universalistic level of politics, which instead requires a more abstract treatment of groups in a so-called public domain, in which people must be regarded as abstractly equal as a condition for their being treated justly. Arendt's approach, although unreasonably narrowing the concept of empathy and therefore rejecting it, in fact suggests to us an important interpretation of the sort of empathic understanding that is required.

We need, I would say (following her), an enlarged thought that cultivates a general perspective by critically working through particulars, and this by imaginatively taking individuals into account, thinking about them, bringing them close to one, and presenting the other's perspective – seriously, although sometimes critically – to oneself. As to whether or not the general standpoint is rightly called impartiality is a difficult question. But I believe that such a transformed appropriation of Arendt helps to illuminate how an empathic perspective in fact can generate a more general perspective. On my own view, this more general perspective is actually one of equality (including an equality of rights) in a sense that recognizes differences, rather than impartiality. I would suggest, too, that beginning from empathy and care, and proceeding in the way proposed, we can in fact arrive at a recognition of common humanity and equality of rights.

Arendt herself suggests how this judgment of particulars moves toward a conception of common humanity, in Kant's version at least. She poses the issue this way: "The chief difficulty in judgment is that it is 'the faculty of thinking the particular'; but to think means to generalize, hence it is the faculty of mysteriously combining the particular and the general."[15] But since "I cannot judge one particular by another particular, in order to determine its worth I need a *tertium quid* or a *tertium comparationis*."[16] She proposes that Kant sometimes finds this in "the idea of an original compact of mankind as a whole and derived from this idea the notion of humanity, of what actually constitutes the humanness of human beings, living and dying in this world, on this earth that is a globe, which they inhabit in common, share in common, in the succession of generations."[17] She also favorably notes Kant's other solution to this problem,

[15] Ibid., 271.
[16] Ibid.
[17] Ibid.

namely, the idea of the "exemplary validity" of a particular, "which in its very particularity reveals the generality which otherwise could not be defined. Courage is like Achilles, etc."[18]

This suggests, then, that the kind of thinking or judging that is morally and politically required is a humanistic reflection, or what Arendt also regards, following Kant in this Third Critique, as "common sense" (*sensus communis*, the sense of a human community), in which the other's similarly human perspective is taken into account, but where difference can also be noted. The crucial thing for Arendt is the mental act of imaginatively presenting others and the perspective of others to oneself, and it can be noted that this process has only global limits and does not stop short with those most like oneself or with whom one personally interacts. In this context, we can speak not only of empathy but also of solidarity, as discussed earlier in this work. Although it is unreasonable to suppose that people will feel a solidarity with all the interests of other individuals or groups, particularly inasmuch as some of these conflict with their own, nonetheless a sort of human solidarity is certainly possible and necessary, where this suggests an empathic understanding of the common needs and interests of others and a standing with them in view of these. It is also possible to feel a solidarity through differences, where the distinctive situation of the others is empathically understood, including their unique challenges and conflicts, or again where the growing interdependence with these different others comes to be recognized.

In terms of the concept of empathy as developed here, one can go on to propose that those engaging in certain extreme terrorist acts may, in fact, suffer from a lack of political imagination and a narrow interest in their own concerns. While they clearly identify with a community of their own, it seems incorrect to hold, as Bruce Hoffman does, that "[t]he terrorist is fundamentally an altruist."[19] On the contrary, as the September 11th case suggests, terrorists can strikingly fail to consider and to identify with their victims, in view of their common human needs. Of course, one could object that this is the case for those engaged in wars as well, especially those in which "innocents" are targeted. Indeed, the lack of empathy of the sort characterized here is widespread. But terrorism – whether nonstate or state – seems especially problematic in this respect, to the degree that it is understood to involve deliberately aiming to kill noncombatants.

---

[18] Ibid., 272.
[19] Hoffman, *Inside Terrorism*, 43.

But what about responses to terrorism? Does empathy or an enlarged understanding play an important role there? To address this question, we need to introduce a further analysis of the concept of empathy. First, it is worth noting again that this usage departs from the usual one in which empathy is held to be applicable in a one-on-one sense; in Meyers's terms, "To empathize with another in this sense is to construct in imagination an experience resembling that of the other person. . . . [It involves] imaginatively reconstructing another's feelings."[20] In contrast to this sort of empathic thinking, which is possible only between single individuals, the Arendtian-influenced model of political imagination, like the conception of solidarity, broadens this understanding of others to involve a consideration of diverse viewpoints, including social standpoints.

Another useful analytical distinction between aspects of empathy is that between an identification with the humanity and the common needs of others, on the one hand, and a more cognitive interpretation in which what is stressed is empathy with the perspective of others, with their point of view. In either of these senses, though, empathy or the representative thinking discussed here does not entail an uncritical and fully accepting identification with the viewpoint of others. Meyers writes along similar lines that

empathy by no means entails sharing the other's point of view or endorsing the other's state of mind. Although we usually reserve our empathic exertions for people whom we like and with whom we hope to maintain relationships, nothing in principle bars one from empathizing with someone for whom one feels no affection. Psychotherapists and social workers do not always like their clients. Indeed, they may find a client's values or conduct repugnant.[21]

Yet, to the degree that empathy begins with concern for another, as Meyers and others have it,[22] it may seem inapplicable to our relation to the terrorists themselves. Nonetheless, this analysis certainly points to the relevance of empathy and representative thinking in regard to the people for whom terrorists often claim to speak. When people are experiencing economic and social deprivation or humiliation, empathizing with their suffering, or imaginatively reconstructing their experiences and their points of view, is clearly in order. And it has been argued by Lloyd Dumas, for example, that although terrorists themselves are often middle class, those from whom they may be able to draw support are

[20] Diana T. Meyers, *Subjection and Subjectivity* (New York: Routledge, 1994), 32–33.
[21] Ibid., 34.
[22] Ibid.

often themselves oppressed.[23] Furthermore, it is undoubtedly useful to attempt to understand the other's perspective from the inside, as well as the conflictual context out of which it emerges, which in this case might give some insight into the causes of, and sources of support for, the terrorist acts. This sort of understanding allows us to construct for ourselves an idea of how the people themselves, and those around them, perceive what they're trying to do.

But this use differs from the primary ethical use of the idea of empathy or of political imagination that I have emphasized here. To the degree that it involves identification with the humanness of other people, rather than with the particulars of their perspective or outlook, what is primarily required by way of a response to terrorism is to address the needs of impoverished or humiliated populations; in this way, we might help to obviate the terrorism that may sometimes make use of these factors and thrive in their midst. In this sense, supporting economic, social, and political development in currently authoritarian and subjugated countries is required, both on practical grounds and on grounds of the value of empathy and care itself, as discussed here. And as I argue next, beyond this attention to social and economic needs, what is necessary is also democratic participation, in a specific sense.

Before turning to some of the connections between terrorism and democracy, it may be useful to reflect on the empathy–democracy connection. Empathy is a concept that derives from the interpersonal realm and, even if necessary to a degree in politics, is not sufficient, even for taking others into account. Rather, the ideal way of doing that in politics is somewhat different, at least from Arendt's analysis of representing others to oneself in imagination. It involves instead actually listening to others' own accounts of themselves and their needs, concerns, and interests, and having a dialogue with them. And the political form of such listening is, in fact, *democracy*. Although we clearly cannot require that we hear from everyone affected by any given potential course of action in order to imaginatively consider their point of view (contra Habermas), it is a desideratum to consider the views, if not of all who are possibly affected (which will extend through the generations), then of all who are coparticipants in the networks of engagement, with respect to issues that concern life in common. Where possible, then, it is essential to actually hear from these others and, where this is not possible, to responsibly

---

[23] Lloyd J. Dumas, "Is Development an Effective Way to Fight Terrorism?" in *War after September 11*, ed. Verna V. Gehring (Lanham, MD: Rowman & Littlefield, 2003), 65–74.

present their interests to oneself in imagination. This quasi-Arendtian account thus supplements the earlier discussion of the role of participation in decisions concerning common activities and of the requisite democratic input by those more widely affected by these decisions.

Inasmuch as a cosmopolitan perspective is implied here, it will have to be one built up from particulars, as the discussion of Arendt has already suggested – what I previously called a "concrete universality," rather than an abstract one. What is needed, moreover, is not simply the empty generality of the concept of the human, but a universality

1. constructed from the various particular social relations in which people are engaged, without arbitrary barriers, and
2. in which attention is given to the real human needs and desires of these others, in a way, moreover,
3. that is nondominating, by actually taking seriously the others' own presentation of these needs and interests. Hence,
4. where otherness is preserved and seen as the ground for an equality that recognizes and respects differences.

This sort of interaction can also perhaps usefully be extended to the dialogue about the interpretation of values and norms, including such crucial ones as human rights themselves, as I propose in Chapter 2. This conception of universality also has the potential for a certain practical impact, in the support it lends to an intercultural perspective, as discussed in Part II, and to new crossborder or intersociative democracies, considered in Part III.

On the view developed here, then, we can discern an integral connection between empathy and equal rights (as between care and justice, discussed previously). This goes beyond the more standard observation that caring within families is a precondition for people to appreciate and respect equal rights in politics. Rather, the proposal is that the recognition of equal rights – say, of human rights – grows out of a sort of empathic and reflective understanding of others, including those globally situated, as alike and yet as different from oneself, based in part on the emergence of increasingly universalistic social relations in practice.

It is worth clarifying that the sort of empathy and enlargement of thought that is needed is not the unique preserve of women, although it has been a main concern of women in their family relationships. Clearly, the emergence of a caring and empathic outlook in both sexes would be salutary, with caring fathers as much as mothers needed as role models for both boys and girls. On a more public level, such an outlook toward those at a distance has shown itself in antiwar movements, with women often playing especially vital roles. At the same time, we need to be careful of too easy a move from the idea of women's caring to an antiwar perspective. Along these lines, while calling on women to redefine security as something like what is now being called "human security" in place of the traditional masculinist military interpretation, Ann Tickner (perhaps too hastily) dismisses as a "myth" the association of women with peace, noting the evidence of women's support for men's wars in many societies.[24]

Likewise, we need to acknowledge the growing equal opportunity for women in the field of terrorism itself. From the female cadres in domestic terrorist groups of the 1970s to the recent female Palestinian suicide bombers, terrorism has not been the sole province of men, although they predominate in it. (According to Morgan, 80 percent of terrorists have been male.[25]) Yet women's motives seem often to be different from those of men. In addition to Morgan's proposal that women sometimes seek to please the terrorist men they are involved with, others have suggested that women in oppressed or alienated communities may come to support militarism and even terrorism, if not actually planning it themselves, because they see it as a way to protect their families, homes, and communities. By contrast, in such societies – often characterized by economic or political insecurity – men's support of and participation in terrorist activities are rarely justified in these terms, but rather by a rhetoric of building a society based on religious or political ideals.[26]

Yet it is also clear that many women respond to terrorism or militarism by becoming activists for peace, again often on the grounds of their responsibilities to protect their families' well-being. As Caiazza observes, "In the Middle East, Latin America, and Northern Ireland, for example, women have fought state-sponsored and non-state-sponsored terrorism through their activism."[27] Sometimes also, as she points out, women strive for peace not only to protect their own but also all children, and they come to see that overcoming their own situation of political or economic insecurity requires addressing a larger set of conditions. Because

[24] Ann Tickner, *Gender in International Relations* (New York: Columbia University Press, 1992), 59.

[25] Morgan, *The Demon Lover*, xviii.

[26] See the discussion in Amy Caiazza, "Why Gender Matters in Understanding September 11: Women, Militarism, and Violence," IWPR Publication, #I908 (November 2001), http:www.iwpr.org/pdf/terrorism.pdf.

[27] Ibid.

of this, these women's peace movements may in turn demand greater responsiveness and accountability from their own governments and other institutions, and in this way the women come to be activists for democracy as well. In view of the antithesis suggested earlier between democracy and terrorism and the correlative need for greater democracy in order to alleviate the conditions in which terrorism can emerge, this observed connection between peace activism and democratic activism should not surprise us and is, in fact, quite necessary in my view. These observations further suggest, as Caiazza also stresses, that women's peace movements themselves should be supported by the United States and other governments as a countermovement to terrorism.

Terrorism and Democracy

The preceding section proposes a connection between empathy and democracy. But now the contrast of democracy and terrorism can also be made clear. This contrast has two distinct aspects: First, to the degree that democracy can be interpreted more substantively as applying to participation in a variety of associations beneath and beyond the level of traditional political communities, it becomes evident that terrorism is the conceptual antithesis of democracy in this fuller sense. Whereas terrorist acts undermine political democracy, they are opposed to an authentically democratic approach involving listening to others and engaging in reciprocal decision making concerning contexts of joint activity and considering the impact of these decisions on those more widely affected. Yet the other side of this terrorism–democracy opposition is perhaps more significant, especially to the question of a proper response: Terrorism appears to come to the fore where opportunities for democratic participation are lacking. Evidence for this can be found in the recent case of Saudi Arabia, an authoritarian regime and breeding ground for most of the 9/11 terrorists; and in the case of the Palestinian Occupied Territories, where democratic avenues for change are notably missing. Along these lines, it is plausible to suppose that where there are effective democratic means for expressing positions and contributing to social and political change, justifying a belief in these possibilities, there might well be less resort to, and far less support for, terrorist acts.

These points can be distinguished from the usual considerations of the connection of terrorism and democracy in practice, which have tended to focus on one of two points: (1) that terrorism is the biggest threat

to democracy or (2) that the fight against terrorism itself endangers
democracy by curtailing liberties and infringing basic human rights. Indeed, the curtailment of due process, removal of privacy protections in
the name of security, detention and prosecution of noncitizens (and now
even some citizens) using different standards and military tribunals all
pose a serious danger to a democratic society.

But I want here to highlight instead the way the lack of democratic
possibilities may contribute to the conditions for terrorism, and the issue of democratization in the response to it. While many commentators
have, in fact, pointed to inequality, poverty, and the general lack of economic, social, and cultural development, along with the frustrations and
deep resentments that these cause, as conditions preparing fertile ground
for terrorists or extremists, not enough serious attention has been paid
to the lack of opportunities for genuine democratic self-determination
in the locales from which terrorism often emerges. To say this is not
to deny the importance of conditions of immiseration, where large
numbers of people without adequate resources for their well-being feel
hopelessness concerning their struggle and may come to support violence
against the powerful – or even against the entire society they perceive as
responsible for it. Experiences of humiliation also play a role, as in the
Palestinian case, among many others. Emphasis can also rightly be placed
on geopolitical factors, such as the U.S. requirement of access to Middle
East oil – and the military presence that it has given rise to – as contributing to generating currents of extremist opposition. In addition, concerns
for self-determination of nationalities and the requirements of cultural
identity are significant and lend support to a more substantial application of cultural human rights than at present, a concept that I analyze in
Chapter 5.

To explore further the relations between democratic participation and
the prevention of terrorism, we need to analyze a bit further both the
specific contrast between terrorist acts and democratic forms and also
the conditions that would permit the replacement of the former with
the latter. First of all, then, the practical oppositions between terrorism and democracy are easily observed. There is, of course, often an
absence of democratic modes of decision making in militant religious
fundamentalisms, which are cited as potentiating, or causing, terrorism. Whether the religious groups exemplifying such fundamentalism
are Islamic, Christian (as among certain of the militias or "patriots" in
the United States), Hindu, or orthodox Jewish, it is noteworthy how often
the fundamentalist believers tend to be organized in strict hierarchies.

While there may be highly effective cooperation among them (harking back to Plato's famous observation in the *Republic* of the honor and justice that often pervade a band of thieves), it is generally the relatively well-off and powerful leaders who undemocratically instruct the foot soldiers what to do, sometimes urging them to sacrifice themselves. Such leaders may also place strict limits on those who have rights to interpret their religious standpoints (most often excluding women). Thus, an additional undemocratic factor is the severe gender inequalities that often permeate the background societies from which terrorists emerge, as well as the oppressive relations toward women that male terrorists themselves sometimes display.

Furthermore, people engaging in terrorist acts may not in actuality be true representatives of the people in whose interests they claim to be acting. They are often self-appointed representatives – not elected, even implicitly. Yet the people for whom they claim to speak may well be deprived of the opportunity to express their will politically. Furthermore, when terrorists claim to represent people who do not in fact support them, their terrorist acts may nonetheless provoke a retaliation that affects everyone in their social group or community. Despite this lack of representativeness, some terrorist groups may nonetheless gain genuine support among local populations by providing basic welfare and health services that governments fail to provide.

To determine the sort of democratization that is required to meliorate this situation, we might look more closely at the conceptual connection I introduced at the start of this section: between the lack of democratic channels and terrorist acts. This connection is implicit already in some of the definitions of terrorism considered at the outset of this chapter. Gordon Graham's definition is especially relevant in this regard. For him, "[t]error consists in the causing of widespread fear and alarm by means of violence as a way of unsettling and hence controlling other people.... The point of terror is to ensure that the *will* to oppose is broken, by breaking the will itself."[28] This definition points again to the connection in question by emphasizing the subordination of the will of others that is involved. Of course, it may be that the coerciveness of violence itself is *eo ipso* undemocratic, except in rare instances when it is in the service of just laws. But if Graham is right that the goal of terrorism is to control or coerce, then it clearly stands opposed to the autonomy of the will, which, as a principle of

[28] Gordon Graham, *Ethics and International Affairs*, 123–124.

self-determination that applies equally to all, is central to the conception of democracy.[29]

Certainly, we can say that if substantive democracy involves listening to and taking reciprocally into account the positions of others (as discussed in connection with empathy), then terrorism appears as antithetical to democracy. Clearly, too, terrorism as political violence stands opposed in principle to the forms of liberal political democracy – majority rule, voting, and so forth. However, it is important to observe that terrorist acts seem quite capable of existing alongside such democratic forms. For example, in the United States itself, one need only mention Timothy McVeigh, abortion clinic bombers, and the Ku Klux Klan some time ago; in Europe, the Red Brigades in Italy and the ETA in Spain; Baruch Goldstein and Yigal Amir in Israel; and terrorist acts against Muslims and others in India, among other possible cases. This observation gives further credence to the idea that deeper and more substantive forms of democracy, along the lines proposed earlier, are what is really required and that political democracy alone is insufficient to ever provide freedom from terror.

Correlatively, it is evident that the absence of local forms of democracy, as well indeed as of more global ones, in which people can participate in jointly directing their everyday lives is one of the conditions sustaining the resort to terrorism. In this context, the inadequacy mentioned earlier of purely formal modes of political democracy is clear in that they tend to involve rule by elites without real opportunities for participation or deliberation. Yet, even fuller and more substantive political democracy would not seem to be enough, as can be seen from the role played by group hatreds and efforts to redress social grievances in terrorism. As Frank Cunningham has argued, an important factor in dealing with such group hatreds is the introduction of substantively democratic procedures across a range of extrapolitical contexts, including informal associations and small-scale interpersonal interactions.[30] It cannot be supposed that these hatreds and the oppressive structures in which they exist can be adequately addressed using purely political modalities; social and personal openings are crucial as well. And in terms of the forms of political

---

[29] Although Graham's account holds for most cases, it is worth mentioning that there may well be certain cases of terrorism – although a minority – that are merely expressive rather than being aimed at control and coercion.

[30] Frank Cunningham, "Antioppressive Politics and Group Hatreds," in *Race, Class and Community Identity*, eds. Andrew Light and Mechthild Nagel (Amherst, NY: Humanity Press, 2000), 182–198.

democracy itself, it often would seem necessary to introduce types that explicitly permit the recognition of group differences and that are accompanied by rights for minority cultures. In this connection, too, it would be a mistake to suppose that traditional American forms of democracy suffice everywhere, whatever their effectiveness in the local context may be.

Finally, it is important to observe that the dearth of local empowerment that I have emphasized is bound up with global inequalities as well. Communities are disenfranchised not only by lacking political democracy but also by having little say in the economic decisions that affect them, deprived of their economic human rights. Global corporations may play a role in this process, not only in their everyday functioning but also by supporting authoritarian regimes out of corporate self-interest. And the U.S. government has historically sometimes followed suit – for example, in the often-noted case of Saudi Arabia and the pursuit of oil interests.[31] If so, then it is not only the commercialism and markets that Benjamin Barber, for one, has strongly criticized[32] that are a problem here, but also the sort of corporate imperialism that has accompanied the largely unbridled globalization of recent years. This dominance, together with the authoritarian regimes themselves, has tended to undercut local – and global – democratic processes, while providing some of the conditions for the extension of democracy, as discussed earlier. These various considerations thus suggest the need to support not only formal but also informal democracy at local levels, as a way of giving people productive and more equal means of expressing their frustrations and implementing their will for change. Remedies for global inequalities and for the antidemocratic practices thus have to go hand in hand.

A final observation can be made in this connection: The interrelation of global distributive justice and economic development, on the one hand, with opportunities for democratic participation, on the other, suggests again the interdependence of political rights to democratic participation and economic rights to means of subsistence. Each of these is a condition for the other, and they are both among the basic human rights.[33] We can say that people need democratic participation to gain and

---

[31] Another example along these lines is the UNOCAL pipeline in Afghanistan, which was originally supported by the Taliban, and which in turn obtained U.S. support until the recent war. Indeed, a substantial number of military bases line its route.

[32] Benjamin Barber, *Jihad vs. McWorld* (New York: Ballantine, 1996).

[33] See also Henry Shue, *Basic Rights* (Princeton, NJ: Princeton University Press, 1980).

protect their economic human rights, which in turn facilitate both the maintenance and the extension of democratic participation. It is clear that both of these preconditions, along with the empathy and cultural recognition discussed earlier, are essential in order to reshape the political, economic, and social landscapes of what is currently fertile ground for the emergence of terrorism.

Thus a fundamental synthesis between democratic participation, going beneath and beyond traditional forms, and the human rights – including the very basic right to live – can be made concrete in their application to the challenge of terrorism. Indeed, our increasingly globalized and sometimes terrorized world, as I have argued here, requires a framework in which an expanded vision of democracy and a broadened conception of human rights are essential, and essentially intertwined.

Index